Peirce

Charles Sanders Peirce (1839–1914) is generally regarded as the founder of pragmatism, and one of the greatest ever American philosophers. Peirce is also widely known for his work on truth, his foundational work in mathematical logic, and an influential theory of signs, or semiotics. Albert Atkin introduces the full spectrum of Peirce's thought for those coming to his work for the first time.

The book begins with an overview of Peirce's life and work, considering his early and long-standing interest in logic and science and highlighting important views on the structure of philosophical thought. Atkin then explains Peirce's accounts of pragmatism and truth, examining important later developments to these theories. He then introduces Peirce's full accounts of semiotics, examines his foundational work on formal and graphical logic, and introduces Peirce's account of metaphysics, the least understood aspect of his philosophy. The final chapter considers Peirce's legacy and influence on the thought of philosophers such as John Dewey and Richard Rorty, and highlights areas where Peirce's ideas could still provide important insights for contemporary philosophers.

Including chapter summaries, suggestions for further reading and a glossary, this invaluable introduction and guide to Peirce's philosophy is essential reading for those new to his work.

Albert Atkin is a senior lecturer in the Department of Philosophy, Macquarie University, Australia. He is the author of *The Philosophy of Race* (2012).

Routledge Philosophers

Edited by Brian Leiter

University of Chicago

Routledge Philosophers is a major series of introductions to the great Western philosophers. Each book places a major philosopher or thinker in historical context, explains and assesses their key arguments, and considers their legacy. Additional features include a chronology of major dates and events, chapter summaries, annotated suggestions for further reading and a glossary of technical terms.

An ideal starting point for those new to philosophy, they are also essential reading for those interested in the subject at any level.

Available:

Forthcoming:

Plotinus
Eyjólfur Emilsson

Berkeley
Lisa Downing and David Hilbert

Levinas
Michael Morgan

Cassirer
Samantha Matherne

Kierkegaard
Paul Muench

Anscombe
Candace Vogler

Marx
Jaime Edwards and Brian Leiter

Sartre
Kenneth Williford

Albert Atkin

Peirce

Routledge
Taylor & Francis Group

LONDON AND NEW YORK

First published 2016
by Routledge
2 Park Square, Milton Park, Abingdon, Oxon OX14 4RN

and by Routledge
711 Third Avenue, New York, NY 10017

Routledge is an imprint of the Taylor & Francis Group, an informa business

British Library Cataloguing in Publication Data
A catalogue record for this book is available from the British Library

Library of Congress Cataloging in Publication Data
Atkin, Albert.
Peirce / by Albert Atkin.
pages cm. — (Routledge philosophers)
Includes bibliographical references and index.
1. Peirce, Charles S. (Charles Sanders), 1839–1914. I. Title.
B945.P44A85 2015
191—dc23
2015003883

ISBN: 978-0-415-48831-0 (hbk)
ISBN: 978-0-415-48832-7 (pbk)
ISBN: 978-1-315-69640-9 (ebk)

Typeset in Joanna MT and DIN
by Swales & Willis Ltd, Exeter, Devon, UK

Printed and bound by CPI Group (UK) Ltd, Croydon, CR0 4

For Chris Hookway

Contents

Acknowledgements

There are far too many people to thank individually, but to mention a few, I would like to thank Louis Gregory, Stephen Gadsby, Angus Hamilton, Charlie Wiggins, Jeff Zaroyko, David Parissi-Smyth, Yu Fai Lam, Chris Masia, Ali Aziz, and all the students who have studied Peirce with me at one time or another. I would also like to thank the various colleagues who have talked with me about Peirce over the years, in particular Cathy Legg and Richard Menary. However, special thanks must go to Chris Hookway, who has inspired and encouraged my work on Peirce from the very beginning. I am deeply grateful to him.

On a much more personal level, this book took far longer to complete than I had initially intended, in large part because, following the births of my children, I took extensive breaks from philosophy and academia to be with them. I feel very fortunate to have been able to do this and still be allowed to produce this book, especially in a time when academic employment is so precarious for so many and the need of a separate personal life frequently given little regard. Thankfully, unlike very many others, I have not in the end had to choose between a philosophy career and being a parent, and I owe my colleagues at Macquarie University a huge debt of gratitude for their support in this. Such attitudes are contributing to a steady but welcome change in the academic climate. I would also like to thank Adam Johnson and Tony Bruce at Routledge for their patience and encouragement throughout. Finally, thanks go to my partner, Hannah, for her unwavering faith and support, and to my children, Tristan and Iris, who have caused delays, distractions, chaos and stresses for which I shall remain forever thankful.

Abbreviations

CP *Collected papers of Charles Sanders Peirce.* Volumes 1–6 (1931–1936). Eds. Charles Hartshorne and Paul Weiss. Volumes 7 and 8 (1958). Ed. Arthur Burks. Cambridge: Harvard University Press. Referencing by Volume/Paragraph/Date – e.g. CP1. 192 (1903) reads *Collected papers, Volume 1, Paragraph 192, dated 1903.*

EP *The essential Peirce: selected philosophical writings.* Volume 1 (1867–1893). (1992). Eds. Nathan Houser and Christian Kloesel. Volume 2 (1893–1913). (1998). Eds. The Peirce Edition Project. Bloomington: Indiana University Press. Referencing by Volume/Page/Date – e.g. EP2. 201 (1903) reads *Essential Peirce, Volume 2, Page 201, dated 1903.*

W *Writings of Charles S. Peirce: a chronological edition.* (1982–). Eds. Max Fisch, Edward Moore, Christian Kloesel, Nathan Houser *et al.* Bloomington: Indiana University Press. Referencing by Volume/Page/Date – e.g. W2. 57 (1867) reads *Writings of Charles S. Peirce, Volume 2, Page 57, dated 1867.*

SS *Semiotic and significs: the correspondence between Charles S. Peirce and Victoria Lady Welby.* (1977). Ed. Charles Hardwick. Bloomington: Indiana University Press. Referencing by Title/Page Number/Date – e.g. SS 197 (1906) reads *Semiotic and significs, Page 197, dated 1906.*

MS *The Charles S. Peirce papers, microfilm edition.* (1966). Cambridge: Harvard University Photographic Service. Referencing by MS number as listed in Robin (1967) and date (where available) – e.g. MS 325 (c1907) reads *Manuscript 325, dated circa 1907.*

L Correspondence in the Harvard University Peirce papers. Referencing by L number as listed in Robin (1967) and date (where available) – e.g. L387 (1895) reads Letter 387, dated 1985.

NEM The new elements of mathematics by Charles S. Peirce. Volumes 1–5 (1976). Ed. Carolyn Eisele. The Hague: Mouton. Referencing by Volume/Page/Date – e.g. NEM4. 238 (1904) reads New elements of mathematics, Volume 4, Page 238, dated 1904.

RLT Reasoning and the logic of things. (1992). Ed. Kenneth Ketner. Cambridge: Harvard University Press. Referencing by title and page number; all lectures are dated 1898 – e.g. RLT 110 (1898) reads Reasoning and the logic of things, Page 110, dated 1898.

Chronology

1872	Starts the Cambridge Metaphysical Club with William James and Oliver Wendell Holmes, Jr.
	Benjamin Peirce promotes him to assistant at U.S. Coastal Survey and places him in charge of pendulum experiments
1874	Benjamin Peirce retires from the U.S. Coastal Survey due to ill health
1876	Peirce and his wife, Zina, are separated
1877	The important *Popular Science Monthly* papers begin to appear
	Elected to the National Academy of Sciences
1878	Publishes *Photometric Researches* from his work at the Harvard Observatory
1879	Begins as lecturer in logic at Johns Hopkins University
1880	His father, Benjamin Sr., dies
1883	Divorces his first wife, Zina, and marries his second wife, Juliette, shortly afterwards
	Publishes *Studies in Logic* with his Johns Hopkins students
1884	Dismissed from his Johns Hopkins University post
1887	His mother, Sarah, dies
1888	Buys a farmhouse in rural Pennsylvania, names it 'Arisbe'
1889	His wife, Juliette, is diagnosed with tuberculosis
	His friend William James is appointed to an endowed professorship in psychology at Harvard
1891	Resigns his position at the U.S. Coastal Survey
1891	The important *Monist* metaphysical papers begin to appear
1892	Gives a series of Lowell lectures on 'The history of science'
1895	Sinking under debts, puts Arisbe up for auction, but Peirce's brother, James Mills Peirce, helps with debts and mortgages
1898	Gives the important Cambridge conference lectures on 'Reasoning and the logic of things'
	William James, in a paper delivered to the Philosophical Union at Berkeley, credits Peirce with inventing pragmatism
1902	Submits a strongly supported application for funds from the Carnegie Institution to write a complete statement of his philosophy, but it is rejected

1903	Gives Harvard lectures on 'Pragmatism'
	Gives Lowell lectures on 'Some topics of logic'
	Begins his correspondence with Victoria Lady Welby
1905	Begins (but does not complete) publishing a series of papers in *The Monist* on 'Pragmaticism'
1906	His brother James dies
1909	Diagnosed with cancer
1910	William James dies
1912	Victoria Lady Welby dies
1914,	
19 April	Dies of cancer

Preface

> The reader has the right to know how the author's opinions were formed.
>
> (C.S. Peirce, CP1. 3 (1897))

As an undergraduate, having stumbled across passing mentions of Peirce in various books on truth and meaning, I made some knowing references to his ideas in a tutorial. My assumed expertise obviously failed to impress my tutor who, as I recall, said, 'If you want to understand what you're talking about, you'd better read Chris Hookway's book on Peirce'. I followed his advice, which was enough to make me realise that I wanted to study Peirce, and that I wanted to study Peirce with Christopher Hookway.

A couple of years later, I arrived at Sheffield to undertake a PhD on Peirce under Chris's supervision, with a view about how one might make best use of Peirce's ideas – take a contemporary philosophical problem, sprinkle on some Peirce (preferably semiotics), bake for a few thousand words and voilà. Those who know Chris Hookway's work will be aware that he is a subtle and careful thinker who finds interesting nuances and remarkable depths in Peirce's philosophy. Thankfully, Chris is also a patient and generous teacher who helped me to see that treating Peirce as sharing the concerns of analytic philosophy is a defensible approach to take, but that my ham-fisted procrustean project needed to show some respect for the complexity of Peirce's thought – my naive 'shake and bake' methodology simply wasn't up to scratch.

Many supervisions during this time would involve Chris respond-ing to some idea of mine with 'that seems . . . right. But here's a thought . . .'. I quickly learned that 'seeming right' wasn't the same as being insightful, and that to understand Peirce's work, one has to mine the depths below the surface; that's where the real treas-ures are. My inclination to see Peirce as solving or dissolving many of the concerns of contemporary analytic philosophers has never really waned since that time, but having formed many of my opin-ions under the subtle scrutiny of Chris Hookway, I realised that the surface level solutions are far less interesting than the subterranean complexities they rest upon.

The approach to Peirce's work used in this book sees him through the lens of contemporary analytic philosophy. Importantly, however, it sees contemporary analytic philosophy as missing a trick in passing over Peirce's thought too quickly. The view taken here is that with-out understanding the connections that exist between Peirce's various philosophical theories, we simply cannot understand the development of his ideas or the important implications that follow from them. The finer details of my approach are outlined in Chapter 1, where I emphasise that key for understanding Peirce is to acknowledge that he saw himself as a scientist and logician and that he had an important vision of how different areas of philosophy are connected. At its heart, though, this view attributes to Peirce quite familiar 'analytic' sensibili-ties – logic and science are crucial – but also an influential if unfamiliar view of the structure of philosophical thought – his architectonic. It barely needs saying that this is not the only way to approach Peirce's work – we might foreground his categories or his cosmology or deny his 'analytic' sensibilities altogether – but my hope is that the picture of Peirce's thought that emerges in this book is clear and compelling enough to justify taking this approach. To be clear, the opinions of the author are that Peirce answers many of the familiar analytic philosoph-ical problems in a way that 'seems . . . right'. But more importantly, the author thinks that the underlying complexities that lead to these answers are the real reason that Peirce is so insightful, and so impor-tant. It should, I hope, be clear to the reader how these opinions were formed.

One
Life, work, and interpretation

Life and work

It is never clear to what extent familiarity with biographical details is necessary for a greater understanding of a philosopher's work. Does knowing the figure's personal characteristics lead to a considerably more refined comprehension of his or her philosophy? The question may not matter enough for us to devote much effort to working it out, but in many cases it is apparent that knowing more can lead us to an additional appreciation of the philosopher's work. In the case of C.S. Peirce, it is clear that it does.

As we shall see, Peirce was, by all accounts, an awkward and irascible man who nonetheless inspired considerable affection and devotion in those close to him. Such a description will no doubt resonate with many Peirce scholars; his work displays precisely the same characteristics. But more to the point, these characteristics, along with a series of events beyond his control, led a man with undoubted genius and potential into a life of academic isolation and penury. The effect on his work and its reception, even today, is telling. Lacking a ready academic community to force him into clear expression and help him focus his ideas, he was often terse where explanation was required and prolix where it was not. His technical terminology can be alien and awkward. He frequently dismissed or ignored objections to his work that would readily occur to those working within a larger academic community. This means that understanding Peirce takes patience and persistence. But it is not all negative, at least not from our point of view.

Given that some of Peirce's philosophical breakthroughs pre-empted important twentieth-century theories or were contemporary with work of which his isolation made him ignorant, we can appreciate the power of his thought. Consequently, when faced with one of his seemingly obscure or even irrelevant ideas, knowledge of his achievements in adversity may give us the sense that it is we, and not Peirce, who are missing something, and further investigation often proves that this assumption of intellectual humility is correct. Of course, Peirce's life was interesting in its own right, but for the reasons just cited a relatively detailed grasp of his biography is useful in understanding his work and why it takes the form it does.

Early influences and promise

Charles Sanders Peirce was born on 10 September 1839 in Cambridge, Massachusetts, into a position of status and privilege. His father, Benjamin Peirce, was a famous professor of mathematics and astronomy at Harvard, and his mother, Sarah Hunt Mills, was the daughter of Elijah Hunt Mills, senator for Massachusetts. Peirce was the second of five children and one of four talented brothers. His elder brother, James Mills Peirce, followed their father to a mathematics professorship at Harvard. Another brother, Herbert Henry Davis Peirce, carved out a distinguished career in the Foreign Service, whilst Peirce's youngest brother, Benjamin Mills Peirce, showed promise as an engineer but died young. The Peirce family was descended from John Pers, an early Puritan settler from Norwich in England, and it is from John Pers that the family got the unorthodox pronunciation of their name; 'Peirce' is pronounced 'Purse'.

Peirce's early life appears to be one of precocious intellect and ready parental indulgence (the Peirce children were never disciplined). Peirce's younger brother Herbert described him as

> [...] forever digging into encyclopaedias and other books in search of knowledge upon abstruse subjects, while discussions with his learned father upon profound questions of science, especially higher mathematics and philosophy, were common

matters of astonishment, not only to his brothers and sister, but to his parents as well. (Herbert Henry Davis Peirce, *Boston evening transcript*, 16 May 1914)

The Peirce family home was host to numerous eminent intellectual figures. Frequent visitors included the English mathematician and founder of the *American Journal of Mathematics*, J.J. Sylvester; the famed 'fireside poets' Henry Wadsworth Longfellow, James Russell Lowell and Oliver Wendell Holmes, Sr.; scientists Asa Gray and Louis Agassiz; and feminist journalist Margaret Fuller. It is little wonder that the young Peirce's intellectual curiosity was always stoked. However, by far and away the greatest influence on the intellect of Peirce, both as a child and arguably for the rest of his life, was his father, Benjamin Peirce.

Benjamin Peirce was a remarkable man who did much to transform the state of American mathematics and science and place it on a respectable international footing. He lobbied Washington for funding for scientific causes, often convincing Congress to part with considerably more than it normally would by arguing for his conviction that the greatness of a nation is measured by its commitment to science, education and the arts. In 1847, when aiding in the foundation of the Lawrence Scientific School at Harvard, he secured funding from Abbott Lawrence, the well-known businessman and one-time candidate for Vice President under President Zachary Taylor. Along with fellow men of learning such as Louis Agassiz, Benjamin Peirce founded the National Academy of Sciences, and in a role that was to prove important in Charles Peirce's life, he served as superintendent and consultant to the U.S. Coast and Geodetic Survey from 1867 until his death in 1880. As an academic, he took a professorship in mathematics at Harvard in 1833 and made contributions in the fields of linear associative algebras, where he developed terminology that is still in current use,[1] and in number theory, where he proved that there is no odd perfect number[2] with fewer than four prime factors.

The influence of Benjamin Peirce on all his sons is obvious, but with Charles, undoubtedly his favourite, the effects on both intellect and personality were profound. Benjamin is reported to have been a difficult teacher who had little patience for those too slow to keep up with his explanations, and so he frequently insisted that students work out problems for themselves. With his children, his teaching methods were also largely heuristic, but for Charles this inspired a love of science and commitment to rigorous and careful inquiry. This steady, unrelenting persistence with intellectual problems (which the young Charles called 'pedestrianism') gave Peirce the remarkable drive to continue with his work in circumstances that would have left others with little inclination towards logic and philosophy. More corrosive, however, was the manner in which the elder Peirce cultured his son's approach to philosophy and philosophers. As Peirce recalled:

> [W]hen I was reading Kant, Spinoza, and Hegel, my father [. . .] would induce me to tell him the proofs offered by the philosophers, and in a very few words would almost invariably rip them up and show them empty. He had even less mercy for such philosophers as Hobbes, Hume and James Mill. (MS 823 (1892))

This manner of teaching, coupled with Peirce the elder's insistence that his son was a genius, was in many ways a destructive influence on Charles. Peirce struggled for the rest of his life trying to understand himself in light of the nature of men of genius. He was often arrogant, quick to dismiss the intellect of others, and focused to the exclusion of all else – even in times of unimaginable adversity – on his philosophical and logical work. Joseph Brent, a Peirce biographer, puts the negativity of the influence thus:

> It must be corrosive of character to be placed, at the age of sixteen, in the unlikely position of believing that your own philosophical abilities are demonstrably superior to those of some of the most respected and revered philosophers of the past. (Brent 1998, 57)

Whilst this is clearly an exaggeration – Peirce was a diligent and respectful student of philosophy with a deep knowledge of its history – there is a kernel of truth in the assessment: Peirce was always quick to rate himself amongst philosophers of the first rank.

There were other significant influences on the young Peirce. He famously recounted his first encounter with logic in 1851, when he was twelve years old:

> I remember picking up Whately's *Logic*, in my elder brother's room, and asking him what logic was. I next see myself stretched on his carpet, devouring the book; and this must have been repeated on following days, since subsequent tests proved that I had fairly mastered the excellent and charming treatise. From that day to this, logic has been my passion. (MS 905 (1907))

Peirce remained devoted to the study of logic for the rest of his life, and many of his most interesting philosophical contributions are to that discipline. There were, however, less pleasant influences.

Peirce appears, from early on in his life, to have been prone to a variety of illnesses, two of which seem to have been significant. From a young age, he was prone to fits of depression and violent outbursts coupled with highly erratic and irrational behaviour. This was something that continued throughout his life, and Peirce frequently suspected that he was prone to insanity. This has led to speculation that he may have suffered from some form of manic-depressive disease. He also suffered from a painful and debilitating disorder known as trigeminal neuralgia, an inflammation of the trigeminal facial nerve which, when aggravated, causes excruciating pain and leaves the sufferer confused and distracted. This disorder is often triggered by nothing more damaging than a cold draft, and its onset is incredibly difficult to predict.

Peirce's ill health had two important consequences. First, to treat his pain he became a user of opiates, ether and, later, cocaine, and it seems likely that he developed some degree of dependency. Second, so fearful was he of the effect a bout of trigeminal neuralgia would have upon his productivity that he often worked feverishly and obsessively in an attempt to complete work before his illness laid him low again.

This mix of influences nonetheless appears to have started Peirce on a path headed for considerable success. Some early problems in school and a rather poor performance at Harvard, where he finished in the lower quarter of the graduating class of 1859, seem to have been the consequence of Peirce's erratic behaviour, indifference to the work and disdain for the intellectual requirements asked of him. Despite this, he remained at Harvard as a resident for a further year, eventually receiving a Master of Arts degree. He enrolled in Harvard's Lawrence Scientific School to study chemistry, graduating in the 1863 class with the first Bachelor of Science degree awarded *summa cum laude*.

Thanks to the influence of his father, Peirce quickly secured employment with the U.S. Coast and Geodetic Survey, although an academic position teaching logic was closer to his desire. Peirce also married his first wife, Harriet Melusina Fay. Zina, as she was called, was a feminist campaigner of good Cambridge patrician stock, and although the marriage was considered hasty by both sets of parents, it was hoped that she would exert a settling influence on Peirce, who had continued to display erratic extremes of behaviour throughout early adulthood. The marriage and the post seemed to give Peirce enough of the grounding and support he needed to concentrate on his first love, logic, and by 1865 his devotion to the subject appeared to be paying dividends.

In 1866, he gave a series of talks on the logic of science for the prestigious Lowell Institute. He published early, well-received responses to Kant's system of categories in 1867 and to Descartes' account of knowledge, science and doubt in 1868. Meanwhile, his father took over as superintendent of the U.S. Coast and Geodetic Survey, where Peirce was employed. Peirce was given greater responsibility and oversaw experiments to ascertain the shape of various landmasses by measuring small variations in gravitational effects on swinging pendulums.[3] In an attempt to elevate the status of American science and to tie the U.S. Coastal Survey findings to those in Europe, Benjamin Peirce arranged for his son to travel to England, Germany, Italy, Spain and Greece to conduct experiments. Whilst in England, Peirce took the opportunity to visit the English logicians Augustus De Morgan and W. Stanley Jevons and to circulate his recent paper 'Description of a notation for the logic of relatives', a work which made important developments to Boole's algebra of logic. This paper made a marked impression upon the English logicians, and Peirce was held in some repute as a consequence.

From late 1869 until 1878, Peirce also began extra work at the Harvard Observatory, where he was chiefly responsible for cataloguing and recording the relative brightness of stars. Whilst there, he proposed a method of using this information to chart the shape of solar systems, the results of which were published in his 1878 *Photometric Researches*. During his time at the Harvard Observatory, Peirce also developed a spectrometer through which he proposed to make a precise definition of the length of the standard meter in terms of the wavelength of sodium light. His work in philosophy continued with the publication of the now legendary *Popular Science Monthly* series in 1877 and 1878. This series, which included 'The fixation of belief' and 'How to make our ideas clear', marked a continuation of his earlier anti-Cartesianism and gave his first developed accounts of inquiry and pragmatism. Moreover, by 1879 his deep desire for an academic position in logic where he could pursue his preferred specialism looked as though it might be realised. Peirce's father had suggested him for the position of logic lecturer at the recently founded Johns Hopkins University in Baltimore, and the president of the university, Daniel Coit Gilman, agreed that Peirce should be appointed to a post with an eye to tenure after a few years of successful service.

At this point in his life, then, Peirce was a promising young man of science and philosophy making groundbreaking contributions to measurement and logic and helping to spearhead his father's deeply cherished ambition of placing American science on a par with the best of Europe, and now he had landed a post as lecturer with the promise of tenure. All looked well for Peirce, but from this position of unquestionable potential, things went badly awry.

Change in fortunes

The problem for Peirce was that despite this period of relative success, the seeds for his downfall had already been sown. Peirce had continued to behave erratically, which seemed to distance him from his wife. His devotion to his work and Zina's corresponding devotion to her feminist and charitable causes seem to have put some pressures on the couple, leading her to suspect him of having affairs with the wives of his U.S. Coastal Survey colleagues. During a second Coastal Survey trip to Europe in 1875, Zina left him and returned to her parents in Cambridge. Peirce fell into a considerable depression, which culminated in an attack of what is now known as conversion disorder, the primary symptom of which is temporary paralysis. Peirce continued to suffer relapses for the next year or two, and whilst he initially harboured some hope of reconciliation with his wife, their continued separation was a source of gossip amongst the patrician families of Cambridge, with Zina largely considered the wounded party.

Peirce's working life also began to turn sour. His appointment and promotions at the Coastal Survey were largely nepotistic and not immediately justifiable, given the time and money required to overcome his lack of knowledge and training in geodesy. In time, this began to create some tensions with colleagues who were passed over or who considered funds spent on training Peirce as misappropriation. Further, his role at the Harvard Observatory led to considerable tension with President Charles Eliot of the Harvard Corporation. With some justification, Eliot suspended Peirce's salary whilst Peirce conducted U.S. Coastal Survey work in Europe, and he continued to press Peirce for the results that were later published as the *Photometric Researches*.[4] Peirce became indignant and spiky, and although the issue was eventually resolved, this episode rather coloured Eliot's opinion of Peirce as an unstable man.

At Johns Hopkins, Peirce had made a considerable impression and taught a difficult though successful class on logic. This culminated in the publication, with his students, of the 1883 book *Studies in Logic*. In a review of the book for *Mind*, John Venn, the famous British mathematician and logician suggested that the collection contained a 'greater quantity of novel and suggestive matter than any other recent work on the same or allied subjects' (Venn 1883, 594). But even here, Peirce's behaviour came to cause problems. Peirce caused repeated troubles with the mathematician J.J. Sylvester, who was now heading the mathematics department at Johns Hopkins. Further, upon the death of his father in 1880, Peirce fell into a depression and resigned from the university, even selling them his personal library, only to reconsider and ask for reappointment a few weeks later. Understandable though his grief was, these actions coloured the opinions of the Johns Hopkins president and board of trustees, who saw Peirce as unstable, erratic and capricious.

All of this need not have mattered excessively, since most of these men of influence considered Peirce's intellect beyond reproach, and many agreed with his father's estimation of him as a genius. They had concerns about his volatile personality, but he was employed for his mind. Unfortunately, after it became clear to Peirce that his difficulties with Zina were irreconcilable, he lived openly and quite publicly with a mistress, Juliette Pourtalei, whom he married in 1883 within seven days of being awarded a divorce. This made Peirce a social pariah, and to have offered him employment in the light of such controversy would undoubtedly have tainted his employer by association.

His second wife, Juliette, was, and remains, a mysterious character. A French divorcee (although no record of her first marriage exists), she claimed to be a member of the Habsburg family in exile. It has also been claimed that she was possibly a former prostitute or was descended from 'gypsies'.[5] What seems clear, though, is that Peirce met Juliette within a year or two of Zina's desertion of him and soon engaged in a very public affair, traveling with her on survey work as though she were his wife. In 1881, he filed for divorce in preparation for his marriage to Juliette. It appears that marrying a mistress whom you had publicly flaunted in front of your wife, estranged or not, was too much for Peirce's Cambridge contemporaries, and he was decried as a man of depraved morality. His own maiden aunt, Elizabeth, wrote that she wished Charles and Juliette would not return to Cambridge and that she 'did not doubt of her [Juliette's] badness, and [. . .] of his also'. Strangely, Peirce seemed oblivious to such opinion, with his mother observing that he was 'like a child about conventionalities and has no idea that anything stands in the way of her being received everywhere!!'[6]

In light of such moral outrage, the decision of President Gilman and the board of trustees at Johns Hopkins not to grant Peirce tenure or renew his contract on a temporary basis was never in doubt. The manner in which the decision was executed, however, was unpleasant for Peirce. All temporary contracts were withdrawn for the year

1884 and no tenures granted; all contracts with the exception of Peirce's were then re-instated. This plan was designed partly to save Peirce some embarrassment, but mainly it was meant to allow the university to dispense with Peirce's services without publicly citing his perceived immorality as a cause. Peirce displayed his usual obliviousness and thought the cause of dismissal was misplaced dissatisfaction with his teaching, and he did not leave without some protest. This was to no avail, of course, and by 1884 he had lost the only academic post he was ever to hold.

Sadly, his remaining source of income, the U.S. Coastal Survey, was also to fall through. With his father's death, he had lost his most powerful backer for the post, and in 1885 the survey was subjected to a government audit amidst accusations of widespread financial impropriety. Peirce was exonerated but the new climate was made unworkable for him, and he eventually left the post after the new superintendent demanded his resignation in 1891. During this time Peirce had purchased a Pennsylvanian farmhouse with his inheritance, and he and his new wife increasingly withdrew to a life of solitude as a response to the professional pressures he was facing. In the space of less than ten years, Peirce had gone from a position of considerable professional and academic promise to that of an untouchable, distinguished only in his instability and immorality.

The remaining years of Peirce's life were marked by incredible hardship and suffering. Peirce was unemployable, and during the ten years following his resignation he became embroiled in numerous failed get-rich-quick schemes with all manner of snake oil merchants. The little steady income that he did generate came from writing reviews and dictionary definitions for various sympathetic publishers and editors. He even managed to publish some interesting academic articles in The Monist on his theory of evolutionary cosmology, for which he was remunerated. Occasional well-paid lecture series were organised by his friends and sympathizers William James and Josiah Royce, but so fearful was the Harvard establishment of his personal reputation that a series given by Peirce in 1898 had to take place in a private home. His potential to corrupt the morals of the young was considered reason enough for refusing him permission to lecture on campus.

That Peirce struggled to find money to live on was bad enough, but a strange attempt to create the impression that he and his wife were living the life of rural gentry caused him to incur huge debts by altering and improving his Pennsylvania home, which he named 'Arisbe'. These unpaid debts, along with assault charges levied for a physical attack on a woman he employed, meant that Peirce was a fugitive from the law for two years in the mid-1890s. Peirce went into hiding in New York, during which time Arisbe was claimed by the courts and his wife became seriously ill. He wandered the streets, went without sustenance or shelter for days at a time, and was even reduced to stealing food. Remarkably, though, he continued to work on his philosophy and logic. As he stated in a letter to his friend Francis Russell:

> My wife was turned out of hospital, as I supposed. I paid them the next day. But she is now in imminent danger. I do not leave her bedside for half an hour at a time; and as I am the only nurse, am pretty thoroughly done up. Still, I write my logic just the same. (L387 (1895))

The threats to Peirce's home and freedom were settled with the intervention of his elder brother, James, who helped to pay off debts on the house, and two friends, George Morison and George Plimpton, who helped to arrange out-of-court settlements for the case of assault and other unpaid debts. By this time, Peirce had begun to realise that no redemption from his position was likely. William James had made numerous attempts to bring him into the philosophical mainstream, including naming him as the progenitor of pragmatism and organising popular lecture series, all to no avail. Peirce's health was failing, and his wife was by now a frail and sickly consumptive in need of constant care and attention. Following a well-supported[7] but failed attempt to secure money from the Carnegie Institute in 1903, Peirce became resigned to his fate. Poor, struggling with health, and desperately trying to give a full statement of his philosophical work, he realised quick wealth or an academic position would never come his way. By 1907, James wrote to Peirce's many friends and family:

> The time has come to recognize that he can't make his living. The makeshifts of the last few years are played out, and he must be kept going by friends and relatives. I am representing the friends and trying to get enough pledges of a certain sum yearly to make an aggregate of 400 or 500 dollars. [. . .]
>
> Will you [. . .] possibly, in memory of auld lang syne and in consideration of C.S.P.'s genius (if not of his character) add your own name to the subscribers? (Quoted in Brent 1998, 306)

This fund managed to raise $1000 or so a year from around twenty anonymous sources, and the money was released in fortnightly remittances to Peirce's wife. The Peirces took this in varying ways. Juliette was shamed by it but saw that they had little choice and accepted the fund with gratitude. Charles, on the other hand, made frequent complaints that he was short of money and objected to being kept in the dark about the identity of his benefactors. However, he was now able to concentrate more readily on his philosophical work. For the remainder of his days he lived on at a steadily decaying Arisbe. Racked with frequent episodes of depression and pained by increasing bouts of trigeminal neuralgia, he tried to work out the causes of his failure. He constantly spoke of suicide and his fear for his wife's health, and whilst his published work petered out into a series of rejections and incomplete projects, he did not stop writing, desperate to leave a complete and finished statement of his work. In April of 1914, Peirce finally succumbed to the bowel cancer he had been struggling with since 1909. He died isolated and largely unappreciated, feeling that his genius was beyond question but that his flawed nature had seen its promise squandered and lost.[8]

The Peirce papers

As his life suggests, academic isolation and hardship were no bar to intellectual toil, and along with work published during his lifetime, Peirce also left around eighty thousand pages of unpublished manuscripts, incomplete drafts and lecture notes. It might have been that Peirce's published work was all that was left to us, with his manuscripts burned along with the other remnants of his estate left at Arisbe after Juliette's death. Thankfully this did not happen, and in seeking a fitting memorial to her husband, Juliette gave Peirce's papers and library to Harvard. Josiah Royce was instrumental in arranging this donation and showed real enthusiasm for organising it into a scholarly edition. The Harvard philosophy department, too, seems to have been keen to see Royce realise this ambition and allocated space and funds. Royce and his graduate student W.F. Kernan worked on organising the horrendously muddled collection of papers, initially for cataloguing purposes, but with an eye on making this previously unpublished material available to a wider audience.[9] Unfortunately, Royce died in 1916, too soon to accomplish anything with the disorganised manuscripts, but by bringing the papers to Harvard and showing a commitment to a scholarly edition, Royce without question effectively secured the long-term influence of Peirce beyond his own lifetime.

In respect for Royce's wishes to do justice to the Peirce papers, J.H. Woods, the head of Harvard's philosophy department, sought another editor for the Peirce papers but had little initial success. Bertrand Russell was approached and both Victor Lenzen and Henry Sheffer did some work with the papers, but very little progress was made in this period and Harvard's interest waned. Indeed, during this time, publications of Peirce's work not connected with the Harvard manuscripts were beginning to appear. In 1923, Morris Cohen edited and published *Chance, Love and Logic*. This work collected together Peirce's early statements of pragmatism and inquiry, previously published as *Illustrations of the Logic of Science* in 1877/1878, and his later statements of evolutionary cosmology, previously published in *The Monist* between 1891 and 1893. Also in 1923, an appendix in C.K. Ogden and I.A. Richard's *The Meaning of Meaning* used quotes from correspondence between Peirce and Ogden's former teacher, Victoria Lady Welby, to give an account of Peirce's theory of signs.

Eventually a young C.I. Lewis was charged with the editorship of the Peirce papers, but he quickly found the task cumbersome and not to his taste. It seems that prior to his appointment, whatever organisation Royce and Kernan had imposed on the papers had been undone and the manuscripts simply placed in large and randomly ordered piles in the Houghton Library basement. Although contact with the papers seems to have been philosophically fruitful for him, Lewis was unable to re-organise the papers. Editorship was passed on to Charles Hartshorne and Paul Weiss, whose editorial work culminated in six volumes of the *Collected Papers of C.S. Peirce* between 1931 and 1935. In the late 1950s, this edition was completed with a further two volumes edited by Arthur Burks.

Given the size and state of the collection, organising the Peirce papers for publication was a significant achievement, and the *Collected Papers* has been of inestimable importance for Peirce scholarship. Indeed, the boom in secondary studies and the surge of interest in Peirce's work following the publication of the initial six volumes, and again with the Burks addenda, is testimony to the value of the edition. However, the editorial policy used in producing them was, in retrospect, unwise. The work was arranged thematically, and single articles were split, lecture series divided and paragraphs written thirty or forty years apart used to construct a single paper. This has the unfortunate effect of making the work seem jarring and disjointed. Sometimes, Peirce appears to change opinions over the course of a page, when what we are actually witnessing is a change of opinions over the course of thirty years. For all its worth, this makes the *Collected Papers* a problematic resource. As Nathan Houser puts it:

> As a compendium of hitherto unavailable writings of America's greatest philosopher the *Collected Papers* is invaluable, but as a dependable resource for the critical study of Peirce's thought as a whole it is notoriously inadequate. (Houser 1992, 1263)

An attempt to overcome this problem has been underway in various forms since the 1970s. The Peirce Edition Project,[10] based at Indiana University at Indianapolis and working from microfilms of the original Harvard manuscripts as well as copies of Peirce's work deposited in the National Archives, is attempting to provide a complete chronological edition. *Writings of Charles S. Peirce*, as this edition is known, currently consists of eight volumes and is projected to run to more than thirty. It includes material from the entire range of Peirce's intellectual endeavours, not merely his philosophy. When completed, the *Writings* promises to provide the best means we have of understanding Peirce's work and philosophical ideas in the context of his broader intellectual interests and writings. The task facing the Peirce Edition Project is no less difficult than that facing Hartshorne, Weiss and Burks, and it has many obstacles peculiar to it because of its scope. However, the slow and steady appearance of the *Writings* is proving to be the source of a second boom in Peirce scholarship which will no doubt ensure that, despite his fears, Peirce's genius will certainly not be lost.

Interpreting Peirce's philosophy

Interpreting Peirce's work is by no means straightforward. As we have seen, his intellectual output covered a period of around fifty years, and like those of any good philosopher, his theories developed, changed and matured across that period. Moreover, as the history of his papers shows, this output was prolific and polymathic and is still to be made easily available in its entirety. Also, as anyone already familiar with any of Peirce's work will know, he was not a clear writer and tended towards unfamiliar terminology. Indeed, by the time of his death, the years of academic isolation had concentrated his terminological willfulness. Understandably, then, there are various interpretations of his work, some of which we shall examine below, but for this book there are three key interrelated elements that we will use as a backdrop for examining Peirce's philosophy: he was a systematic philosopher; he was a scientist; he was, and saw himself as, primarily a logician.[11] Let's look at each one of these in turn.

Systematicity

Largely under the influence of Kant, one of his philosophical heroes, Peirce thought of himself as a *systematic* philosopher. He believed all of his philosophical work hung together as a systematic whole, with work in one area being connected to, informed by and informing other areas of his work. As with almost everything else, Peirce's opinions on the details changed throughout the course of his life, but two particularly useful descriptions of the shape and structure of his philosophical system come from his failed 1902 application to the Carnegie Institute and an accompanying syllabus to a Lowell lecture series from the following year. In this work, Peirce positioned his philosophy within a broader hierarchical classification of all sciences, which exist in relations of sub- and super-ordinacy to each other. Our concern here, though, is more narrowly focused on the structure of philosophy and those disciplines most directly pertinent to it.

1. MATHEMATICS

2. PHILOSOPHY

    which consists of

    a) Phenomenology
    b) Normative science

        which consists of

        i)   Aesthetics
        ii) Ethics
        iii) Logic

             which consists of

             α) Philosophical grammar
             β) Critical logic
             γ) Methodeutic

    c) Metaphysics

        i)   Ontology
        ii) Religious metaphysics
        iii) Physical metaphysics

3. PHYSICAL AND PSYCHICAL SCIENCES

Figure 1.1 The architectonic structure of philosophy

The structural relationship apparent in Figure 1.1 is important to seeing how Peirce viewed the nature of philosophy and philosophical research. Indeed, the whole architectonic of Peirce's philosophy is governed by relationships of sub- and super-ordinacy. Mathematics is super-ordinate to philosophy, which is subordinate to mathematics and super-ordinate to the physical and psychical sciences. Similar relations of super- and subordinacy exist within the branches of philosophy identified by Peirce: the normative sciences are subordinate to phenomenology but super-ordinate to metaphysics. Indeed, the same relationships exist even within these branches: ethics is subordinate to aesthetics but super-ordinate to logic, and so on.

The first thing to be clear about here is that the notion of super- and subordinacy is quite specific. A super-ordinate discipline provides general laws or principles for subordinate disciplines, which in turn provide concrete examples of those general laws. This means that the various branches and sub-branches in this structure are all topically independent – logic draws no content from ethics, for instance – but rely on super-ordinate disciplines to provide them with principles of inquiry or general rules for organising their research. To illustrate the notion of super- and subordinacy, consider a somewhat contrived example.

Let's suppose that psychology provides general principles that suggest that human beings have emotional responses to music. Leonard Meyer (1956), for example, famously suggested that an emotional response to music is no different to any emotional response and relies on expectations and desire management. Within music, we have similar expectations about which sounds will follow which sounds, and through managing these expectations a musician can manage our emotional responses to her composition. Using minor keys allows the musician to invoke sadness amongst listeners. Confounding our expectations that some chords or sounds will be resolved by another chord or sound, the musician may invoke anger or frustration or anxiety in her listeners by leaving chords unresolved and so on. Most important, though, is that this represents an instance where musical practice provides a concrete, confirming phenomena of general psychological principles about emotion and expectation. Psychology, then, is super-ordinate to music in this example, in so far as it *provides* general principles for musical practice: *emotion is expectation.* Music is subordinate in so far as it provides a concrete instance of the general rules derived from psychology: *emotional responses to music are secured by expectation management.*

When we start to think of super- and subordinacy as applied more specifically to Peirce's view of philosophy as we find it in Figure 1.1, mathematics provides general laws, which Peirce often called *guiding* or *leading principles,* for philosophy. Philosophy in turn provides concrete or confirming cases of those laws. Similar relations exist within philosophy itself and between philosophy and the empirical sciences. Indeed, the connections between the different strands of philosophy in Peirce's system are what are so important to us in our understanding of Peirce as a systematic philosopher, and in the rest of this book we will return frequently to these systematic relations. For the time being, however, we shall look briefly at one example that is especially helpful for seeing why we need to interpret Peirce as a systematic philosopher.

Peirce's cosmological metaphysics is perhaps the most interesting of his metaphysical writings, and within his system it falls generally under the rubric of physical metaphysics. We shall examine it in some detail in Chapter 6, but briefly, according to Peirce's cosmology, the universe grows from a state of nothingness or chaos to a state in which time and space exist through the emergence of habit, and from there to a state where everything is completely governed by fully determined habits and laws. The universe does this not in a mechanistic or deterministic way, but instead by tending towards habit and a law-like nature through chance and spontaneous transition. In a sense, laws, rules, order, nomological principles and so on evolve spontaneously. These ideas, often attributed to a mystical experience and crisis of faith he underwent in the 1890s, may sound hopelessly obscure, even a little mysterious, and they led some of Peirce's friends to fear for his sanity. What's more, this evolutionary cosmology has left many commentators uneasy about its relation to the rest of his work and has led to particular interpretations of Peirce's work.

For example, important early secondary studies by Thomas Goudge (1950) and W.B. Gallie (1952) claimed to see a schism between Peirce's hardheadedly scientific theories of pragmatism, truth and inquiry and this more metaphysical, even mystical, evolutionary cosmology. Goudge thought that Peirce's metaphysical work was essentially, perhaps irreconcilably, in conflict with his more scientific work and that study would be more fruitful if these two strands of Peirce's thought were kept apart. W.B. Gallie expressed similar views about these strands and famously noted the commonly held view that these elements of Peirce's metaphysics were the 'black sheep or the white elephant' of his philosophy. In many ways, this 'schismic' interpretation is understandable given the lack of availability of Peirce's papers in the early 1950s and the influence of Cohen's *Chance, Love and Logic*, which presented Peirce's papers in two distinct and contrasting groups. From that position, Peirce's cosmology would have seemed as though it came from an entirely separate line of thought to his pragmatism. What we now know is that such a view is wrong and comes from failing to realise that the work on cosmology must be viewed in light of its place in Peirce's broader systematic vision.

Viewed as part of a systemic philosophy, cosmology is meant to act as a confirming instance of a general principle which Peirce derives from the super-ordinate discipline of aesthetics, namely the *ultimate aesthetic ideal*. Peirce says very little about aesthetics, treating it as a study of what is *unconditionally admirable*, and identifies the ultimate aesthetic ideal as the growth of reason and order or, as he describes it, 'the development of concrete reasonableness' (CP5. 3 (1898)). His cosmological metaphysics, then, simply takes this aesthetic ideal, this growth of concrete reasonableness, and examines or illustrates how it is realised through the growth of habit and law in the universe at large. Peirce's cosmology looks to be a simple logical upshot of the normative sciences and logic, which show the nature and desirability of the growth of reason. So, as we can see, understanding the work on cosmology in light of the broader system helps us to a better understanding of just what Peirce is doing. In fact, as we shall see in Chapter 6, a systematic approach to the cosmological metaphysics allows us to see that it is in accord with the hardheadedly scientific approach to philosophy which Peirce employs elsewhere. There really is no schism in his views.

Hopefully, it should be clear that interpreting Peirce's work against the backdrop of his systematic view of his philosophy is an important tool in getting to grips with his work. When we look at Peirce's theories in detail in coming chapters, we will often make reference to the systematic relations between his ideas in order to gain a clearer understanding of his work.

Peirce as scientist

The second element we shall use as a backdrop for interpreting Peirce's work is his commitment to science. As our brief biographical sketch above shows, Peirce was a practicing scientist throughout much of his life. Indeed, it is hard to imagine what would have sustained him had he not been engaged in practical science. We shall touch upon his views on the methodology and progress of science in more detail in Chapter 3, but here it will suffice to say a little about how his experience and views of science manifested themselves in his philosophical work and why this aids our interpretation of his philosophy.

First and most simply, Peirce's methodology, examples and terminology all resonate with his scientific background. He frequently referred to his approach as 'laboratory philosophy', and he often adapted terminology from chemistry, mathematics and physics for philosophical purposes.[12] His best-known theory, pragmatism, centres squarely on the claim that philosophical import is measured by practical consequences, and in that respect it is unabashed in its scientific background. Further, Peirce's well-known theories of truth and inquiry look to science and scientific progress as the measure of our knowledge and grasp of the world around us. As we shall see in Chapter 3, scientific methodology is a cornerstone of his account of how purposive inquiry arrives at the truth. Indeed, so committed was Peirce to the view that science is central to philosophy that he even suggested on occasion that to understand his theories fully, we, his audience, should assume the role of scientist and seek out experiences of the phenomena of which he spoke.[13] In this respect, then, seeing Peirce as a philosopher who brings the armoury and approach of an accomplished practicing scientist to bear is essential in helping us to make sense of his individual theories and ideas. Such an approach may also settle an important interpretative issue when viewing Peirce's work as a whole.

As we have already noted, Peirce was a systematic philosopher. However, there has been some disagreement about how many systems of philosophy Peirce attempted to make, or, rather, how many times he abandoned an attempt at philosophical system building and started another. For instance, Murray Murphey (1961) suggested that Peirce made no less than four separate attempts at building a philosophical system, each of which he abandoned when various insurmountable theoretical problems emerged. Murphey's work is an influential and groundbreaking study, not least because it draws attention to important and subtle differences between early and later versions of Peirce's theories. Arguably, however, Murphey is wrong that there exist multiple systems with distinct attempts at creating accounts of, say, pragmatism or inquiry. Rather, it seems likely that Peirce simply moved between the various elements of his system, taking one theory as far as he could given what he had established within his system at that point, returning to it later when some other element had been developed enough to clear ground for progress to be made in the first area once again. To make the point a little clearer, consider the following example of scientific progress.

As early as 1904, Sir Gilbert Walker, a British meteorologist working for the Indian Meteorological Service suggested that changes in sea temperature and rainfall in South America were linked to raised air pressure in the South Pacific. Walker felt convinced that there existed some meteorological connection between droughts in India and Australia, Asian monsoons, the inexplicable depletion of fish stocks on the South American Pacific coast, and even mild Canadian winters. Sadly, Walker had limited data and he fell short of filling out the details of this conjecture. Lacking the requisite means to make accurate measurements of barometric pressure, sea temperatures and high altitude wind patterns, his conjecture was dismissed and abandoned. Some fifty years later, however, Norwegian meteorologist Jacob Bjerknes, armed with technological and theoretical advances, was able to return to Walker's early conjectural work and confirm that the connection Walker had posited did in fact exist. What Walker had identified is what we now know as the El Niño Southern Oscillation or the El Niño effect, but it was only after technology had progressed that this phenomenon could be confirmed and investigation into it advanced to the state in which it stands today. Clearly, Bjerknes did not simply abandon Walker's earlier work and start again. Rather, the early work remained, waiting for necessary advances before it could be made more precise, honed and definite. Of course, such tales are common within the annals of science.

As a practicing scientist, Peirce was familiar with developments such as these. For instance, he went to great lengths in his account of his own developments in geodetic work to show how this work refined and corrected earlier developments (CP7. 1–7.20 (1883)). Indeed, his brief retelling of the history of the kinetical theory of gases (CP7. 216 (1901)) shows awareness of just this kind of theory development. More importantly, his use of this example as an illustration of the importance of induction shows his embracing of such facts in his own philosophy and supports the claim that he is more likely to have worked within one system, making various elements clearer as and when developments supported such work, rather than abandoning earlier work and starting afresh. His views of scientific and theoretical development, then, are more in keeping with the idea that theories develop when and as far as resources and background work are able to support them. They must then wait for other developments that enable further refinement of those theories to make them more precise and 'to make the formal hypothesis represent better what was really supposed to be the case, but which had been simplified' (CP7. 216 (1901)). Given Peirce's reflectivity of his own work as a scientist, he is more likely to have viewed his work in the same vein, as something to be developed and made precise when the right supporting work has been done and the theoretical resources are in place.

Of course, this is not an outright refutation of Murphey's view that Peirce simply gave up earlier attempts and started afresh, but the view that Peirce had a single system whose elements he worked on and returned to when the conditions were right for making the underlying hypotheses clearer and more precise is more in keeping with his status as a scientist, and for such reasons it is certainly the favoured view of many current leading Peirce scholars.[14] In this book we will interpret Peirce the philosopher in light of Peirce the scientist, and for those same reasons we shall view him as having a single system which he worked on and refined, rather than as having many systems which he started afresh in light of earlier failures.

Peirce the logician

Peirce described himself as a logician, and logic was undoubtedly his major philosophical preoccupation. Apart from naming his profession as logician in the Marquis *Who's Who in America*, he also described himself there as having 'always been devoted to the theory and art of reasoning' and as having in 1887 'retired to Pike County, Pa., to devote himself completely to logic'. However, Peirce's notion of logic is much broader than our treatment of that subject today. Of course, Peirce was interested in the narrower body of work that we think of as formal and mathematical logic, and as we shall see in Chapter 5, some of his most interesting, important and long-lasting contributions are to that discipline, but his broader conception of logic also includes subjects such as knowledge, rationality, science, inference and language. In this respect, we can see that a proper description of Peirce would include 'philosophical logician', 'philosopher of language and mind', 'epistemologist' and 'philosopher of science', as well as his preferred 'logician'. But why should this matter to our interpretation of his philosophy?

Given what we know of Peirce's systematicity, we know that he saw these various areas of his broad notion of logic as connected. Indeed, in crucial ways what draws these sub-disciplines together is inquiry, the growth of knowledge and the pursuit of truth, a connection clearly influenced by his commitment to science. For

Peirce, a proper treatment of language and rationality is key to appropriately explaining measured inferences in our inquiries, all of which contribute to the growth of knowledge and rational thought and lead us steadily towards the truth. For this reason, an account of logic, as Peirce saw it, is the core of any philosophical account of human intellectual progress. Of course, as we shall see in coming chapters, just what the proper treatments of language and rationality are, or what makes some inference appropriate, or precisely what rules and standards we should employ in our pursuit of knowledge and truth, were all subject to development and clarification over the course of Peirce's philosophical life. Nonetheless, seeing Peirce as a logician is crucial to seeing what drives his philosophical work and understanding his philosophy.

A final word on interpreting Peirce's work

In the rest of this book, we shall look at a variety of Peirce's theories and ideas, dealing with a separate topic in each chapter. In the next chapter we shall look at pragmatism; in the third, truth and inquiry; in the fourth, Peirce's sign theory; in the fifth, his work on logic; and in the sixth, his account of metaphysics. This topic-by-topic treatment is certainly conducive to understanding what is interesting and distinctive about Peirce's work, but it is worth sounding a word of caution and emphasising why we have just identified three important features for interpreting Peirce's work.

A topic-by-topic approach can sometimes lead to the impression that these topics are self-contained. Of course, all that we have seen above about the interpretation of Peirce's work shows that they are not self-contained and it is not profitable to view them as such. In the coming chapters we shall look at the core elements of Peirce's theories, but we will also be especially interested in the problems those theories faced and how those theories developed over time to accommodate and overcome those difficulties. It is here that the three elements we have just introduced as background to interpreting Peirce's work will become involved. We will note frequently how Peirce's views of science and scientific progress led him to change some feature of his work. Or how developments in his views about precisely what guides our acquisition of knowledge, say, refined his views about, for instance, meaning. Or how an altered appreciation of the systematic connections between inquiry and meaning led to developments and refinements in his account of signs. Needless to say, we shall draw attention to the causes of these developments as and when we discuss them, but bearing in mind at all times that Peirce was a systematic, scientific logician (in the broad sense) can only assist us in appreciating just how deep the ideas we will encounter run.

Summary

Peirce was precocious, was raised in an intellectual environment, and his early life was one of promise. He achieved early successes in the sciences and philosophy, securing work with important scientific institutions and with Johns Hopkins University and publishing important, well-received work.

- After the mid-1880s, he lost employment and sank into increasing isolation and penury. Nonetheless, he continued to produce work and publish where he could. At his death in 1914, he left 80,000 pages of unpublished manuscripts, which were donated by his widow to Harvard.
- The history of Peirce's papers contributes to our understanding of his work since the availability of his work in its most complete and useful form is still an ongoing process.
- Interpreting Peirce's work can be difficult, but the approach in this book will be to look at core areas of his work – his pragmatism, his account of truth and inquiry, his semiotic, his logic and his metaphysics – and see how his ideas developed across his intellectual life.
- We will also use three guiding principles in examining the development of Peirce's thought: that he was a systematic philosopher, that he was for much of his life a practising scientist, and that he saw himself as a logician.

Further reading

The secondary literature on Peirce is broad, and the suggestions for further reading in this and other chapters are of necessity highly selective. However, all suggestions for further reading are representative of the best Peirce scholarship available. I have tried to limit the number of suggestions made for each chapter since one could easily suggest very many excellent works, but this would risk being daunting to those coming to Peirce for the first time. This of course means some excellent scholarship is not mentioned.

Before moving on to suggestions for further reading, I think it is worth drawing attention to a journal which has been publishing the best work on Peirce for the last fifty years. The *Transactions of the Charles S. Peirce Society* contains seminal papers and contributions in the study of Peirce's work and is essential reading for anyone interested in a proper or prolonged study of C.S. Peirce.

Although it is often controversial, Joseph Brent's *Charles Sanders Peirce: A Life* (1993) is the only full-length biography of Peirce. It provides an interesting and useful resource for understanding the context of Peirce's life and character and their influence on his work.

A detailed and insightful overview of the early history of Peirce's unpublished manuscripts and the often difficult and troubled process of creating a complete and accurate scholarly edition of his works is given in 'The fortunes and misfortunes of the Peirce papers' by Nathan Houser (1992). This account of the Peirce papers sometimes makes painful reading – for example, in its description of the treatment of Peirce's *Nachlass* at Harvard – but it also gives genuine insight into the early reception of Peirce's work and the ongoing effort of the Peirce Edition Project to produce a definitive work.

For those looking to familiarise themselves with Peirce and explore the relation between his life and his philosophy, it is also worth reading Nathan Houser's excellent introductions to the two volumes of *The Essential Peirce: Selected Philosophical Writings*. These introductions are better suited to more advanced scholars, but I would contend that they are profitable for anyone.

For anyone interested in exploring Peirce's architectonic further, Chapter 2 of Douglas Anderson's *Strands of System:The Philosophy of Charles Peirce* (1995) is a short but detailed and clear introduction.

Notes

1 *Indempotence*, or the algebraic law that xn = x (for m ≤ 2), and *nilpotence*, or the description of an algebraic element, x, such that xn = 0 (where n is a positive integer).

2 A perfect number is a number which equals the sum of its distinct proper divisors.

3 It seems that Peirce was very good at this and detected a critical flaw in pendulum designs which could lead to a serious undermining of geodetic results. The redesigned pendulum built to eradicate this flaw bears his name, the Peirce Pendulum.

4 Unbeknownst to Eliot, Peirce had a pre-standing agreement with the director of the observatory, Joseph Winlock, about the time scale for the *Photometric Researches*. Sadly, just prior to these tensions between Peirce and Eliot, Winlock died. Peirce, however, never informed Eliot of this arrangement, thus allowing the tensions and misunderstandings to continue.

5 There is no evidence for any of this, but even a recent historical novel, *The Queen of Cups* by Mina Samuels, takes her as its heroine and expands widely and wildly upon these myths.

6 From the Harvard University C.S. Peirce papers, quoted in Brent (1998, 145).

7 The usual men of letters, William James and Josiah Royce, supported the application, but Andrew Carnegie and President Theodore Roosevelt also expressed support for Peirce's claim on funds.

8 Shortly before his death, Peirce drew an informative parallel between himself and the hero of Georges Ohnet's *Le Grande Marnière* – the wasteful, egotistical, daydreaming Honoré de Clairefont – whom he described as 'C.S.P. to a dot'.

9 It seems that, contrary to Juliette's wishes upon donation, the library was merely integrated into the main Harvard collections without anything to distinguish Peirce's books from any others. According to Nathan Houser (1992), although they refused Juliette's wish of a separate Peirce collection, Harvard did promise to paste a name plate in his donated books.

10 A group of important Peirce scholars which includes (or has included) Max Fisch, Edward Moore, Nathan Houser, Andre de Tienne and Cornelis de Waal, amongst others.

11 It is an often cited fact that Peirce is the first person to enter his profession as 'logician' in *Who's Who*.
12 For example, in his accounts of semiotics, when looking to mark a distinction between indexical signs which rely on causal connections with whatever they represent and indexicals which rely merely on convention, Peirce calls the former 'reagents', a term borrowed straight from chemistry.
13 For instance, when discussing his phenomenological categories, firstness, secondness and thirdness, Peirce gave just this advice.
14 For example, Hookway (1985, 2000), Houser (1992), Kent (1987) and Anderson (1995).

Two
Pragmatism

Introduction

If people know anything about Peirce, it is usually expressed in some platitudinous observation about his relation to the pragmatist movement – he was its inventor, or founding father. It is true that pragmatism, in some sense at least, begins with Peirce, but the birth and blossoming of the movement is more complex, and Peirce's version of the pragmatic method far richer and more interesting than such simple platitudes can capture. Pragmatism is a very broad church, but it is roughly characterised by an interest in practical consequences, real experiences, actions and so on. Whilst his work shows a genuine concern for these issues, the question of Peirce's pragmatist credentials has rather polarised opinion amongst contemporary card-carrying pragmatists. Some, like Richard Rorty, think Peirce a marginal figure whose 'contribution to pragmatism was merely to have given it a name, and to have stimulated [William] James' (Rorty 1982, 161).[1] Others, Nicholas Rescher for instance, see Peirce as the pragmatist visionary and much that bears the name 'pragmatism' as 'an ill-advised departure from the original Peircian concern' (Rescher 1997, 47). The question of Peirce's place at the heart or foundation of the tradition, then, is fraught. So much for platitudes.

Despite questions about whether Peirce really is the founding father contemporary pragmatists desire, or whether pragmatism is the legacy Peirce would want, what cannot be doubted is that Peirce exerted an important influence over his friend, contemporary and indubitable founding father of pragmatism, William James. James, who was responsible for the rise to philosophical prominence of pragmatism in the early part of the twentieth century, famously attributed the movement's central philosophical tenet – the pragmatist principle – to Peirce. What James was referring to was a methodological principle that Peirce proposed in his 1878 paper 'How to make our ideas clear'. That principle, which later became known as the *pragmatic maxim*, was the source of the central pragmatist insight that we can judge the meaning and importance of concepts by the differences they make to our experiences or lives. How that insight is explored and developed varies from one pragmatist to another, but given that Peirce's pragmatic maxim is arguably the source of that insight, its importance is clear. Consequently, we shall spend much of this chapter examining in some detail Peirce's maxim as we find it in 'How to make our ideas clear'.

A further interesting relation between Peirce and James is that the pragmatism that James developed on the basis of Peirce's maxim was, in many ways, something that Peirce did not think of kindly. From Peirce's point of view, he developed a heuristic principle for clarifying the meanings of concepts as part of a series of papers on science and logic in the 1870s. This principle then re-emerged some twenty or so years later in the work of William James and found its way into a broader, increasingly influential philosophical programme. As we shall see, Peirce was not entirely at ease with what his heuristic principle had become in the hands of James, and it was with a renewed sense of vigour that, at the turn of the twentieth century, he set about refining his own views and ensuring that his relation to the better-known theories of his pragmatist contemporaries was clear. So, as well as examining the maxim as we find it in Peirce's early work, we shall also spend some time examining the later developments that he made. As we shall see, the differences are profound.

In the remainder of this chapter, then, we shall look in some detail at Peirce's early influential pragmatic maxim and draw out its role as an account of meaning and a tool for clarifying concepts. We shall also spend some time discussing the often-made comparison between the pragmatic maxim and the verificationist criterion of meaning. We shall then turn to the details behind Peirce's later development of the maxim in light of his need to differentiate his own views from those of his fellow pragmatists and to handle certain deficiencies that he perceived in his earlier account.

The early account of pragmatism

Peirce's first important contribution to pragmatism comes from his 1878 paper 'How to make our ideas clear'. This paper forms part of an important series of five papers that are collectively known as *Illustrations of the Logic of Science*, and in it Peirce outlines what he takes to be the means for ensuring we have the fullest, most comprehensive understanding of any concept we employ. The means of attaining what Peirce calls the 'highest grade of clarity' require that we take the following into account:

> Consider what effects, which might conceivably have practical bearings, we conceive the object of our conception to have. Then, our conception of these effects is the whole of our conception of the object. (EP1. 132 (1878))

This became known as the pragmatic maxim, and it is the principle that William James identified as the source of his own pragmatism. Indeed, the maxim as it is expressed here is important not only for its influence on William James but also because it remains something like the canonical statement of the principle, even for Peirce when he returns to re-examine and refine his pragmatism in later life. However, it is unclear just what Peirce's pragmatism is supposed to mean thus far or quite what its deeper implications are, and more detail is certainly required. There are two ways in which we can get clearer about the pragmatic maxim: first, by looking at the maxim as a response to and development of rationalist notions of clear and distinct ideas, and second, by attending to the philosophical role and purpose that Peirce intends for his maxim.

The pragmatic maxim: clear and distinct ideas

Recall that Peirce describes his maxim as the highest grade of under-standing or apprehension of a concept. An important element in understanding Peirce's maxim is seeing just why he does this. To this purpose, we need to look to an earlier series of papers pub-lished in the *Journal of Speculative Philosophy* in the late 1860s,[2] since the rudiments of the 1878 pragmatic maxim emerge from these articles.

A predominant theme in the *Journal of Speculative Philosophy* papers is an anti-Cartesian account of thought and cognition, and it is this anti-Cartesianism that proves to be important here. In particular, Peirce makes four key claims designed to contrast with the ortho-dox Cartesian idea that some introspective method (the method of doubt) can provide us with a self-evident foundation (the *cogito*) for our knowledge (EP1. 30 (1868)). First, Peirce argues that we have no powers of introspection; our access to the life of the mind is not somehow special, privileged or insulated from our understanding of the world (EP1. 22–23 (1868)). Second, he claims that we have no intuitive knowledge; there is no basic, somehow self-evident, knowledge that we are simply given *ex nihilo* (EP1. 11–18 (1868)). Third, he claims that all thought is in signs. Much here rests on Peirce's notion of what a sign is, but the important claim is that signs are essentially external to minds and inferential, so this claim is a simple corollary of the denial of introspection and intuition (EP1. 23–24 (1868)). Finally, Peirce argues that there are no incognisa-bles; the way the world is cannot outstrip our ability to know it (EP1. 24–25 (1868)). These early anti-Cartesian sentiments re-surface in many other areas of Peirce's work, and we shall draw attention to them when they do, but what we are interested in here is how this earlier work leads to and emerges in Peirce's pragmatic maxim.

Returning to 'How to make our ideas clear', Peirce takes up the earlier anti-Cartesian strain in his philosophy by questioning the adequacy of what he thinks of as a rationalist criterion of meaning and apprehension, the notion of *clear and distinct ideas* (EP1. 124–126 (1878)). According to Peirce, rationalists, and in particular Descartes, recognise two modes of apprehending some concept or thing. The first of these is *clearness*.

To apprehend something *clearly* is simply to have an immediate unreflective apprehension of it (EP1. 124 (1878)). Peirce takes the idea of clearness to mean something like having such familiarity with a concept that we show no hesitancy in applying it. For example, we are all familiar enough with the concept 'solid' that we open doors rather than attempting to walk through them closed. Of course, a simple lack of hesitancy in applying a concept does not mean we have a full understanding of it. The unreflective clarity displayed in *clear apprehension* in no way suggests or even requires any deeper reflective clarity. I might show a considerable lack of hesitancy in observing or recognising solid things, but I may be at a total loss when it comes to explaining what, if anything, I take 'solid' to mean. Instead, the rationalist proposes an additional mode of apprehending a concept, *distinctness.*

To apprehend something *distinctly* is to understand it so no element of it is unclear to us. Peirce characterises this mode in terms of our being able to 'give a precise definition of it, in abstract terms' (EP1. 125 (1878)). For example, by being able to define 'solid' as 'unyielding and resistant to deformation or penetration', we display a deeper grasp of the concept than our mere unreflective tendencies to apply the concept suggested. For the rationalist, this is all there is to understanding some concept – unreflective, unhesitating application (clearness) and the ability to provide a definition of the concept (distinctness). For Peirce, however, this is inadequate, and a third grade of understanding is required. It is here that Peirce proposes the pragmatic maxim quoted above, which requires us to look to the 'effects' and 'practical bearings' of some concept in order to fully apprehend it.

The pragmatic maxim is, in fact, far deeper and richer than this simple rendering may suggest, and we shall examine its finer details shortly, but it is worth pausing to address two questions: why does Peirce take clearness and distinctness to be insufficient, and why does he think we require the pragmatic maxim with its focus on effects and practical bearings in order to have a full understanding?

First of all, the insufficiency of clearness is already apparent, even to the rationalist. Unreflective clarity requires nothing deeper of us, and given that all it requires is a lack of hesitation, it does not even seem to ask that our application of some concept be correct. The insufficiency of distinctness, though, is that it seems to allow for the possibility of our providing a precise definition of some concept yet remaining ignorant of where, when and, more importantly, if that concept applies to anything. Indeed, this is no abstract worry. Examples of definitions under which nothing falls are plentiful: place-holder definitions such as Le Verrier's description of Vulcan, mythical creatures, and definitions of 'absurd' objects such as the squared-circle. For Peirce, such possibilities run dangerously close to the worry he expressed in his earlier papers about incognisables – that nothing of their sort occurs in experience – but with the added and more important worry that nothing in a mere definition allows us to see that this is so. Indeed, matters are worse; by taking distinctness as the highest grade of apprehension, we are not even compelled to go further and ask whether the concept we have defined exists. Having a definition to hand is enough.

For Peirce, then, 'the doctrine of clearness and distinctness [. . .] may be pretty enough, but it is high time to relegate to our cabinet of curiosities the antique bijou, and to wear about us something more adapted to modern uses' (EP1. 126 (1878)). But why does he propose the pragmatic maxim? Why the focus on effects and practical bearings?

There are two related reasons. First, it is obvious that the insufficiency of distinctness comes from the failure to see how our definitions apply in the real world (EP1. 126 (1878)). For Peirce, this is to miss something important. Unless we know how some concept will feature in our experiences, what its practical consequences are, we simply do not have a full or complete apprehension of the concept in question.

Second, and relatedly, looking to practical bearings is precisely the kind of response that Peirce's anti-Cartesianism calls for. As Cartesian mainstays, clearness and distinctness provide space for the kind of introspective and intuitive knowledge to which Peirce's earlier work is so resistant. Take Descartes' cogito, for instance. I quite unreflectively grasp, and unhesitatingly act in accord with, the idea that I am a sentient and existing being. Further, definitions of the terms involved for 'thinking' and 'existing' mean that the argument turns out to be analytic.[3] Of more importance, though, is that Peirce's objection to this kind of Cartesian argument is that it ignores what he takes to be a fundamental scholastic insight: we study the mind by studying the body.

For Peirce, Descartes ignores the connection between the human mind and the external world. Consequently, self-evident introspective knowledge, such as the cogito, is gained only by illegitimately limiting ourselves to clear and distinct apprehension and by ignoring the external world and our experiences of it. Obviously, then, if we are to correct the Cartesian error we must re-instate our scholastic commitment to examining the physical universe and the effects and bearings our concepts have within it. This is precisely what the pragmatic maxim is supposed to do.[4]

The purpose of the maxim

Whilst the maxim as a development of clear and distinct ideas may seem straightforward enough, it can also seem like a rather esoteric, even parochial, concern. Descartes and Leibniz advanced these ideas, but as interpreted by Peirce, their ideas are deficient. But really, why does any of this matter? Why does a rather simple, even obvious, addendum to rationalist notions of understanding manage to exert such an influence over James and other pragmatists? The answer may well seem opaque given the simple statement of the maxim we have so far. However, attending to just why Peirce thought his maxim was needed and the valuable philosophical work he thought he could do with it is instructive and helps us to see the real import of this simple methodological principle. Here we shall focus on two connected features of the pragmatic maxim that Peirce thought made it such an important development: the maxim as an account of meaning and the maxim as tool of inquiry.

The pragmatic maxim and pragmatic meaning

Peirce saw the maxim as providing what we might think of as a pragmatic account of meaning. Attaining the highest grade of clarity or level of apprehension about some concept is to have a full grasp of its meaning. To see this, let us look at one of Peirce's better-known examples, the concept 'hard'. Peirce asks what we mean by calling something hard. His suggestion is that by calling something hard we mean that we will be unable to scratch it with very many substances. Now, what Peirce is driving at with this suggestion is that for any such concept we will be able to suggest a number of experiences which we will encounter in any worldly interaction with any object which exemplifies it. We find that hard things don't scratch easily, are often impermeable, aren't easily punctured and so forth, and when we describe something as hard, these are exactly the things which we are claiming we will experience when we interact with that object. These experiences, for Peirce, exhaust the meaning of the concept.

Although there is nothing explicit in 'How to make our ideas clear', many Peirce scholars suggest that these experiences take the form of a list of indicative conditional statements that exhaust the experiential outcome of any interactions we have with objects falling under the concept which the list of conditionals clarify.[5] To remain with Peirce's example of 'hard', we might end up with a clarificatory list of conditionals that includes, amongst others, *If X is hard, then X will not be scratched by many substances; If X is hard, then X will not be easily punctured; If X is hard, then X will likely be impermeable;* and so on. This list of conditional statements exhausts the meaning of a concept.

As an account of meaning, the maxim, or at least what emerges from Peirce's illustrations of it, is very interesting, not least because it shows remarkable similarities to the verificationist criterion of meaning that emerged from the work of the Vienna positivists and was made famous by Carnap, Schlick and Ayer (amongst others). We shall look at this connection shortly, but there is another aspect of this pragmatic account of meaning that we must examine first since it is more pertinent to our current task, that is, identifying just what Peirce saw the power and import of the maxim to be.

The first thing we should note about the pragmatic account of meaning that emerges from Peirce's maxim is that it is quite strictly empirical and nominalistic. What we mean by this is that Peirce wishes to limit the kinds of experience and effects that count as clarifying a concept to *actual* occurring experiences and effects. To make the point clearer, we should note that, in compiling our lists of clarificatory conditionals, there are three types of conditionals that we might be inclined to use: indicative conditionals of the form *If X is* φ*, then X will behave* Ψ *ly;* subjunctive conditionals of the form *If X were* φ*, then X would behave* Ψ *ly;* and counterfactual conditionals of the form *If X had been* φ*, then X would have behaved* Ψ *ly.* At first blush, there seems to be no obvious reason why all three of these conditional types could not form part of the clarificatory lists which exhaust the meaning of some concept. For example, we might think the following three sentences all count as clarificatory of the concept 'British Monarch' in some sense:

1   If Elizabeth II is *British Monarch*, then she is also Defender of the Faith.
2   If Prince Charles were to become *British Monarch*, he would also be Head of the Armed Forces.
3   If Princess Margaret had been *British Monarch*, she would have also been Head of State.

In combination, these three sentences seem to tell us that the British Monarch is also head of the church, defence forces and government, respectively. And, of course, they tell us this in different ways. Sentence 1 tells us what is the case and uses an indicative conditional; Sentence 2 tells us what might be the case should certain circumstances obtain and uses a subjunctive conditional; and Sentence 3 tells what would have been the case had things been different and thus uses a counterfactual conditional. For Peirce, however, only indicative conditionals, such as in Sentence 1, can play any part in the pragmatic clarification of a concept.

We know that Peirce is resistant to subjunctive and counterfactual conditionals forming part of the pragmatic meaning of a concept because, in 'How to make our ideas clear', he quite explicitly rejects the idea that subjunctive and counterfactual circumstances are at all pertinent to our understanding of some concept. For example, in his discussion of 'hardness' he asks us to imagine the following case:

Suppose, then, that a diamond could be crystallized in the midst of a cushion of soft cotton, and should remain there until it was finally burned up. Would it be false to say that that diamond was soft? [. . .] [Or we might] ask what prevents us from saying that all hard bodies remain perfectly soft until they are touched, when their hardness increases with the pressure until they are scratched. [. . .] This leads us to remark that the question of what would occur under circumstances which do not actually arise is not a question of fact, but only of the most perspicuous arrangement of them. (EP1. 132 (1878))

So, Peirce is resistant to the idea that anything but *actual effects* should count towards meaning. A diamond, or any hard thing which we never test for scratchability, permeability and so on, either because we never bother to or because the object is no longer available to us for such testing, cannot contribute to the meaning of 'hard'. Only those hard bodies which we have somehow brought to the test can count. Whilst this may seem like a simple rejection of certain kinds of evidence and a resistance to certain ways of framing clarificatory conditionals, what it amounts to is that Peirce's pragmatic view is, as we suggested, very strictly and literally empirical and quite clearly rejects *possible* experiences in an account of meaning. Peirce is, in simplistic terms, nominalistic about possibility; subjunctive and counterfactual circumstances cannot contribute to pragmatic meaning because the effects or experiences that such circumstances describe are *not facts*. As we shall see, Peirce was to change his opinion about this later, but in its early form the pragmatic maxim, as an account of meaning, does not count possible experiences as real experiences and thus excludes them from making any contribution to a concept's meaning.

The second thing to note about the pragmatic account of meaning that emerges from the maxim is that, as we might well expect, it focuses on the practices of language users. We can see this in a couple of respects. On the one hand, it treats *understanding* as central to meaning, and on the other, it focuses on the *use* to which language users put these concepts. We already know that the maxim is a development of rationalist notions of understanding, but the focus on understanding is made even more apparent by the idea that our understanding of the experiential upshots of taking some concept to be true exhausts the meaning of that concept; or, as Peirce puts it, 'that our conception of these effects is the whole of our conception of the object' (EP1. 132 (1878)). Such a view of meaning is not uncommon, and in many respects Peirce's emphasis upon understanding is prescient of some rather interesting and influential views on meaning. For instance, Michael Dummett thinks that providing a theory of meaning involves providing an account of understanding; a meaning-theory is an account of speaker knowledge, and speaker knowledge is described in terms of how speakers manifest their knowledge or understanding. Peirce's views suggest a very similar thing in some sense; meaning is an account of language users' understanding of the practical consequences of taking some concept to be true.[6]

The use element of the pragmatic account of meaning we find in Peirce's maxim should also be unsurprising. If we look to his illustrations of the maxim, we find him asking what we mean by calling something 'hard' or what we are really saying when we call something 'heavy', and from these questions we raise lists of clarifying conditionals which frame our experiential expectations. Clearly, what Peirce has in mind here is that we come to the meaning of a concept such as 'hard' by applying it to objects, like diamonds, and asking if such objects exemplify it. Again, this is an obvious outcome of Peirce's introduction of the pragmatic maxim as the development of lower grades of meaning. We can define 'hard', but only when we start using the concept in our interactions with worldly objects can we be said to truly understand the concept and its meaning.

The pragmatic maxim as a tool of inquiry

Aside from being the basis for a pragmatic account of meaning, Peirce also sees the maxim as a tool for fruitful philosophical inquiry. We shall examine Peirce's views on inquiry as part of the next chapter, but here we shall illustrate Peirce's conception of the maxim as a tool of inquiry by, again, turning to his illustrations and examples of the maxim in action. First of all, Peirce sees that in our scientific inquiries we often employ various concepts, but we are not always entirely clear about those concepts. The pragmatic maxim is a tool that allows us to make these concepts clearer. As an extended example, Peirce discusses the concept of 'force' as a unifying or underlying concept for such notions as 'acceleration', 'velocity' and 'gravity'. He is critical of scientists who suggest that, whilst we can see the effects of forces, the concept of 'force' is itself mysterious,[7] and he instead asks what use we might have for thinking about such a concept. His answer is that we use 'force' in order to account for changes in the states of motion of bodies and that 'whoever will take the trouble clearly to apprehend [this] [. . .] perfectly comprehends what force is' (EP1. 136 (1878)). For Peirce, once we have grasped what we use the concept 'force' to *do*, it does not matter what we think force *is*. Thus, descriptions of force itself are irrelevant, and by looking at practical effects we have a clearer idea about the concept we use. As a clarificatory tool, then, the pragmatic maxim allows us to make the concepts of our scientific inquiries precise by making clear just what the concepts we are talking about mean.

A second use for the maxim as a tool of inquiry is to show where certain disputes are merely illusory. Peirce's discussion of the notion of transubstantiation – the idea that the bread and wine of the Holy Sacraments are the body and blood of Christ – is useful here. The Holy Sacraments in the Catholic Church are taken, quite literally, to be the body and blood of Christ; the characteristics of the sacraments remain indistinguishable in appearance from bread and wine, but nonetheless they are the flesh and blood of Christ. Post-Reformation Protestant churches, on the other hand, tend to treat the Holy Sacraments as being only metaphorically the body and blood of Christ. Now, in what do the differences between these two approaches to the sacrament consist? Despite differences in the way both denominations describe their sacraments, is there really any practical difference between the two?

From the Protestant position, taking the sacrament will mean drinking a substance with all the sensible qualities of wine and eating a substance with all the sensible qualities of bread. From the Catholic position, the same thing holds – the body and blood of Christ retain all the 'accidental' qualities of bread and wine. In terms of the pragmatic maxim, then, Catholics and Protestants would compile the same list of conditional expectations about the objects of their sacraments and, when understood in their clearest terms, would employ the same concepts of transubstantiation. There are no practical differences between them, so there are no differences at all. As Peirce puts it:

> It is foolish for Catholics and Protestants to fancy themselves in disagreement about the elements of the sacrament, if they agree in regard to all their sensible effects, here or hereafter. (EP1. 132 (1878))

Once we have a pragmatic clarification to hand, we can see that the debate is empty. For Peirce, this lesson is transferable to philosophy, and clarity about the pragmatic meanings of the concepts involved in any debate will allow us to see whether some philosophical dispute is actually substantive or merely reveals a difference in how we choose to speak of the same phenomenon.

Related to this example is what we might think of as the third feature of the maxim as a tool of inquiry: namely, it allows us to see when some concept is empty or without meaning. Clearly, the reason why the debate about the sacraments is illusory, according to Peirce, is because the Catholic concept of transubstantiation is pragmatically empty, but this type of analysis is useful for looking at other concepts too. If some concept has no experiential consequences, or 'effects', then we should be suspicious of it and ultimately reject it as a contributor to, or object of, worthwhile inquiry. For Peirce, this means that we should reject a whole raft of propositions that make up what he calls 'ontological metaphysics' – the kind of philosophical endeavour that treats the essential or true characters of things as being transcendental or beyond experience and direct observation. Similarly, a great deal of ethics appears to be philosophically unfruitful since it is difficult to see what distinctive pragmatic clarifications there could be for our normative ethical judgments. If we ask, as we did for 'force', what we mean by calling a set of actions morally permissible or impermissible, it is not clear that we can formulate a set of conditionals which frame obvious experiential or observational outcomes.[8] Consequently, ethics, like metaphysics, looks as though it will not make for fruitful philosophical inquiry. Many, if not most, of its concepts have no experiential effects and so are pragmatically meaningless.

By treating the maxim as a tool of inquiry, then, it looks as though clarifying concepts would reveal many of them to be pragmatically empty, and it would mark much of metaphysics, ethics and so forth as unsuitable for fruitful philosophical pursuit. As it happens, matters are not quite so clear, and Peirce is not so resistant to the view that some kind of metaphysics should form part of our philosophical concerns or that there is nothing important or useful to say about ethics and aesthetics. Indeed, as we saw in the previous chapter, ethics and aesthetics become central to Peirce's more mature view of philosophy. However, given the emphasis upon experience and 'sensible effects' that we find in the early statements of the pragmatic maxim, it should be obvious why the pragmatic maxim as a tool for identifying worthwhile inquiry would seem to rule out much of mainstream traditional philosophy.

The pragmatic maxim and verificationism

Earlier we mentioned that there is a perceived and frequently asserted connection between Peirce's maxim and the verificationist account of meaning and approach to philosophy. Given what we've just said about Peirce's maxim as an account of meaning and tool of inquiry, it seems appropriate to comment upon this connection in a little more detail, especially since it helps us to a deeper understanding of Peirce's early statement of pragmatism.

There are various reasons for thinking that the maxim's pragmatic account of meaning and the view of philosophy that it gives rise to is a close cousin of verificationism. The first reason is that many of the central and well-known figures of the logical empiricist movement see Peirce's maxim as progenitor to the insights that their own philosophical approach offers. For example, Herbert Feigl, in his survey paper 'Logical empiricism', describes the movement's criterion of meaning with specific reference to Peirce's early statement of the maxim:

> If we possibly conceive of what would have to be the case in order to confirm or disconfirm an assertion, we would not be able to distinguish between its truth and falsity. [. . .] C.S. Peirce's pragmatic maxim, formulated in his epoch-making essay, 'How to Make Our Ideas Clear', has essentially the same import. We may paraphrase it crudely: a difference that is to be a difference (i.e. more than merely a verbal or an emotive one) must make a difference. (Feigl 1949, 9)

Similarly, A.J. Ayer, probably the best-known verificationist, in his 1968 introduction to pragmatism describes Peirce's account of meaning as 'closely akin' to the logical empiricist position and asserts that the 'pragmatic maxim is indeed identical, for all practical purposes, with the physicalist interpretation of the verification principle' (Ayer 1968, 55). Of course, most of the canonical statements of logical empiricism predate any real awareness of Peirce's pragmatism,[9] and the identification of the pragmatic maxim as an affiliate of the verification principle is largely *post hoc*. Importantly, though, it is a *post hoc* ascription of affiliation by adherents of logical empiricism and those most sympathetic to verificationism.

Secondly, both the pragmatic maxim and verification principles look to observation and experiential effects in order to ground the accounts of meaning to which they give rise. The pragmatic maxim, as we have seen, asks us to consider the experiential effects that come from treating some object as falling within a concept. The standard reading of the verificationist view of meaning is that a statement is meaningful/meaningless if that statement is conclusively verifiable/falsifiable, where verifiability/falsifiability depends on there being a set of observation sentences that logically entail the statement or its negation. Of course, observation sentences or statements are simple sentences or statements about an object that are framed in terms of experiential or observable effects. 'This diamond is hard', for example, is an observation sentence. Clearly, then, the verificationist principle and the pragmatic maxim look to empirical, observable data to ground the meaningfulness of language. In that respect, it is unsurprising that the two should seem to be affiliates.

Third, both verificationism and the pragmatic maxim are what we might call 'scientistic'; both form part of an attempt to apply science and scientific processes to philosophical ends. Verificationists, for instance, make frequent reference to 'scientific inquiry', 'scientific methodology' or 'scientific standards of testing'. Indeed, in many respects, verificationists see themselves as continuing an Einsteinian turn in science, best captured by the operationalism of P.W. Bridgman,[10] by applying it to philosophical questions in the hope that philosophy might somehow be reinvigorated and shake off old dogmas. For example, Moritz Schlick describes his project thusly:

> The most famous case of an explicit formulation of our criterion is Einstein's answer to the question, What do we mean when we speak of two events at distant places happening simultaneously? This answer consisted in a description of an experimental method by which the simultaneity of such events was actually ascertained. Einstein's philosophical opponents maintained [. . .] that they knew the meaning of the above question independently of any method of verification. All I am trying to do is to stick consistently to Einstein's position. (Schlick 1936, 342–343)

Similarly, Peirce explains the power and import of his maxim by reference to scientific concepts such as 'weight' or 'force' before suggesting that using the maxim to philosophical ends will help usher philosophy out of its preoccupation with Cartesian dogma and towards an appreciation of the advances a scientific approach can reward us with:

> How to give birth to those vital and procreative ideas which multiply into a thousand forms and diffuse themselves everywhere,

advancing civilization and making the dignity of man, is an art not yet reduced to rules, but of the secret of which the history of science affords some hints. (EP1. 141 (1878))

For Peirce, then, it is clear that the pragmatic maxim forms part of his notion of science and scientific progress. Of course, as we suggested in the last chapter, Peirce was primarily a man of science who viewed philosophy as an extension of scientific inquiry. It is unsurprising then that his pragmatic maxim and the view of philosophy to which it gives rise should be so intimately connected to his view of science.

Finally, and related to the 'scientism' apparent in both views, similarity is seen in the proposed domain of legitimate philosophical inquiry that seems to arise from the pragmatic maxim and the verificationist principle. As we noted above when looking at the maxim employed as a tool of inquiry, metaphysics and ethics seem not to fall within the purview of legitimate philosophy, or at the very least not to admit of the kind of pragmatic clarifications that would make them appropriately meaningful. The only kind of philosophical questions worth pursuing, or indeed that can be pursued in a manner which will yield true conclusions, are those whose concepts can be made meaningful in accord with the pragmatic maxim and its requirements of experiential effects. Similar constraints hold for verificationist views. Consider, for example, A.J. Ayer's discussion of the concept of 'the soul' in questions of the self or personal identity:

> [I]t is self-contradictory to speak of a man as surviving the annihilation of his body. For that which is supposed to survive [. . .] is not the empirical self, but a metaphysical entity – the soul. And this metaphysical entity, concerning which no genuine hypothesis can be formulated, has no logical connection whatsoever with the self. (Ayer 1936, 198)

We cannot find or formulate any set of observation sentences about the soul; it is, in Ayer's words, a 'metaphysical entity'. Consequently, our philosophical inquiry into the self should eschew as empty or meaningless, and thus not philosophically legitimate, talk of the soul. Of course, this represents the general verificationist attitude towards metaphysics, ethics, aesthetics and many areas of traditional philosophy: there can be no set of observation sentences that conclusively entails the truth or falsity of the statements these domains employ, so their statements are unverifiable and thus meaningless.

Given the four factors that we've just mentioned, it is totally unsurprising that many should see such parallels and similarities between the pragmatic maxim and verificationism. Indeed, Peirce's early statement of the maxim in 'How to make our ideas clear' is quite clearly of a positivistic stripe, and examining the parallels with verificationism is definitely instructive. However, we must be cautious about drawing too strong a conclusion from this and reading more into the parallels than we should. For instance, some see the connections to be so close that problems which mark the decline and fall of logical empiricist accounts of meaning are problems that, by extension, also affect the pragmatic maxim. To give an example, Israel Scheffler's introduction to the classical pragmatists, *Four pragmatists*, contains the following comment:

> Peirce's idea [the pragmatic maxim] was certainly a pioneering conception, but it has not survived the process of logical clarification and intensive examination of the past several decades. This process has revealed critical weaknesses both in positivistic meaning criteria and in the concept of operational definition. (Scheffler 1974, 80)

To paraphrase, the demise of verificationism is the demise of the pragmatic maxim. But it is precisely because of this kind of assumption that a word of caution about the strength of the affiliation is due.

The parallels between the maxim and verificationism are apparent, but in a very important sense they result from our filling in the gaps in Peirce's maxim. Yes, the reliance on experience is there, the scientific background is there, the antipathy towards 'empty' metaphysics is there, but the pragmatic maxim, as we find it in 'How to make our ideas clear', is in very many ways under-explained and underdeveloped. First of all, the maxim, if we look at it more closely, contains two components, only one of which supports our drawing strong parallels with verificationism. The first of these components is the mention of effects, and it is this that really prompts the affiliation with verificationism, especially since, in his examples and illustrations, Peirce talks of 'sensible effects' and 'what affects the senses'. But the maxim also makes mention of 'practical bearings'. These two components of the maxim, the verificationist component and the practical component,[11] are important because it appears from the way the maxim is expressed that the latter should in some way modify or qualify the former. Yet Peirce says very little about the practical component in 'How to make our ideas clear' and his early discussions of the maxim, but what Peirce thinks of as practical bearings will naturally greatly influence just how sensible effects and experiences constitute the meanings of philosophical concepts. If we lack an understanding of what Peirce has in mind when he speaks of practical bearings, we seem to lack a full understanding of exactly which effects the maxim is asking us to consider. In the current discussion of how far we should take the parallels between Peirce's pragmatic maxim and the verificationist criterion of meaning, this matters for the following two reasons.

First, unless we understand what effects we are being asked to consider, we cannot really judge just how severe Peirce's stripe of meaning-positivism is. To illustrate, think again of Ayer's comments on the self and the soul; there are no observation sentences or experiences that we can have concerning the soul or of the self separate from the body. But Ayer's fellow logical empiricist, Moritz Schlick, sees matters differently:

> I think we may agree with Professor [C.I.] Lewis when he says about this hypothesis [that the self may survive after death]: 'Our understanding of what would verify it has no lack of clarity'. In fact, I can easily imagine e.g. witnessing the funeral of my own body and continuing to exist without a body [. . .]. We must conclude that [this hypothesis] should not be regarded as a metaphysical problem, but as an empirical problem because it

possesses logical verifiability. It could be verified by the following prescription: 'Wait until you die!' (Schlick 1936, 356)

It seems, then, that what you are inclined to count as experience, what you're prepared to admit as an 'effect', will rather influence what you are prepared to count as legitimate philosophy. Schlick's notion of verifiable experience looks more accommodating than Ayer's here, and a question that Ayer seems to put off as metaphysical Schlick is prepared to address as legitimate. Some approaches to verification seem stricter than others, and this should of course be a lesson we apply to Peirce. Peirce's maxim could be rather strict about experience or rather liberal, but we have little idea just how strict Peirce's views are from the reading of the pragmatic maxim as it is stated in 'How to make our ideas clear'. We know that Peirce wants no truck with metaphysical extravagances, but as we can see from Schlick's comment above, what counts as 'metaphysics' depends on what counts as 'experience'. More importantly, without some elaboration on practical bearings we cannot know for sure just what Peirce counts as experience, and so we cannot be sure if his pragmatic maxim mirrors the verificationist delineation of legitimate and non-legitimate philosophy that many attribute to it. We should be cautious, then, about how strongly we assert the parallels between Peirce and verificationists.

We might object that being unsure about how Peirce views practical bearings in his early statement of the maxim – and thus being unsure how broad his view of experience is – in no way excuses him from the verificationist fold or the arguments which effect its demise. Whether Peirce's view of experience is broad or narrow, it is still put to the service of what is essentially a positivistic account of meaning. However, this brings us to the second reason why we need to be cautious about the attribution of affiliation between the maxim and verificationism: Peirce's account may well look like meaning-positivism regardless of his account of experience, but it is still too quick a move to think that the arguments that count against verificationism automatically apply to the maxim. Again, the lack of clarity we have about practical bearings seems to be important here. To illustrate, consider one of the problems of many of the stronger verificationist accounts of meaning, universal generalisation.

The problem for verificationism is that universal generalisations are not, or cannot be, conclusively verified. How could we construct a conclusive set of observation sentences for a sentence such as (i) below?

(i)   All bodies will fall unless they are supported.

That such a sentence would seem to require a potentially infinite set of observation sentences seems problematic. Without such a set of sentences, (i) cannot be verified or falsified and is thus meaningless,[12] but providing an infinite set is impossible.

Does this same concern manage to undermine the pragmatic maxim too? It is actually difficult to say. Sentences such as (i) will certainly be a part of Peirce's concern since such generalisations look like scientific laws. Indeed, (i) sounds similar to the kind of thing Peirce takes us to mean when we call something 'heavy' or when we give the meaning of 'weight'. And it may be that the list of conditionals required to give this sentence pragmatic meaning, like the set of observation sentences, is potentially infinite. But it is not clear just what Peirce requires of the list of clarificatory conditionals. Must they exhaust all and every experience and thus be potentially infinite, or can we get away with a much smaller list? And if we can, what could justify our allowing a much smaller list to provide meanings?

We would expect that the call for practical bearings would militate against an infinite list since this would be impractical. Indeed, we might expect that a list of clarificatory conditionals need be large enough only to have a pragmatic upshot, a practical bearing. If this were so, then the concerns which affect the verificationist criteria don't seem to have the same impact upon the pragmatic maxim, and the demise of the former certainly need not herald the demise of the latter. Of course, this is speculation since Peirce says very little in his early statements of pragmatism that indicate his position one way or the other. This much is clear, though: the pragmatic maxim has a positivistic strain or verificationist element, and in that respect it is certainly an account of meaning of the same stripe as verificationism. However, there are other elements to Peirce's maxim that, early on at least, are under-explored and not emphasised. Depending on how these elements are explored and developed, there may be some marked differences between the maxim and the principle of verification which are enough to mean that the maxim really is the pragmatist baby that too many people have unwittingly insisted be thrown out with the verificationists' bath water. So, whilst the parallels are instructive, they can also be destructive unless we are careful how much weight we give them.[13]

The later account of pragmatism

The early statement of the pragmatic maxim that we have just examined proved to be influential, as we said. In an 1898 address to Berkeley University, William James outlined his pragmatist philosophy and named Peirce's pragmatic maxim as a key principle of the movement. Indeed, James' own explanations of the *pragmatist principle* are simply paraphrases of Peirce's original maxim:

> [A]t the root of all our thought-distinctions [. . .] is that there is no one of them so fine as to consist in anything but a possible difference of practice. To attain perfect clearness in our thought of an object, then, we need only consider what conceivable effects of a practical kind the object may involve – what sensations we are to expect from it, and what reactions we must prepare. (James 1907/1975, 29)

However, James' use of the pragmatic maxim varies from that which Peirce had in mind. In particular, James is much more explicit about how he sees the notion of practical effects; for James, we must look to the conduct that arises on the basis of belief about some object. This move to looking at the kinds of conduct and effects upon our lives that arise from treating some concept to be true changes the focus from *objects* in Peirce's maxim – what does it mean to call something 'hard'? – to individual believers and particular cases in James' version – what does it mean to *me* to call *this* object 'hard'? This is quite a subtle turn in James' reading, but it is also a crucial marker of other differences between James and Peirce regarding pragmatism more generally.

As we have seen, the pragmatic maxim for Peirce is primarily an account of meaning and a tool of purposeful scientific inquiry. James does not share these sensibilities. For James, pragmatism must be more than a simple account of meaning and scientific procedure. In his own philosophy, James shows some scepticism about the power of logic and science, distrusting the extent to which we can answer the important human questions with a materialistic and scientific approach to understanding the universe and our place in it. Consequently James tends to see pragmatism as the approach that we must take up when materialist and purely intellectualist sciences have failed to answer our questions about which beliefs are justifiable. Religious and moral questions require a separate criterion of justification, and this is where a pragmatic method determines what difference I take some such belief to have and why it is reasonable to hold that belief. For Peirce, philosophy in general and the pragmatic maxim in particular should never stray this far from scientific inquiry. The important philosophical questions, and those with which the pragmatic maxim are concerned, remain firmly within the realm of scientific and intellectualist inquiry. As far as Peirce is concerned, the questions to which James is inclined to apply a pragmatic method are largely beyond the realm of fruitful philosophical inquiry. For Peirce, pragmatism is strictly within the realm of scientific sensibilities; for James, it begins at the point where our scientific explanations fall short.

The uptake of his idea by James and others seems to have been something of a surprise to Peirce. 'Who originated the term "pragmatism", I or you?' (CP8. 253 (1900)), he asked William James in a letter. And in his first public reassessment of his pragmatism as part of a series of papers delivered at Harvard in 1903, Peirce clearly states, 'I sent forth my statement in January 1878 [in 'How to make our ideas clear']; and for about twenty years never heard from it again'. However, and much more important, this surprise is overshadowed by some real concern on Peirce's part over what his maxim had become in the hands of James. As we saw above, James had made pragmatism into an approach to philosophy with a focus on the beliefs of individuals. This is at odds with Peirce's original intentions for the maxim:

> The new pragmatists seem to be distinguished for their terse, vivid and concrete style of expression together with a certain buoyancy of tone as if they were conscious of carrying about them the master key to all the secrets of metaphysics. [...] I make pragmatism to be a mere maxim of logic instead of a sublime speculative philosophy. (EP2. 134 (1903))

From Peirce's point of view, his simple maxim of pragmatic meaning, with its scientific aims and simple clarificatory objectives, had turned into something which he did not recognise as his own. Moreover, Peirce clearly sees the Jamesian version of pragmatism taking hold in the public idea of what pragmatism was. For example, Schiller's 1911 description of pragmatism for the *Encyclopaedia Britannica* names Peirce's maxim, but it describes the main principle of the movement as asserting that 'the real difference between two conceptions lies in their application in the different consequences for the purpose of life which their acceptance carries', thus describing a Jamesian, not Peircian, reading of the maxim.

James' public acknowledgement of Peirce's role in creating pragmatism, along with his unease at what it had become, presented Peirce with two urgent reasons to return to his pragmatic maxim and re-examine its content. On the one hand, he was receiving public recognition for his philosophy, and given his academic isolation by the turn of the twentieth century, he would do well to exploit such recognition. On the other hand, he was keen to rescue his own ideas from those of his fellow pragmatists. For a man such as Peirce, it must have been frustrating and disconcerting to be given credit for views which, on closer inspection, you don't think you ever espoused. Unsurprisingly, then, around the turn of the century, Peirce sets about re-examining his original statement of the maxim and looking again at its meaning for his views of philosophy and philosophical endeavour. The resulting view of the pragmatic maxim and pragmatism is deeply interesting and markedly different to the account we examined in the first part of this chapter, and it is to the details and results of this later re-examination that we now turn.

The later view: pragmaticism

Although Peirce makes numerous efforts to examine his pragmatism after 1900, what follows draws heavily on two important series of papers: the first, a series of lectures delivered at Harvard in 1903, and the second, a series of papers written for The Monist around 1905. The account of pragmatism which Peirce develops in these papers he names *pragmaticism*, a term which he suggests is 'ugly enough to keep it safe from kidnappers' (EP2. 335 (1905)). What is particularly interesting about this work, as we shall see, is that Peirce believes, for the most part, that his original formulation of the maxim was correct. Nonetheless, this later work shows many differences from the original 1878 maxim. We shall examine the newer formulations that Peirce offers of the maxim, but first, in order to make sense of those formulations, it is instructive to look at those issues which impress themselves most forcefully upon Peirce when he returns to the question of pragmatism after 1900 and which prompt him to make the developments he makes.

We shall examine three interrelated issues: first, a cluster of problems which Peirce feels his early version of the maxim faced; second, the effect that Peirce's clearer sense of the architectonic structure of his philosophy has upon the requirements of the pragmatic maxim; and third, Peirce's conviction that his version of the maxim could be made 'precise'.

Three problems with the early maxim
NOMINALISM

As we mentioned above, James' reading of the 1878 maxim marks a change in the focus of the maxim towards the effects on individuals. Although we also suggested that this change marks some deeper differences between Peirce and James' philosophy, it is also a simple upshot of James' understanding of practical effects. Recall that we noted how Peirce's original maxim has two elements, one of which, the practical component, is largely under-explored. In James' reading of the maxim, the nature of this practical component is filled in to some degree and then given a central role in pragmatist philosophy. The interpretation that James gives to the practical component is, as we suggested, that we must look to particular reactions and expectations in individual cases to gauge the practical effects and, thereby, the meaning. Of course, this is to say no more than we have already said about James' rendering of Peirce's maxim. So why should this matter? Why should this be a problem for Peirce's early account and thus provide an impetus to change the maxim?

The answer is simply that in many respects James' reading of the early maxim in terms of particular effects and individual cases is entirely in accord with Peirce's early statement: we look at particular cases to ask of particular objects if they exemplify some property and then see what sensible experiences follow. And this is precisely what troubled Peirce. The way that James put it made Peirce realise that his earlier statement was *too* nominalist, *too* focused on individuals and particulars and shy of any genuine commitment to generalities, laws or rules.[14] For Peirce, this was an error in his earlier account.

The easiest way of seeing Peirce's discomfort and reaction to the nominalist character of his early pragmatism is to look again at the clarifying conditionals that are supposed to express the meaning of a concept. Recall that in our discussion above we noted that Peirce countenances only indicative conditionals, since he feels that the circumstances expressed in subjunctive and counterfactual conditionals do not express *facts* but merely possible states of affairs. In his later view, Peirce recants this restriction:

> Another doctrine which is involved in Pragmaticism [. . .] is the scholastic doctrine of realism. This is usually defined as the opinion that there are real objects that are general, [. . .] real vagues and especially real possibilities. [. . .] The article of January 1878 ['How to make our ideas clear'] endeavoured to

gloss over this point as unsuited to the exoteric public being addressed; or perhaps the writer wavered in his own mind. He said that if a diamond were to be formed in a bed of cotton wool, and were to be consumed there without ever having been pressed upon by any hard edge or point, it would be merely a question of nomenclature whether that diamond should be said to have been hard or not. No doubt, this is true, except for the abominable falsehood in the word MERELY, implying that symbols are unreal. [. . .] [T]he question is, not what did happen, but whether it may have been well to engage in any line of conduct whose successful issue depended on whether that diamond would resist an attempt to scratch it. (EP2. 354 (1905))

Whilst it may seem that the point here is that Peirce is now prepared to allow subjunctive conditionals to form part of the clarification of concepts – conditionals which express what *would* happen *were* we to act thus and so – the point is actually a little deeper. Peirce has committed himself to the view that possibilities, generalities, laws, are *real*, not merely modes of expression.

The reason Peirce makes this commitment is due in no small part to his status and perspective as a scientist. Recall that in Chapter 1 we said that Peirce's life as a practising scientist had a strong effect upon how he developed his philosophical views; his changes in emphasis between earlier and later versions of pragmatism represent a fine example of this. In his early elaboration of the maxim, Peirce suggested that a quest to find the meaning of a concept such as 'hard' involved asking 'what we mean by calling a thing *hard*' (EP1. 132 (1878)). From the point of view of a scientist, this is to ask a single experimental *instance* to bear the weight of providing meaning. The correct manner in which to ascertain meaning here is to look to the general phenomenon, of 'hardness' for instance, and realise that its meaning comes not from 'any particular event that *did* happen to somebody in the dead past, but what surely will happen to everybody in the future who shall fulfil certain conditions' (EP2. 340 (1905)). The import of a concept, for Peirce, lies in its general applicability to current and future instances, and any reformulation of the pragmatic maxim must serve to express this commitment to the importance of laws and generalities and the secondary status of individual and particular effects.

INDIVIDUALISM

The second problem that Peirce seems to have spotted in his early statement of the pragmatic maxim is what we might call its *individualism*. As we have just mentioned, Peirce's early statement of the maxim lends itself to a focus on particular effects and consequences for individuals, and we know that Peirce is keen to remove these nominalist features. However, there is a further consequence of the possible particularist/individualist reading of practical consequences. The worry is simply that a concept may, to all intents and purposes, have no readily perceivable practical consequences for us at all yet still have some pragmatic import for others a long way off into the future.

In many ways, such a worry is tied up with Peirce's account of inquiry, which we shall turn to in the next chapter, but here we can give a simple illustration of the concern. Take as an example imaginary numbers, that is, any complex number involving a real number and the imaginary unit i, whose square is less than zero. These were defined by Rafael Bombelli in the sixteenth century but were thought not to exist. Indeed, Descartes, who coined the term 'imaginary number', was rather disparaging of them. From the point of view of Bombelli and his contemporaries, these numbers could be given a relatively simple definition, yet it seemed that no practical consequences were to be had from them. By the pragmatic maxim, they seem to be empty. Yet after work by Euler and Gauss in the eighteenth and nineteenth centuries, mathematicians came to see uses and applications for imaginary numbers, some of which are really quite concrete. For example, by using real and imaginary numbers, electrical engineers are able to give the value of two combined alternating currents, a task that is impossible to do with precision otherwise. Obviously, this looks like a practical effect.

Hopefully, the moral, and thus the worry, is clear: concentrating on the pragmatic maxim from the point of view of individuals might render pragmatically meaningless concepts which over the longer term have clear practical bearings. Arguably, the earlier reading of the maxim with its focus on individuals permits just such a reading. Any later reformulation of the maxim, then, must allow for a broader, less individualistic notion of practical import.

PSYCHOLOGISM

Aside from an unpalatable nominalism and individualism, Peirce's re-examination of his pragmatism also led him to think he had been too *psychologistic* in explaining his maxim and that this posed problems. Peirce's worry, in essence, is this: there is something undesirably exclusive about the way in which he tried to explain the utility of the maxim in 1878. To be clearer, the problem seems to be that the effectiveness of the pragmatic maxim as an account of meaning comes from the fact that these meanings are explicated in terms of practical consequences and, thus, effects upon our actions – my interactions with hard things will presumably be coloured by my knowledge of the pragmatic meaning of 'hard'. But in his 1878 account, the power of the maxim to affect our actions comes as a simple corollary of the way in which we are psychologically composed – a belief is something upon which we are prepared to act. My belief that diamonds are hard underpins, in part, my preparedness to use them when I need something hard. The utility or power of the maxim, then, seems to be grounded in facts about the ways in which we form and respond to our beliefs. This seems to make the maxim without utility to anyone or anything which doesn't form and respond to beliefs in this way, and this was not what Peirce had intended for the maxim; rather, its utility should be universal. Peirce expresses this worry thus:

> I do not think it satisfactory to reduce such fundamental things to facts of psychology. For Man could alter his nature, or his environment would alter it if he did not voluntarily do so[.] (EP2. 140 (1903))

Whilst Peirce's concern here is that simple changes in the way we form or respond to beliefs, or the possibility of creatures whose doxastic modes differ radically from our own, might undermine the broader utility of the maxim, that is not all there is to the point. The thought instead is, why shouldn't creatures radically different to us in doxastic terms be able to utilise the pragmatic maxim too? After all, the maxim, as a means of clarifying our concepts, clearly has a normative or prescriptive element. If we want to attain the highest level of understanding or clarity, then we *ought* to look to the practical bearings of our concepts. Creatures who do not respond to beliefs with an automatic preparedness to act upon them can nonetheless benefit from knowing that they should act if they wish to achieve certain desired outcomes. The problem is that explaining the power of the maxim in terms of *facts* about our doxastic states seems to leave no room for this normative feature of the maxim. Any reformulation of the pragmatic maxim, then, must generate room for this normative dimension.

As we said earlier, these worries about the 1878 statement of the pragmatic maxim – its nominalism, individualism and psychologism – are not the only things that drive Peirce's reformulation of his pragmatism. His increased sense of the architectonic structure of his philosophy and his belief that the maxim could be made precise are also important in understanding the developments he makes. We turn to them now.

The effect of the architectonic

As we saw in Chapter 1, Peirce was an 'architectonic' philosopher – he believed important systematic relations existed between all types of knowledge and between particular branches of philosophy. By the time he comes to re-examine his pragmatic philosophy after 1900, his architectonic vision is very sophisticated and well worked out. This is due in part to a serious application he made for funds from the Carnegie Institute in 1902 in which, intending to give a definitive statement of his philosophy, Peirce laid out his systematic vision in full. Moreover, at the time when his return to pragmatism was at the forefront of his research in 1903, he outlined the systematic connections between various elements of his philosophical work in a pamphlet he created for the audience of a series of lectures at the Lowell Institute in Boston. So, at the time of returning to his pragmatic maxim, Peirce's sense of the overarching structure of his thought is readily worked out and quite apparent to him, and seeing the precise place of pragmatism within this structure means that the original statement of the maxim would need to change.

We have already seen in Chapter 1 some of the general structure of Peirce's philosophy and the principles by which it is organised. However, for our purposes it is worth recapping and developing the important areas in the architectonic since they came to have an important bearing on the developments Peirce makes to his pragmatism and pragmatic maxim. As we saw, philosophy is divided into three main branches: phenomenology, the normative sciences and metaphysics. The pertinent area for us is the normative sciences, which Peirce further divides into aesthetics (the study of what is unconditionally admirable), ethics (the study of what is admirable in the way of human conduct) and logic (the study of what is admirable in the way of reasoning). Further, we saw that Peirce thinks a super-ordinate discipline provides guiding principles for a subordinate discipline and that the guiding principle of aesthetics is to pursue the growth of concrete reasonableness. Realised in terms of ethics, this becomes a pursuit of the right forms of human conduct aimed at securing the growth of concrete reasonableness. For ethics, the right form of conduct is self-controlled and deliberate. For the subordinate discipline of logic, the pursuit of which forms of rational conduct will secure the growth of concrete reasonableness becomes a matter of how self-controlled and deliberate reasoning secures the growth of concrete reasonableness. This much we are already familiar with, but what is interesting for us is that Peirce develops this structure even further, and it is within his development of logic that we find the proper place for the pragmatic maxim.

Just as with the normative sciences, Peirce also divides logic into three branches: speculative grammar (the theoretical explanation and exploration of the nature of signs), critical logic (the study of forms of argument and reasoning) and methodeutic (the study of how signs and argument generate habits and forms of rational conduct conducive to achieving the growth of concrete reasonableness). Also, just as the division of the normative sciences sees logic taking the aims and principles of aesthetics and ethics as tools for a particular application, namely reasoning, so the methodeutic takes speculative grammar and critical logic (or semiotic and forms of reasoning) as tools for showing the process of inquiry and methods by which we increase our knowledge and understanding. The proper place of the pragmatic maxim on this view, then, is within logic more generally and within the methodeutic branch more specifically, where it functions within the process of inquiry by contributing towards the ultimate aesthetic ideal through aiding self-controlled and deliberate reasoning.

In many ways, this architectonic view of certain elements of Peirce's philosophy can seem abstract, unnecessary and rather heavy going, but this 'clearer' view of where pragmatism sits in the overall landscape of Peirce's philosophy makes for two important features of his later account of pragmatism. First of all, and related to Peirce's worry about the psychologism of the 1878 account, pragmatism has a strong normative element; it is a key part of how the third branch of the normative sciences is able to achieve its purpose and contribute to the growth of concrete reasonableness through self-controlled and deliberate reasoning. Any reformulation must make the normativity of the pragmatic maxim more readily apparent.

Second, and again related to the issue of normativity, the precise service to which the maxim is to be put within Peirce's view of philosophy will place certain constraints upon it. To be a little clearer, making the pragmatic maxim a key part of the process of inquiry certainly emphasises Peirce's anti-Jamesian insistence that pragmatism is a methodological tool or principle and not an approach to philosophy – but it also does more than this. As a tool for self-controlled inquiry aimed at contributing to the ultimate aesthetic ideal, the pragmatic maxim has to do more than simply clarify concepts and show up empty terms and disputes. Rather, it has to clarify concepts in such a way as to enable the self-controlled conduct of inquirers. Again, this draws on the normativity of the pragmatic maxim; it must help us to decide what to do in the course of inquiry and provide some guidance on how we ought and ought not to act in the process of philosophical investigation.

In summary, Peirce's stronger sense of the place of pragmatism within his architectonic philosophy seems to suggest two further requirements upon any reformulation of his earlier maxim: it must reflect that the maxim is part of the *normative sciences*, and it must reflect the role that the maxim plays in helping guide our deliberate, self-controlled, rational inquiries.

Making the maxim precise

As we mentioned earlier, Peirce renamed his pragmatism 'pragmaticism' in order to 'keep it safe from kidnappers'. However, Peirce's choice of name was also meant to make a point about precision. For Peirce, philosophy could learn a lesson from science by introducing specialised technical terminology in order to mark fine-grained distinctions and subtle conceptual differences. His tendency towards new terminology is, as mentioned before, rampant, but pertinent here is his suggestion that the suffix 'ism' be used to denote the name of a doctrine and the suffix 'icism' be used to denote 'a more strictly defined acceptation of that doctrine' (EP2. 334 (1905)). Hence, Peirce's 'pragmaticism' is a more strictly defined version of the broader doctrine of 'pragmatism' and is thus a more defined, logically respectable version of the doctrine than the looser readings of James and Schiller. The impetus that this places upon the later reformulation of the maxim is clear: it must be more clearly defined and more precise. However, we can break this call for precision down into two separate requirements, only one of which we shall pursue further.

First, and of the greatest long-term importance for Peirce, the call for greater precision requires that his logically respectable, more defined version of the maxim be provable. Of course, Peirce's belief that there must be a respectable proof of pragmatism relates to his discomfort with the psychologism of his earlier maxim. It is fine for his earlier self, James and others to justify the use of the maxim on the grounds of its utility to us, but a more refined version, especially one clearly worked out within the structure of his philosophy as a principle of logic, must admit of a proof. As it happens, Peirce was never able to provide a proof with which he was entirely happy, and reconstructing a proof from his manuscripts is very difficult. In some ways, this is because it is not altogether clear what Peirce demanded in the way of proof for his pragmatism, and there are various attempts to 'prove' pragmatism using, amongst other things, his theory of perception, his theory of signs and his account of diagrammatic logic, none of which seem to have worked. How we should try to work out Peirce's proof is interesting, but we shall not examine it further since the nature of the proof is something that must come after the maxim is restated, and our concern here is with what leads to the reformulation of the maxim rather than what further work the reformulation leads to.

The second requirement that emerges from the call for precision is simply that we must be given a greater sense of what a practical effect or bearing is. Recall that we noted at the end of our discussion of the 1878 statement that the early version of the pragmatic maxim leaves the notion of practical effect too vague and undefined. Arguably, Peirce's idea that his account of the maxim be made precise comes from wanting to place his version of pragmatism on a more scientifically and logically respectable footing than that of James. Of course, James' reading comes from filling in the gaps that Peirce's early expression of the maxim leaves open and making practical effects and bearings a matter of individual interests. To close this gap and make his maxim more precise therefore requires filling out some of the details regarding practical bearings. Any reformulation of the pragmatic maxim must therefore give us a clearer sense of what Peirce had in mind when he spoke of practical effects and bearings.

In summary, re-examining his earlier maxim in light of his need to provide an account distinct from those of James *et al.* impressed upon Peirce that there were problems with his earlier account – it was nominalist, individualist and psychologistic – which needed attention. Moreover, developments in his architectonic view meant his maxim now needed to reflect pragmatism's place as a part of the normative sciences and its role in guiding the self-controlled conduct of inquirers. Finally, the imprecision and vagueness of his original maxim, especially concerning the notion of practical bearings, meant that a clearer, more defined version was called for. Thus, the redevelopments of the maxim between 1903 and 1905 needed to take account of these now prominent elements and features of Peirce's pragmatism.

The later statements

Having cleared some ground with our discussion of what Peirce found pressing in his reassessment of the 1878 maxim, we are now in a position to examine the results. So what do his later versions of the pragmatic maxim look like? As I suggested, Peirce makes two clear and related attempts at reformulating the 1878 maxim: one in his Harvard lecture series delivered between March and May of 1903, and one in a series of articles written for *The Monist* between 1905 and 1906. In one of his 1903 papers, Peirce states his position thusly:

> Pragmatism is the principle that every theoretical judgement expressible in a sentence in the indicative mood is a confused form of thought whose only meaning, if it has any, lies in its tendency to enforce a corresponding practical maxim express-ible as a conditional sentence having its [consequent] in the imperative mood. (EP2. 134–135 (1903))

Immediately after this version of the pragmatic maxim, Peirce restates the original 1878 maxim and reaffirms his commitment to it.

In his 1905 paper 'Issues of pragmatism', Peirce begins by repeat-ing his 1878 maxim and then gives the following version and clarification of his earlier account:

> The entire intellectual import of any symbol consists in the total of all general modes of rational conduct which, conditionally upon all possible different circumstances and desires, would ensue upon the acceptance of the symbol. (EP2. 346 (1905))

These restatements are interesting for a host of reasons, but our con-cern, of course, is with how these two ways of stating Peirce's pragmatic maxim answer the issues we suggested were pressing for Peirce after 1900. So we will examine these statements in light of three questions: how do these developments counteract the nominalism, individual-ism and psychologism of the 1878 maxim? how do these statements reflect the place of the maxim within the normative sciences and as a guide to the deliberate, self-controlled conduct of inquirers? and how do they help to make the pragmatic maxim more precise?

We already noted in our discussion of Peirce's rejection of the nominalism implicit in 'How to make our ideas clear' that he believes that subjunctive conditionals, or 'would-bes', should form part of the clarificatory conditionals for any concept, but we can also see this rejection of nominalism in these developments to the maxim, along with his commitment to the view that generalities and possibilities are real. In the 1905 statement, for example, the 'intellectual import' of a concept consists in a *general* mode of conduct, not any particular instance, and we are interested in all *possible* different circumstances, not just those which actually occur. This reading of the maxim, then, certainly bypasses the nominalism implicit in the 1878 account.

As for the implicit individualism of the early statement of the maxim, this too is resolved, and in a similar manner to the issue of nominalism. The implicit individualism comes from a possible particularist reading of the 1878 statement: what do we mean by calling *this object* 'hard'. But the 1903 and 1905 formulations clearly rule out such a reading. The 1903 reading, for instance, mentions not the imperative that *does* arise but rather those which *tend* to arise. The 1905 formulation is even more explicit and mentions 'the total of all general modes of rational conduct' and 'all possible circumstances and desires'. The pragmatic import of concepts, then, is focused on tendencies (or habits), generalities and possibilities, and not on single instances or individual and particular cases. Of course, this broader focus precludes an individualistic reading of the maxim and suggests that wider practical import and pragmatic meaning must be situated in a wider communitarian setting.

As for the psychologism of the 1878 statement, this also seems to be bypassed here. Recall that the worry was that the utility of the maxim as stated in 1878 implicitly relied on a view of how we form and respond to our beliefs – our beliefs compel us to act. What Peirce needed was to explain the utility of his maxim not via descriptive facts about what we do but by prescriptive facts about what any rational agent ought to do. Clearly, the 1903 and 1905 formulations do this. The 1903 formulation, for instance, provides us with conditional imperatives to action: if we want some outcome, O, then given what we know of X, we should make use of X. This imperative clearly holds whether I am the kind of being whose beliefs compel me to act or whether I am the kind of being whose beliefs are formed in such a manner as to invoke a refusal to act or even paralysis and an inability to act; regardless of my actual response to a belief, the imperative holds. We find the same prescriptive tone in the 1905 formulation. The pragmatic meaning of any concept is found in the kinds of actions it is rational for us to take in light of accepting that conduct. Regardless of how my psychological make-up suggests I will act, the utility of understanding the pragmatic meaning of some concept comes from identifying what would be a rational way for us to act.

Increased awareness of the normativity in later statements of the pragmatic maxim not only handles the issue of psychologism but also meets the requirements imposed by Peirce's architectonic system upon any adequate formulation of the maxim. Since pragmatism is a methodological tool of the third branch of the normative sciences, it had better reflect that and show itself to be a normative principle. Those features of the 1903 and 1905 statements which disarm the psychologism worry are the same features which clearly mark the pragmatic maxim as a normative principle. Concepts are clarified in terms of imperatives which tell us what we *should* do, what the most rational course of action is. But showing sensitivity to the place of pragmatism in the normative sciences is not all that Peirce's architectonic views require of any formulation of the maxim. The pragmatic maxim is a tool of inquiry whose purpose is to help the deliberate, self-controlled conduct of inquirers. So how do these later reformulations reflect that?

The key here is that the 1903 and 1905 formulations suggest that explicating the meaning of a concept involves looking to its practical bearings. This is really no departure or advance upon the earlier statement of 1878. However, the important deepening of the maxim here is that looking to practical bearing means something like issuing or *enforcing* conditionals which contain *imperatives* (as suggested by the 1903 formulation) geared towards *rational conduct* in light of *all possible circumstances and desires*. As committed inquirers, of course, we will presumably aim for the 'growth of concrete reasonableness', or at least harbour a simple desire for a true understanding and account of our concepts. Indeed, Peirce suggests that '[the] first [. . .] rule of reason [is] that in order to learn you must *desire* to learn' (CP1. 135 (1898), *italics added*). More simply, the maxim suggests that I, as an inquirer, reflect upon possible circumstances, C, where my desired outcome is O; note that the rational course of action for achieving O would be A; and affirm that in such cases I must, and therefore will, endeavour to perform A in C in order to achieve O. By doing this, I am simply equipping myself with a tool for self-controlled action in such circumstances – I am using the maxim to work out how I will act. For example, if the occasion arises in which I might need a malleable, non-reactive metal, and the rational choice in such a scenario would be to use gold, then I clearly must use gold, and in such circumstances I will enforce the maxim and do so. It is the rational thing to do.

This kind of tracing out of consequences and courses of action in possible circumstances suggested by the 1903 and 1905 readings is precisely how Peirce saw the maxim as a methodological tool for inquiry:

> The method prescribed in the maxim is to trace out in the imagination conceivable practical consequences – that is, the consequences for deliberate, self-controlled conduct – of the affirmation or denial of the concept. (CP8. 191 (1904))

So not only do the later formulations capture the position of pragmatism within the normative sciences, they also capture the more sophisticated methodological role that Peirce sees for his maxim within the process of inquiry.

As for Peirce's sense that the later formulations should make the 1878 maxim clearer and more precise, we can already see from the manner in which the 1903 and 1905 formulations guide rational conduct that Peirce achieves this. First, as we suggested in Chapter 1, as a scientist, Peirce's method was not to simply abandon earlier work wholesale but to make his statements more precise when appropriate evidence and supporting work enabled him to do so. As we saw, in both 1903 and 1905, Peirce restates his original maxim of 1878 and affirms his commitment to it before offering further clarifying formulations of it. Second, recall that the most pressing requirement of precision for Peirce was to remove the vagueness around the notion of practical bearings that allowed for the kind of reading of the early maxim that we find in James' work. In both the 1903 and 1905 formulations there is some emphasis upon practical bearings. In the 1903 formulation we find that any theoretical judgments, such as 'X is impermeable', enforce *practical maxims* which contain imperatives such as 'if you want to protect Y from water, then use X'. We find a similar result in 1905, except that the practical maxim is expressed in terms of what it is rational for us to do. In simple terms, Peirce's later reformulations and developments attempt to achieve precision by making the practical component of the maxim clearer.

Conclusion

The redevelopment of Peirce's pragmatic maxim and changes between the earlier and later versions are actually quite considerable. The early 1878 statement of the pragmatic maxim is something which Peirce felt throughout his life to be a good general characterisation of the doctrine. Left at this broad, general level, the maxim is easily read in very nominalist terms; the practical bearings which capture the pragmatic meaning of any concept must be actual effects. Similarly, as a clarificatory tool, the broad, early characterisation seems to suggest that the maxim will allow us to look to the actual effects of our concepts and mark out empty terms and empty disputes for exclusion from worthwhile philosophical effort; it looks rather like a tool for dissolving philosophical problems.

By the time Peirce offers us his later more 'strictly defined acceptation of [the] doctrine' (EP2. 334 (1905)), we find a marked difference. Greater definition rules out the nominalist reading; possibilities, generalities, laws and tendencies all feature in the pragmatic meaning of a concept. As an account of meaning, Peirce's pragmatism has moved from a narrow, individualist, static, synchronic account to a broader, communitarian, dynamic and diachronic picture. More importantly, the concomitant realism about possibilities and generalities means that experience and practical bearings are much broader, more inclusive notions than we might previously have thought. So much that would seem to be meaningless becomes meaningful. Of course, a result of this is that as a methodological tool, the later account of the maxim becomes similarly sophisticated. The maxim still clarifies meanings and marks out empty terms and disputes, but the real difference is that the maxim now becomes more clearly a tool for deliberative action. On the later formulations, we, as inquirers, are supposed to use the maxim not only to clear ground and rule out dead-ends but also as a guide to action, even with those concepts we know are meaningful. The maxim is no longer a simple sieve for identifying which inquiries are fruitful; it is also a tool to be used in the course of those inquiries, acting as a normative principle and guide to action. When we put matters this way, the contrast between the earlier and later versions of Peirce's pragmatism are clear. The early statement of the maxim appears to be a nominalist, descriptive account of meaning as a tool for dissolving and excluding certain types of philosophical discourse; the later statement of the maxim is an anti-nominalist, prescriptive account of meaning and a normative tool for guiding inquiry.

One further instructive way to see just how radical Peirce's later formulations of the maxim are is to compare it, very briefly, with the verificationist account of meaning and the logical empiricist approach to philosophy which we outlined earlier. As we noted, the grounds for comparison between the 1878 statement of the maxim and verificationism are really quite strong. Both provide a positivist criterion of meaning as a tool for a more strict account of what is and isn't worthwhile philosophy. But, as we also noted, the notion of practical bearings is under-explored in 1878, and how this notion is fleshed out will influence how far the comparison goes. Arguably, the more strictly defined pragmaticism we find in the 1903 and 1905 formulations fleshes out the notion of practical bearings in a way that makes the comparison untenable.

First, early verificationist accounts of meaning are descriptive and epistemological – we look to how the truth of X is verified to capture its meaning. Peirce's later accounts of the maxim make meaning normative. A crucial feature of the clarifying conditionals which give the pragmatic meanings of a concept is the shift from simple descriptions of what we will do to an account of what we *must* or *ought* to do and what it is *rational* to do in light of the possible practical upshots.

Second, the realism about possibilities, generalities, tendencies and habits that we find in Peirce's later maxim is something that the logical positivists would have been uncomfortable with. In many respects, logical positivism offers a reductionist strategy aiming to reduce 'meanings' to conditions of verification, that is, to observation sentences. Peirce's broadening of what we can experience and what we can observe to include possibilities and generalities would strike most logical positivists as endorsing an unpalatable ontological profligacy. Peirce would, of course, think the logical positivists too nominalistic.

Summary

In his 1878 paper 'How to make our ideas clear', Peirce attempted to extend the rationalist ideas of clear and distinct apprehension of a concept by proposing an additional pragmatic level of clarification and apprehension.

- The maxim, which encapsulates the pragmatic level of clarity, serves as an account of meaning and a clarificatory tool to identify empty terms and disputes. These features have led many to conclude that Peirce's account is a forerunner of verificationism.
- Peirce returned to his early account of the pragmatic maxim around 1900, after William James made it a key feature of his theory of pragmatism. Peirce objected to James turning the maxim from a simple methodological tool into a broader, more thoroughgoing approach to philosophy.

- Peirce's re-examination of the maxim found it to be too nominalist, individualist and psychologistic. These features were made especially apparent to him through James' and Schiller's interpretations of the maxim.
- By the time of his re-examination, Peirce also had a more refined sense of the role and position of the maxim within his overall view of philosophy. It was a methodological tool geared towards helping inquirers contribute towards the growth of knowledge and understanding through deliberate and self-controlled rational inquiry.
- This all led to a deepening (but not abandoning) of the earlier maxim, transforming it from a nominalist, descriptive account of meaning and a clarificatory tool into a normative, anti-nominalist account of meaning and a regulative principle of inquiry.
- Finally, whilst there are clear analogies and comparisons between the early account and the verificationist criterion of meaning, the viability of that comparison collapses under the later developments.

Further reading

Peirce's work on pragmatism really focuses on his pragmatic maxim. As one would expect, Peirce's work is infused with comments and reflections on pragmatism, especially in his later work responding to James and Schiller's adoption of the maxim. It is a worthwhile enterprise to simply contrast the best statements of Peirce's early and late accounts of the pragmatic maxim by reading his early (1878) paper 'How to make our ideas clear' in the *Popular Science Monthly* before turning to his later (1905) paper 'What pragmatism is' in *The Monist*.

The best and most accessible secondary literature includes Christopher Hookway's 'The principle of pragmatism: Peirce's formulations and examples' (2004), which introduces Peirce's earliest formulation of the maxim and traces its development in his later philosophical work, giving detailed discussion of the various formulations and what these mean for Peirce's version of pragmatism. Although we haven't devoted time to Peirce's stated claim that he had a proof for his pragmatism, those with more advanced interest may want to look at Richard Robin's 'Classical pragmatism and pragmatism's proof' (1997), which provides an excellent starting point for delving into these extended questions surrounding the pragmatic maxim.

Notes

1 The irony of this statement, of course, is that as diminishing of Peirce's foundational role as it is, it is still more generous than Rorty might have intended. Strictly speaking, it was James who provided the name 'pragmatism' by famously misremembering seeing the term in Peirce's early published work.

2 This series consists of three famous papers: 'Questions concerning certain faculties claimed for man' (EP1. 11–27 (1868)), 'Some consequences of four incapacities' (EP1. 28–55 (1868)) and 'Grounds of validity of the laws of logic: further consequences of the four incapacities' (EP1. 56–82 (1869)).

3 See Katz (1987).

4 Interestingly, in his earlier criticisms of Cartesian philosophy, and in particular in his insistence on the denial of incognisables, Peirce gives what is largely seen as a prototype version of the pragmatic maxim with its insistence on practical bearings when he says 'there can be no conception of the absolutely incognizable, since nothing of that sort occurs in experience. But the meaning of a term is the conception it conveys. Hence, a term can have no such meaning' (EP1. 24 (1868)).

5 In some ways, the idea that the pragmatic clarification of a concept takes the form of such a list is quite natural; Peirce's illustrations in 'How to make our ideas clear' imply that the clarifications will be conditionals. Moreover, in later work and developments to the maxim, Peirce is quite explicit that the clarifications might take the form of conditionals. However, when we interpret Peirce or explain his maxim, we are often in some ways, I think, a little too quick to suggest that the maxim insists that pragmatic clarifications are in the form of conditionals. Hookway (2004) is an important exception here.

6 Cheryl Misak (1991, 3 fn 2) notes some of the similarities between the insights offered by Peirce's maxim and the central 'manifestationist' arguments of Dummett, Wright and Peacocke.

7 Peirce had in mind his contemporary, the physicist Gustav Kirchhoff, who suggests that force is 'a mysterious entity'.

8 As it happens, Peirce says very little about moral philosophy directly, but his resistance to treating ethics as open to easy pragmatic treatment turns out to be less about there being clear experiential effects for moral concepts and more about his belief that moral decision making requires a different kind of support to that which we would use for 'scientific' concepts. We shall mention such issues again later, but those interested in looking at how Peirce's maxim

accommodates moral and political philosophy should see Cheryl Misak's 'C.S. Peirce on vital matters' (2004).

9 For instance, Schlick and Ayer both published their important work in the 1930s, and in Europe during this period, the pragmatism of James and Dewey was what predominated in their view of American thought and philosophy. However, Carnap makes mention of Peirce in his discussion of verification principles in his 1936 paper, 'Truth and confirmation'.

10 Bridgman's 1927 book, The Logic of Modern Physics, is often cited as an influence on the logical empiricist criterion of meaning.

11 Hookway (2004a) also notes the presence of these two components and calls them the 'verificationist dimension' and the 'pragmatist dimension'.

12 Of course, verificationists can make their requirements for verifiability weaker, and there are weaker versions in light of this kind of problem. The worry, however, is that by weakening the requirements for verifiability, logical empiricists allow many previously meaningless statements to count as verifiable and so meaningful once more.

13 Cheryl Misak's Verificationism: Its History and Prospects (1995) is especially worth mentioning here. Misak places Peirce's maxim as part of a family of verificationist views of meaning but is quick, and I think correct, to point out that the pragmatic account of meaning 'presents an advance' on logical positivism. For those interested in verificationism generally and Peirce's pragmatic maxim as an improved version of it, this book is worthy of attention.

14 Peirce's frequent use of 'nominalism' requires some explanation. 'Nominalism' is more normally associated with the medieval discussion on the existence of universals. The nominalist position in this debate sought to explain universals and general terms as properties of the words or names used (hence 'nominalism' from nominalis, or belonging to the name) rather than as separately existing forms. Peirce, however, uses 'nominalism' to refer to any theory that does not take the real, separate existence of laws, generalities, possibilities and so forth seriously. His early version of the maxim, by ignoring general cases and effects and focusing on individual cases and particular effects, is an example of just this kind of nominalism.

Three
Truth and inquiry

Introduction

Aside from his founding role in the pragmatist movement, Peirce is also well known in broader philosophical circles for a distinctive account of inquiry and the related account of truth. Peirce's account of inquiry, as we shall see, is complex and multifaceted. It relies on a distinctive theory of belief as settled opinion, doubt as a state of irritation and an ongoing interplay between these two concepts. Moreover, it is strongly connected to his ideas on the purpose and process of science, an intriguing cluster of ideas that appears to pre-empt theories from such eminent philosophers of science as Popper, Kuhn and Reichenbach. However, it is his explication of the concept of truth as it emerges from this account of inquiry that has drawn most philosophical attention to Peirce's theory.

Peirce introduced his theory of inquiry in the same series of papers that introduced the now famous pragmatic maxim, the 1877/1878 *Illustrations of the Logic of Science* series. It is unsurprising, then, that this account of inquiry is closely tied to his account of pragmatism. In particular, the account of truth that emerges from, and is so closely connected to, his account of inquiry results from Peirce's attempt to give a pragmatic clarification of the concept of reality. What this means is that the work we shall examine throughout this chapter forms an interconnected cluster of Peirce's philosophical ideas. Although we shall examine the details in much greater depth in what follows, it will be useful to know that in his pragmatic explication of reality, Peirce sees inquiry as leading to a convergence of opinion, that this final opinion is what we mean by truth, and that the facts conveyed by this final opinion are what we mean by reality.

Unsurprisingly, this account, especially Peirce's connection of inquiry and truth, has led to plenty of objections, the most important of which we shall examine below. On the whole, it is fair to say that Peirce's account of truth and inquiry has few admirers and fewer adherents. However, as I shall endeavour to show in the rest of this chapter, very many of the objections raised against Peirce's theory have less bite than they might initially seem to have once we get clearer about what is really going on. In particular, we shall see that, as with his account of pragmatism, these ideas are first introduced in articles written for a popular audience, and there is always a propaedeutic element to such work. Once we fill in some of the details, we can see that Peirce's ideas are more robust than some of the obvious objections would suggest.

A second issue in looking at Peirce's work here, and at the objections that are frequently raised against it, is that later developments to his thinking are crucial in seeing how serious objections and concerns are overcome. It is important that we see just how Peirce's later philosophical developments help him to overcome some of the concerns that are frequently raised against his earlier account of inquiry. Again, we shall pursue these developments in detail later in this chapter, but it is worth noting that the same kinds of development that we saw impacting upon Peirce's account of pragmatism and the pragmatic maxim are again important here. In particular, a growing dissatisfaction with what he saw as the nominalism of his earlier work, a greater sense of the normative dimensions of inquiry, and some independent developments in his thinking about realism lead him to refine some of his stronger claims about the process of inquiry and generate some philosophical distance between the key concepts of his earlier account – namely, inquiry, truth and reality. At the moment, the exact impact of these developments will not be so clear, but as we shall see below, later developments do much to offset the many objections given against his earlier formulation of inquiry.

The way we shall proceed throughout the rest of this chapter is as follows. First, we shall introduce Peirce's earlier 1877/1878 account of inquiry, showing its connection to his theories of science and scientific progress and, most importantly, how it gives us an account of truth when used as part of a pragmatic clarification of the concept of reality. Second, we shall examine the range of worries and objections that are frequently cited against this account. Third, we shall examine a series of developments in Peirce's philosophical ideas, charting just how those developments impact upon his ideas about truth and inquiry and lead to a later, more mature account. Finally, we shall examine just how this later account deals with the most robust and serious problems facing the earlier account.

The early account of inquiry: 'The fixation of belief'

Belief and doubt

In his 1877 paper 'The fixation of belief' (EP1. 109–123 (1877)), Peirce sets about giving an account of inquiry that draws upon a particular conception of belief and doubt. His first task is to draw a distinction between these two states. First, he notes that *belief* and *doubt* are very different sensations, the nature of which manifests itself quite clearly to us. As Peirce puts it, it is clear to us whether we wish to raise a question (doubt), or whether we wish to make a statement or give a judgment (belief) (EP1. 114 (1877)). Second, he notes that belief is a guide to action: it is because I believe the bank has my money that I go to the bank when I need to draw upon that money. Doubt is not at all like this: when I have doubts about the location of my money, I am unsure or unable to act (EP1. 114 (1877)). Third, and finally, he notes that doubt is a state that we find troubling or that makes us uneasy, and it is something from which we seek to free ourselves. When I come to doubt that the bank has my money, I seek to remove or eradicate that doubt and find out where my money is. Belief is not at all like this. When I believe that the bank has my money, I rest quite contented with this state and do not seek to remove or eradicate the belief. Belief, in contrast to doubt, is not a troubled or uneasy state but is instead a settled and satisfactory state (EP1. 114 (1877)). From these three observations about belief and doubt, Peirce sees the basis of an account of inquiry.

Whenever we have a body of satisfactory beliefs that guide our behaviours and capture what we expect of our experiences, we can see that we are in a settled state. We are confident in our opinions and statements and in the way we act in the world. Whenever we are confronted with serious doubts, we find ourselves without any satisfactory guide to behaviour or account of what to expect from our experiences and we are in a troubled enough state to raise questions and try to remove this doubt and find a settled state of belief once more. The drive and compulsion to move from a state of doubt to a state of settled belief is, for Peirce, simply the drive of inquiry. As Peirce says, 'The irritation of doubt causes a struggle to attain a state of belief. I shall term this struggle inquiry' (EP1. 114 (1877)).

To give a simple example, imagine that I confidently believe that I have enough fuel in my car to complete a journey that I intend to take. I will make self-assured statements to this effect and even behave according to this belief. I decline to stop and refuel when presented with a chance to do so since I'm confident I already have as much fuel as I need. However, when my passenger says that she thinks I should buy more fuel, that she suspects the fuel gauge of being faulty, and that it seems to have been a long time since I did refuel, I begin to have some doubts. Perhaps I've been hasty in declaring that I don't need fuel, and a range of questions present themselves. Is my passenger serious? Is the fuel gauge really unreliable? Has it been a long enough time since refuelling to suggest that my belief might not be well grounded? Until I attend to these questions and come up with satisfactory answers, I will no longer be in a settled state of belief, I will not make confident statements about the quantity of fuel in my car, and I will no longer be sure how to act when presented with the chance to refuel. To move from a state of settled belief to a state of doubt and by concerted effort to eradicate that doubt back to a settled state of belief once more is simply to engage in inquiry.

We shall examine some important ideas from Peirce about various methods of inquiry shortly, but it is worth noting two related things about this belief/doubt model of inquiry that make it especially distinctive. First, since inquiry is driven essentially by the need to eradicate doubt and reach a settled state of belief, truth is not immediately central to inquiry. As Peirce puts it:

> With the doubt, the struggle begins, and with the cessation of doubt it ends. Hence, the sole object of inquiry is the settlement of opinion. We may fancy that this is not enough for us, and that we seek, not merely an opinion, but a true opinion. But put this fancy to the test, and it proves groundless; for as soon as a firm belief is reached we are entirely satisfied, whether the belief be true or false. (EP1. 114–115 (1877))

We shall say more about the relationship between truth and this model of inquiry a little later, but the idea that our inquiries are not directly concerned with the truth might seem odd to some. But as Peirce says, simple observation is enough to tell us that our inquiries stop when our beliefs become settled once more, regardless of whether those beliefs are true or not. I may have come to doubt that my money is in the bank and, having set out to resolve the matter of where my money is, been reassured by the manager that it is, in fact, in the bank. She may have taken a solemn vow and even have shown me money in the bank vaults. Reassured, I return to a settled state of belief about where my money is: it's in the bank. I stop in my quest to determine the whereabouts of my money. The inquiry is over. At this point, it matters not one bit whether my money really is in the bank or somewhere else. The manager could be lying and could have shown me someone else's money, but I was reassured nonetheless, my doubts were eradicated and the inquiry duly ended.

The second thing to note about this belief/doubt model of inquiry is that it adds to Peirce's famous dismissal of the Cartesian method of doubt. If the cessation of doubt and the settlement of opinion is the sole object of inquiry, then one cannot conduct a genuine inquiry without a genuine doubt. According to Peirce, artificial or hypothetical doubts, such as those invoked by the Cartesian method, cannot lead to genuine inquiry since they lack the compulsion towards eradication and the settlement of opinion that is a marker of genuine doubt. For inquiry to occur and to be genuine, there must be 'a real and living doubt, and without this all discussion is idle' (EP1. 115 (1877)). In many respects, one can see the weight of this anti-Cartesian sentiment in our pre-theoretical responses to those sceptical arguments that employ systematic doubt. We can see the deductive weight of such arguments, but the doubt required to generate the premises of these arguments is rarely felt and seldom compels us to genuine inquiry.[1]

The methods of inquiry

Having established space for an account of inquiry as the struggle to eradicate doubt and reach a settled state of belief, Peirce goes on to discuss four possible methods of inquiry: *the method of tenacity, the method of authority, the a priori method* and *the method of science*. He notes that only one – the method of science – can be fully successful in the long run. Again, it is important to note that the mark of successful inquiry is the settlement of belief or opinion, and so the mark of a successful method of inquiry is its ability to arrive at a body of beliefs that are not easily disturbed by recalcitrant experience. With this in mind, let us examine Peirce's discussion of the four methods of inquiry.

The method of tenacity

The first method of inquiry that Peirce discusses in 'The fixation of belief' is what he calls 'the method of tenacity' (EP1. 115–117 (1877)). We can think of this method as something like the steadfast refusal to relinquish our beliefs in the face of recalcitrant evidence. I may believe that all swans are white, and when faced with what seems to be a black swan, I may simply refuse to acknowledge that this is evidence against my beliefs. This tenacious and dogmatic commitment to one's beliefs is a common enough phenomenon, and we see exactly how such *tenacious believers* respond to recalcitrance. For example, a commonly held but racially prejudiced belief is that black people are naturally more athletic and make for better sportsmen and women.[2] However, so entrenched are such beliefs in some quarters that even when confronted with compelling evidence to the contrary, these beliefs are retained. White heavyweight champions, white or Asian sprint champions, outstanding white basketball players – these are all somehow written off as anomalies or as exceptions which prove the rule.

Although this kind of tenacious belief is quite familiar to us, as a method of inquiry Peirce is quite rightly circumspect about its efficacy. As Peirce notes:

> A man may go through life, systematically keeping out of view all that might cause a change in his opinions and if he only succeeds [. . .] I do not see what can be said against his doing so. [. . .] But this method of fixing belief, which may be called the method of tenacity, will be unable to hold its ground in practice. The social impulse is against it. (EP1. 116 (1877))

It may be that whenever we are confronted with doubt, we commit ourselves to disregarding or avoiding recalcitrance and cling to our beliefs come what may, but this cannot give us a successful method of inquiry. For Peirce, given that the sole object of inquiry is the settlement of belief or opinion, it seems unlikely that we can avoid noticing that our beliefs are out of kilter with those around us. This ought to be unsettling – we can't all be right. Moreover, such a method will lead, quite obviously, to many different sets of beliefs, each as tenacious as the next. To avoid recalcitrance, then, the tenacious believer would need to avoid others with their differing beliefs, but given the social contexts in which we find ourselves, it is hard to see how such a means of eradicating doubt could ever be functional. As Peirce notes, if we can secure our beliefs against doubt by disregarding and avoiding recalcitrance, then all is well and good given the aims of inquiry, but in practice we cannot live in isolation from others and their beliefs. In that 'social impulse' lies the downfall of the method of tenacity.

The method of authority

The second method of inquiry that Peirce discusses in 'The fixation of belief' is what he calls 'the method of authority' (EP1. 117–118 (1877)).

In many respects, the method of authority is simply a deferral to particular prescribed shibboleths and dogmas, and wherever any doubt
arises through recalcitrance it is allayed or offset by recourse to official doctrine. Again, such a notion is quite familiar to us through,
for example, organised religion or totalitarian states. Whenever we
think of the state prescribing beliefs and attitudes for its citizens, we
think of mass indoctrination, state control of information and even
flat-out manipulation of facts to remove anything that contradicts official views. Indeed, in more extreme cases, people are removed lest
their opinions and beliefs lead to doubt and recalcitrance amongst the
broader population.

Such a method seems to be a superior means of achieving the
aims of inquiry than the method of tenacity. Beliefs are prescribed
across a whole society, and the manipulation of information and
insulation from other societies clearly does much to police potential
recalcitrance. Nonetheless, for Peirce, this method is obviously not
an appropriate means of securing the settlement of opinion in the
long term. As he notes:

> [N]o institution can undertake to regulate opinions upon every
> subject. Only the most important ones can be attended to, and
> on the rest men's minds must be left to the action of natural
> causes. This imperfection will be no source of weakness so long
> as men [. . .] cannot put two and two together. But [. . .] some
> individuals will be found who are raised above that condition.
> These men possess a wider sort of social feeling; they see that
> men in other countries and in other ages have held to very dif-
> ferent doctrines. (EP1. 118 (1877))

The point here is simply that the kind of total control needed to
make the method of authority effective simply cannot be had. We
will notice that amongst the beliefs that the state must leave to each
person to decide for themselves there is disagreement and multifor-
mity. There are always grounds for questioning why such doubt and
unsettlement cannot be extended to 'official' beliefs. Moreover, state
control of information and management of recalcitrance is never

comprehensive enough to leave society free of doubters and, as a result, dissenters. When, in order to preserve the 'correctness' of governmental agricultural policy, a state-induced famine is blamed on farmers' refusal to follow official techniques, it may well be that the majority believe that the state is correct in how food should be grown and distributed. The 'culpable' farmers, however, are less likely to be convinced that the officially sanctioned belief is as stable as all that. The crucial point in Peirce's criticism of the method of authority, though, runs parallel to his complaints against the method of tenacity – there is a social impulse that counts against it.

As Peirce notes, those people who are prone to question official beliefs or to be concerned that state-sanctioned doctrines are not beyond doubt are those with 'a wider sort of social feeling' (EP1. 118 (1877)). Just as the method of tenacity will struggle to keep individual belief systems insulated from each other, the method of authority will fail ultimately to prevent society-wide beliefs from interacting with alternative views from other societies, contemporary or historical. People locate their beliefs, whether acquired individually or officially sanctioned, in the context of other potential beliefs. Whenever we do this there are grounds for raising questions and the possibility of unsettled belief.

The a priori method

The third method of inquiry that Peirce discusses in 'The fixation of belief' is what he calls 'the *a priori* method' (EP1. 118–120 (1877)). In many ways, this method is simply one of allowing systems of belief to develop from simple presupposition without any necessary recourse to reality. Further, such beliefs are simply required to run the tribunal of rational coherence and reason rather than mere empirical correspondence in order to be deemed acceptable. This is the kind of method that sounds most familiar to those of a philosophical bent, and Peirce is quick to point to philosophy for his examples:

> The most perfect example of [the *a priori* method] is to be found in the history of philosophy. Systems of this sort have not usually

> rested upon any observed facts, at least not to any great degree.
> They have been chiefly adopted because their fundamental prop-
> ositions seemed 'agreeable to reason'. [. . .] Plato, for example,
> finds it agreeable to reason that the distances of the celestial
> spheres from one another should be proportional to the differ-
> ent lengths of strings which produce harmonious chords. (EP1.
> 118–119 (1877))

Peirce's observation is that since the chief deficiencies of both the
method of tenacity and the method of authority stem from their
attempts to close down exposure to other sets of beliefs, allowing
other sets of beliefs to exist and be judged by their rational coherence then seems to sidestep these problems.

The problem, however, is that this kind of system building can
accommodate all kinds of belief and offer all manner of theorising without it being at all clear that we are engaged in effective
inquiry. Instead, what seems to be an interesting and useful body
of beliefs will simply give way to some other body of beliefs when
tastes change and fashions in theory-building shift. For example,
Pythagorean ideas about speculative numerology – the notion that
numbers are the core explanatory element of the universe – can be
made coherent with our experiences of the world if we have a taste
for such a view. The presence of good and evil in the world corresponds to the presence of odd and even numbers and so on. But in
the end, such speculative systems will fall aside when our explanatory tastes change. As Peirce observes:

> This method is far more intellectual and respectable from
> the point of view of reason than either of the others we have
> noticed. But its failure has been the most manifest. It makes
> of inquiry something similar to the development of taste; but
> taste, unfortunately, is always more or less a matter of fashion,
> and accordingly metaphysicians have never come to any fixed
> agreement, but the pendulum has swung backward and forward
> between a more material and a more spiritual philosophy from
> the earliest times to the latest. (EP1. 119 (1877))

When we come to see that our theories are influenced in this way, and that taste is an integral part of what we take to be a good theory and fashion a factor in what strikes us as a compelling counter-instance, we come to have some concerns about the solidity of our beliefs. Of course, such concerns are simply doubts. From Peirce's point of view, even as common and familiar a method as this will not secure long-term settlement of opinion. We allow beliefs and theories to flourish and bloom according to the tastes of believers and theory builders. But once we become aware that the prevalence of any belief is subject to the vicissitudes of intellectual tastes, we come to have doubts about the stability of our current beliefs.

The method of science

The final method that Peirce discusses in 'The fixation of belief' is what he calls 'the method of science' (EP1. 120–123 (1877)). Peirce was an accomplished practising scientist for most of his life, and so he had clear ideas about what the practice of science and the scientific method involved. We shall not venture into his theories here but will note instead that Peirce characterises the method of science as, broadly, a commitment to the existence of what he calls 'some external permanency' (EP1. 120 (1877)). The idea is that we have to see our beliefs as arising in relation to an external world with independent objects and properties. As Peirce puts it:

> Its [the method of science's] fundamental hypothesis [. . .] is this: There are real things, whose characters are entirely independent of our opinion about them; those realities affect our senses according to regular laws, and though our sensations are as different as our relations to the objects, yet by taking advantage of the laws of perception, we can ascertain by reasoning how things really are, and any man, if he have sufficient experience and reason enough about it, will be led to the one true conclusion. (EP1. 120 (1877))

There are couple of things to note about this view of science that turn out to be quite crucial to how Peirce views matters here. First, this method is marked out as distinct from the other methods of inquiry by moving away from matters of human interest and towards an external guide to belief. In the methods of tenacity, authority and *a priori* system building, the guide by which we judge whether a belief is settled and a doubt rightfully set aside is a matter of human interest: does it meet with *my current beliefs?* does it meet with the beliefs *prescribed by authority?* does it accord with the *assumptions upon which I've built my system* a priori? If so, the belief is settled and doubt is eradicated, although not for long if Peirce's concerns are correct. The method of science, however, adjudicates the settlement of belief and eradication of doubt in accord with external facts: Is this belief in line with *the way the world is?* Naturally, the way the world is has to be a matter independent of human interest. If the world is as it is, our human interest in its being otherwise is neither here nor there.

A second and related thing to note about this is that only the method of science seems to have anything like a robust element of 'right' or 'wrong' about it, and so it is the only method by which we can judge any set of beliefs as being correct. The other methods all adjudicate the need to retain a belief on matters of comfort, conformity or taste. These are not matters that clearly make my belief on some matter wrong and your belief on that same matter right. It's perfectly acceptable for us to find comfort in different ways, to conform to different authorities or to have different tastes. The method of science is not like this. If my beliefs make less sense of the world and lead to disturbance more often than your beliefs, then I am doing something wrong and you are doing something right.

Interestingly, coupled with the first fact about the appeal to an external permanency made by the method of science, this second point about having a standard by which to judge right from wrong leads us to what amounts to Peirce's famous and important claim that the method of science is *self-corrective.* If we think that the world is as it is independently of human interests and that our beliefs can be right or wrong in how far they accord with this, then we can see that the world will eventually pull our beliefs into line with it. Whenever they are wrong, beliefs will run into conflict with the world at some point, and the only beliefs that won't meet with recalcitrance and lead to doubt will be beliefs that correctly approximate the way the world is. Put this way, the method of science feels very familiar as an account of inquiry. Consider the following example.

Suppose I see the moon shining from the earth and assume that its brightness is due to its reflecting the light of the earth. After all, there is no sun at night, so what else could be making the moon shine? But despite my comfort in this belief, you note a worry: if my belief is correct, why does the moon have phases? There is nothing around that obstructs the supposed light shining from the earth, so the moon should always be bright and full. Perhaps, you suggest, my belief is incorrect. Troubled and convinced by your objection, you and I endeavour to discover what could explain the brightness of the moon *and* its phases. After some thought, we conclude that it is perhaps the sun that shines upon the moon after all, and the phases are explained by the partial obscuring of sunlight by the earth passing between the two bodies. But then our friend notes a worry: if our belief is correct, how come she can see the moon in the daytime (albeit less bright and obvious), but still apparently in phases? Presumably, it wouldn't appear in its phases until we on the earth pass between it and the sun, but here we are, both facing the sun. Perhaps, she suggests, our beliefs are wrong. Troubled and convinced by her worry, we all endeavour to discover what could explain the brightness and the phasing if the earth passing between the moon and the sun isn't a causal factor. After some musing, we conclude that what we are seeing is the sun shining on the moon, that the phasing is caused by our own perspective on this phenomenon, and that depending on where we are, the moon will *seem* to have more or less of its surface illuminated. This would explain its brightness, its phasing and its daytime appearances. This belief leaves us content and settled.

This is all contrived, of course, but it illustrates how our beliefs meet recalcitrance and can be judged as incorrect and fit for replacement by a better correspondence with observed facts. Further, it shows how we can keep doing this until we edge closer to some belief that will not meet with recalcitrance. In short, it shows how the method is self-corrective.

The third and final thing to note about Peirce's account of the method of science is that he thinks that by subjecting our beliefs to sufficient experience and appropriate reasoning, we can arrive at what he calls 'the one true conclusion'. We shall explore this idea further in the next section, but it is worth pointing out that this is a rudimentary suggestion of what is often thought of as the claim that inquiries are *convergent*. The idea is simply that if the world is as it is independently of us, and our beliefs can be judged right or wrong by it, then my inquiries, given time, will accord with the way the world is. The compulsion to avoid doubt will drive this. But similarly, any inquiry into the same question will eventually arrive at the same belief.

Obviously, this method of inquiry, for Peirce, is to be preferred over the others. The reasons are straightforward. Judged by the standards for successful inquiry, namely the eradication of doubt and the settlement of belief or opinion, this method is superior. The first three methods will never take us to a point where our beliefs are immune to recalcitrance. However settled our beliefs are now, there will always be another individual or society with different beliefs, or a change in the tastes that provide starting points for our current theories. Science, on the other hand, will take us steadily towards a state where our beliefs adapt and develop in line with our recalcitrant experiences until we reach a state where our beliefs are in line with the world as it is and so can draw no recalcitrance from it.

Truth and reality

Peirce's discussion of the methods of inquiry is something that we shall return to shortly, since there are important questions to raise and clarifications to make about just what Peirce is trying to achieve with this discussion. At this point, however, we shall turn to what is perhaps the most important and controversial element of Peirce's account of inquiry – that he puts it to service in giving us an account of truth and reality.

We looked at Peirce's pragmatism in the last chapter, paying close attention to his original account in the 1878 paper 'How to make our ideas clear' (EP1. 124–141 (1878)). This is a paper from the same *Illustrations of the Logic of Science* series as 'The fixation of belief', our concern in this chapter. In 'How to make our ideas clear', Peirce shows us how we can attain a third grade of clarity over and above our everyday familiarity with a concept or our ability to offer a definition of it, that is, by showing what practical bearings and expectations follow from our understanding of that concept. Part of his project there is to highlight the power of the pragmatic explication of concepts by giving us examples, one of which is the concept of reality.

Peirce notes that we all show remarkable familiarity with the concept of reality in our daily lives: 'no idea could be clearer than this. Every child uses it with perfect confidence' (EP1. 136 (1878)). Further, he notes that though an abstract definition may be harder to arrive at for most of us, we can still define reality as 'that whose characters are independent of what anybody may think them to be' (EP1. 137 (1878)). Looking to the practical effects of the concept of reality, however, Peirce suggests that 'the only effect which real things have is to cause belief' (EP1. 137 (1878)). But since fictions may also cause belief, the pressing question for us in seeing the practical effects of reality is how we distinguish between true and false belief. This takes us back to the methods of inquiry introduced in 'The fixation of belief'. As Peirce suggests, 'the ideas of truth and falsehood, in their full development, appertain exclusively to the scientific method of settling opinion' (EP1. 137 (1878)). What matters most for the connection between the scientific method and the pragmatic explication of the concept of reality, however, is the way in which Peirce sees scientific progress. To quote at length:

> [A]ll followers of science are fully persuaded that the processes of investigation, if only pushed far enough, will give one certain solution to every question to which they can be applied. One may investigate the velocity of light by studying the transits of Venus and the aberration of the stars: another by the opposition of Mars and eclipses of Jupiter's satellites; a third by the method of Fizeau [. . .]. They may, at first obtain different results, but, as each perfects

his methods and processes, the results will move steadily toward a destined centre. So with all scientific research. Different minds may set out with the most antagonistic views, but the progress of investigation carries them by a force outside of themselves to one and the same conclusion. This activity of thought by which we are carried, not where we wish, but to a foreordained goal, is like the operation of destiny. No modification of the point of view taken, no selection of other facts for study, no natural bent of mind even, can enable a man to escape the predestinate opinion. This great law is embodied in the conception of truth and reality. The opinion which is fated to be ultimately agreed upon by all who investigate, is what we mean by the truth, and the object represented in this opinion is the real. This is the way I would explain reality. (EP1. 138–139 (1878))

This is a rich and dense passage, but in it Peirce gives what is the most important early statement of his view on how the settlement of opinion and account of inquiry intersect with his account of pragmatism and the pragmatic clarification of concepts. In essence, the idea is that the best available method for settling opinion, the scientific method, is guided by its adherence to external permanencies; it depends on something external to humans for a standard of right and wrong. This enables us to judge right or true belief from wrong or false belief, in so far as true beliefs will accord with the external world and false beliefs will, at some point, lead us into recalcitrance and doubt.

The strength of Peirce's claim here comes from his observation that we can commence inquiry from various starting points with very different presuppositions and intellectual dispositions, but so long as we let the scientific method guide our way, we will converge upon the same answer. His example is inquiry for determining the velocity of light, and it is a common phenomenon in the annals of science to find different approaches and programs of investigation converging on the same theories or concepts.[3] The conclusion for Peirce, then, is straightforward: when investigation has converged and no recalcitrance can arise because our beliefs are doubt-proof in virtue of according neatly with the constraints placed upon them by the external permanencies which we let guide our inquiries, we have a body of opinions that are aptly called 'true' and a concomitant description of the external permanencies that is aptly called 'reality'.

This is an intriguing and controversial view of truth and reality, and we shall look at some of the problems with it and objections to it soon. However, it is worth noting two things about this view before we begin examining the many objections given against it.

First of all, it is crucial to note that it is a *pragmatic explication* and not a definitional analysis.[4] As Peirce is keen to note in his discussion of his pragmatic maxim, it is meant to extend our understanding of the meaning of a given concept beyond everyday familiarity or abstract definition. Peirce's explanation of truth and reality, then, is a pragmatic explication of the practical effects of using such concepts (EP1. 127 (1878)).

Second, the concepts of truth and reality are very intimately connected on this view. Peirce's stated aim at the end of 'How to make our ideas clear' is to give a pragmatic explication of reality as the object represented in the body of beliefs that comprises the final opinion. In this explication, Peirce also gives us a corresponding account of truth as the fated or final opinion agreed upon by all who carry inquiry sufficiently far (EP1. 139 (1878)).

The importance of these two features of Peirce's account of truth and reality may not be immediately apparent, but they prove to be crucial, as we shall see. Understanding that Peirce's account of truth and reality is a pragmatic explication rather than a constitutive definition, for instance, heads off a range of complaints against the view. Similarly, understanding that truth and reality are intimately connected on this view makes it easier to see how and why Peirce's views develop in his later work and overcome some of the difficulties which beset this early account. At this point, however, it is enough to note these two features of Peirce's view and move on.

Criticism of the early view

For all the details we have just introduced, Peirce's early picture of inquiry, truth and reality is a rather simple and, to an extent, simplistic view. *Belief* is a settled state of opinion; *doubt* a state of irritation that drives us to find a settled state once more. The attempt to settle our opinions is just the process of *inquiry*, and of the various ways we can soothe our doubts back into a state of belief, the scientific method is best. This is because it offers the only chance of arriving at a permanently settled body of beliefs, and followed sufficiently far it guarantees that we arrive at a final settled opinion on any question. That final fated opinion is the *truth*, and that body of fact it represents is *reality*. Intriguingly, his account was not much challenged in his own lifetime, with his contemporary Josiah Royce offering the most robust critique. Nonetheless, there are clearly some worrying elements to the theory, and as Peirce presents the argument in the *Illustrations of the Logic of Science* papers it has, over time, attracted considerable criticism. We shall examine six of the more interesting criticisms here.

The specious methods are 'strawmen'

When Peirce discusses the four methods of inquiry, it becomes obvious that the arguments given against the methods of tenacity, authority and *a priori* system building are ushered through rather quickly. As Murray Murphey, a leading early interpreter of Peirce, puts it:

> That the scientific method is the only adequate means of reaching agreement and therefore the method which will prevail, Peirce seeks to show by proving that each of the alternatives will fail in the long run, where science will not. But the arguments which are presented for this purpose are barely worthy of the name. To say that the method of tenacity fails because 'the social impulse is against it' (5.378) is hardly adequate, and Peirce's confidence in the impossibility of a completely authoritarian state cannot survive twentieth-century history. In fact, Peirce takes it for granted that his reader will agree upon the inadequacy of these methods without any real proof, and he therefore makes no serious effort to provide one. (Murphey 1961, 164–165)

Murphey then goes on to describe as 'straw methods' the non-scientific means of fixing belief suggested by Peirce. Whilst this is perhaps unduly disparaging – the papers were written for the *Popular Science Monthly* and so were intended for a popular audience – Murphey's worry that the specious methods may be more robust than Peirce gives them credit for still looks like a reasonable first response to this early account of inquiry. It is clear that Peirce's comparison of the four methods in 'The fixation of belief' is not even-handed. The first three methods are judged by their effectiveness in providing a stable belief, yet the method of science is arguably judged by a different set of criteria, including its reliance on an independent reality and Peirce's own experience and confidence in its efficacy. Indeed, even if we were inclined to grant Peirce's claim that, unlike science, the first three methods cannot permanently fix belief, there is also an assumption that these four methods are exhaustive. However, the idea that no other methods of 'artificial' or non-scientific belief fixation are available is not compelling either. So this concern is natural and worth addressing, but it can be answered, I think, by looking at a more recent discussion of just these concerns from another leading Peirce scholar, Cheryl Misak.

In her *Truth and the End of Inquiry* (1991), Misak devotes some time to the question of specious methods and asks why they are unfit to permanently fix belief. Drawing on an objection from Frankfurt (1958), Misak notes that we can easily imagine a case where 'a pill would forever freeze our beliefs' (1991, 46), and that, by his own argument, Peirce would have to concede that it is worth our while to adopt such a method. Crucially, though, as Misak points out, there is something of a definitional stop on such methods. If we understand belief properly, then whatever such specious methods as authority or belief-freezing pills are fixing, it isn't obvious that we should call it 'belief'. At the very least, belief is such that it ought to resign in the face of recalcitrance, and it ought to give way to an awareness that it came about from a questionable method. Considered this way, the 'beliefs' created by the specious methods mentioned by Peirce, or any other more robust methods which we might imagine, will fail to count as genuine beliefs if they remain fixed yet unresponsive to evidence.

Murphey's objection is, I think, more or less put to rest by Misak's reading, especially since she gives us some textual reasons for thinking that such an argument is present beneath the popularist veneer of the *Popular Science Monthly* papers. As Misak notes, Peirce is clear in these early papers that belief must be responsive to evidence (EP1. 119–120 (1877)) and that we ought to be suspicious of those who call such artificially fixed states and propositions 'beliefs' and 'truth' (EP1. 137 (1878)). Murphey's response is perhaps natural, but a more charitable reading of what Peirce says about the deficiencies of the non-scientific methods means we can set such concerns aside.

The opacity of the final state of belief

The view of truth as the final or fated opinion is, in many ways, the area of Peirce's account of inquiry that draws the most fire. A great many of these objections come from the lazy tendency to lump all early pragmatist views together and then systematically misread the claims in order to provide a stalking horse for more 'robust' accounts of truth.[5] However, some who have paid more attention to the details of Peirce's account are worth attending to.

The first such complaint against Peirce's notion of truth is put most clearly by Crispin Wright (1992, 45–47). As Wright notes, Peirce's view of truth is couched in epistemic terms. A proposition is true if, after a sufficiently long and appropriate inquiry, we cannot find any more information to overturn it or undermine our belief in it. However, for Wright, the idea of belief at the end point of inquiry is an epistemic idealisation, which poses problems since it is impossible to see how anyone could be in such a state and know that they had a complete set information relevant to a given question, hypothesis or belief. Having a belief for which there is no more recalcitrant evidence to consider is one thing; knowing that we have attained that state is another. But why is this supposed to matter?

The crux of the worry here for Wright is definitional.[6] If truth is defined in Peirce's picture by giving strict conditions for the truth of a proposition, then it looks as though the conditions are impossible to fulfil. For example, take a proposition, P. Let's say that a necessary and sufficient condition for P being true is that P would be believed were we to conduct and complete an inquiry into P (i.e. knowingly take inquiry into P to its final state). But since we cannot complete such an inquiry – an inquiry is not complete until we know that no more evidence or information can be brought to bear – the anteced-ent of the subjunctive conditional we have just used is false. Truth cannot be satisfactorily defined on such a view.

Wright may be correct that any definition of truth which generates subjunctive conditionals with exclusively false antecedents is going to be in trouble, but there are a couple of simple responses to the kind of concern that we are looking at here. First, it's not entirely clear why Wright thinks Peirce's description of truth as belief at the end of inquiry comes with the epistemic constraint he suggests. Peirce seems only to require that our doubt-proof beliefs underpin actions, not that we are aware we have attained such a doubt-proof state. Second, and more important, is a point we noted above: Peirce does not take himself to be merely giving a definition of truth. Rather, the account of truth we see here stems from his giving us an example of how the third grade of clarity can elucidate key philosophical concepts such as reality. What we are looking at here is a pragmatic elucidation of truth, not a definition of it. The complaint that a final state of inquiry is such that we cannot know when we have entered into it, thus leaving us with problematic definitions of truth, is moot. A definition of truth was neither given nor aspired to in Peirce's early account.

The scientific method doesn't give us belief

Whilst the two criticisms we have just examined are relatively easy to handle, a commonly mentioned concern about Peirce's model of inquiry is more difficult. It seems that there is a conflict between how Peirce frames his model of inquiry and his advocating for the method of science as the most effective means of pursuing it. Christopher Hookway, for instance, puts the concern thusly:

> It turns out that by adopting the method of science we postpone the removal of doubt for the sake of a settlement of belief which

is truly stable. Adoption of the method of science provides no guarantee that we shall settle belief in the short run [. . .]. In that case, it is reasonable to protest, I have not obtained what I was looking for. I sought a method for removing the irritation of doubt; and I triumphantly endorse a method which requires me to put up with it in the hope that when, eventually, it is removed, the removal will be permanent. (Hookway 2000, 34)

Simply put, the model of inquiry that Peirce develops is driven by our compelling need to remove doubt when we find it because it is an irritating state, but the method he advocates for removing it, science, seems to require of us that we accept and embrace doubt. The problem is, essentially, that if inquiry is such that its forward momentum is obtained by our need to remove the felt irritation of doubt, then it is hard to see why it would push us to embrace a method which requires us to willingly embrace that irritation. The removal of doubt is a 'here and now' compulsion, but the method of science is a strategy for the long game. Peirce requires us on the one hand to seek immediate gratification by relieving doubt, and on the other hand to accept delayed gratification by adopting a method that only gives us peace in the long run. We are to be doxastic grasshoppers and methodological ants. It is not a compelling picture.

Not all inquiry is 'problem solving'

A further concern about Peirce's belief/doubt model of inquiry is that it does not provide a very accurate picture of how we arrive at many of our beliefs or of why we engage in inquiry at all. One finds this complaint expressed most clearly by Israel Scheffler (1974, 67–68; 2009, 107–108). For example:

[T]here is, in fact, much thinking that does not originate in doubt. Imagination, recollection, perception, composition – all seem to provide counter-instances. But, it will be said, Peirce speaks of inquiry specifically, not thinking in general, and he is surely concentrating on scientific research as his model. Is it then true, at least, that all such research in fact originates [. . .] in [. . .]

doubt? Does there need to be an active and real irritation [. . .] before scientific research can begin? Does not theoretical curiosity or playfulness have a role in sparking scientific thought? (Scheffler 1974, 68)

The concern that Scheffler expresses here is quite straightforward. For Peirce, inquiry is motivated by the eradication of doubt, but this implies that our doxastic path through the world is driven solely by problem solving. This seems too restrictive, even if we limit ourselves to scientific inquiry. Whilst we may well be motivated for much of the time by problem solving, we are also very often problem seeking. We are often motivated to inquiry by simple curiosity, by nothing more than the urge to work out the upshot of a simple conjecture, and as apocryphal and sanitised as the history of science often is, it is still littered with examples of discoveries and advances in knowledge driven by conjecture, accident and blind curiosity rather than by the kind of compulsive doubt-driven call to action that Peirce has in mind here.

There are various things we might say in Peirce's defence, especially since the epistemological picture present in 'The fixation of belief' is under-described. Perhaps a charitable reading of Peirce's early work here might recast the problem-seeking inquiries in terms of the problem-solving model. After all, Peirce is aware that there are other ways in which philosophers try to generate doubt and thus motivate inquiry, as his urging against the feigned doubt of the Cartesian method makes clear. There is also an implicit prescriptive element to these early arguments, so perhaps we should see his aim as directing us towards a more pragmatically effective method of inquiry. All the same, there are reasons to think that this is a fair complaint against the model of inquiry we find in Peirce's early papers.

Issues with fated or final opinions

As we noted above, it is the account of truth that emerges from Peirce's theory that often draws the most criticism. To finish our survey of the problems facing Peirce's early account of inquiry, we will look at two clusters of criticism that stem from the connection between inquiry on the one hand and, on the other, truth as the fated or final opinion. The second problem, 'the problem of buried facts', is the more serious of the two, and we shall look at that in a moment. Here, we shall quickly introduce a series of worries about just how clear the concept of fated or final opinion really is.

The worry can be broken into two complaints. The first is the rather simple and common observation, often attributed to Peirce's contemporary, Josiah Royce (1899), that if inquiry never actually reaches a 'satisfactory' end – and what reasons have we for thinking that it will? – then it seems that on Peirce's view there can be no true beliefs. If truth is just what we identify with the belief settled at the end of inquiry, then without an inquiry's end there can be no true belief. This seems concerning given our common assumptions about the veracity of many of the beliefs we hold, and even if we are happy to concede that many of our current beliefs might be overturned in the future and that we are none the worse for that, the thought that we might *never* have a fully settled belief, and thus truth, is itself an unsettling thing to countenance. In short, we seem to need an end to inquiry in order to have truth, but it is unclear why we should have any confidence that our inquiries will follow the projection Peirce makes for them and tend towards an end.

The second and related concern, often attributed to Bertrand Russell (1939) in his criticism of John Dewey's account of inquiry, is that by identifying truth and reality as the end point of inquiry, we seem to allow that the opinions held by the last inquirers on earth have some special feature. This seems odd, given that the opinions held by the last humans on earth might very well represent a premature end to inquiry or be held in times of catastrophe. These opinions would represent, in some sense, the final opinion and thereby represent a body of truths. Whilst we have no reason to believe that the last people on earth would hold a very interesting or expansive body of opinions – indeed, Russell thinks that their concerns would be with the rather mundane affair of survival – the more disconcerting feature of this worry is that it takes no great leap of imagination to see how far such a body of 'final beliefs' could be from expressing truths or representing reality.

There are issues with both these complaints, and both ultimately rest on a lack of clarity about what Peirce has in mind when he speaks of the 'final opinion'. Nonetheless, these concerns are still pertinent since, as we shall see shortly, Peirce's means of expressing his view in the *Popular Science Monthly* papers leave him without the tools for handling the Roycian and Russellian worries mentioned here.

The problem of buried facts

Of all the problems for the early view that we have mentioned, 'the problem of buried facts' is by far the most serious. The problem, essentially, is that if there are questions or facts that inquiries could not provide an answer for, then we have no stable beliefs about them at the end of inquiry, and by extension there is no truth to be had in matters concerning them. Moreover, it is far from ludicrous to suppose that there are questions to which no answer would be forthcoming, no matter how far inquiry is taken. It is fruitful to divide this problem into buried facts of three kinds, what we shall call *lost facts, distant facts* and *uninquireable facts*.

Intriguingly, Peirce himself mentions lost facts, but he characteristically shrugs off the problem in 'How to make our ideas clear'. As he puts it:

> I may be asked what I have to say to all the minute facts of history, forgotten, never to be recovered, to the lost books of the ancients, to the buried secrets. [. . .] To this I reply that [. . .] it is unphilosophical to suppose that, with regard to any given question (which has any clear meaning), investigation would not bring forth a solution to it, if it were carried far enough. (EP1. 139–140 (1878))

Peirce clearly states the problem here. It does not seem perverse to think that there are obscure facts in the past that are now irrevocably 'lost' to history and for which no amount of inquiry, no matter how well conducted, could settle an opinion one way or the other. For instance, how many hairs did the first human to cross the landbridge between Asia and North America have on his or her right arm? I have no idea how to set about answering such a question, and Peirce's confidence that such a question could be answered with enough investigation seems misplaced and unsatisfactory. It's true, of course, that the forward process of inquiry recovers all kinds of facts that we may never have thought it possible for us to know. For example, how did the insects of the Jurassic period sound? It seems incredible to imagine that we could settle on an answer, yet by modelling the kind of sounds crickets and insects recovered from the appropriate portion of the fossil record would make, we can deliver an answer and perhaps settle opinions on such an obscure matter.[7] All the same, such wonderful and surprising recoveries of information don't do much to alleviate the worry, and it seems only the most naive Pollyanna of science would believe that *every* such dim and dwindling fact of the past is recoverable through inquiry. And as we said, facts lost behind the veil of history are not the only type of case that seems to threaten Peirce's picture here.

The problem of distant facts — that is, circumstances that would require inquiry across vast physical distances — could leave our inquiries just as frustrated as historically lost facts. It is easy to imagine facts buried by our physical and spatial remove, minute and hidden occurrences at some corner of the universe lost to us by virtue of distance. Indeed, Peirce would have been aware of just such concerns from the history of science. For example, the great French positivist Auguste Comte confidently stated:

> Of all objects, the planets are those which appear to us under the least varied aspect. We see how we determine their forms, their distances, their bulk, and their motion, but we can never know anything of their chemical or mineralogical structure; and much less that of organised beings living on their surface. (Comte 1858/2009, 137)

The problem for Comte's prediction, of course, was that it was wrong. Discoveries by Gustav Kirchhoff and William Huggins using spectrum analysis did within a few short years of his prediction exactly what Comte said would never happen. As an employee of the Harvard Observatory making important discoveries of his own in the field of spectroscopy,[8] Peirce was completely aware of this:

> Auguste Comte said that it was clearly impossible for man to ever learn anything of the chemical constitution of the fixed stars, but before his book had reached its readers the discovery which he announced as impossible had been made. (W2. 64)

It is little wonder that Peirce expresses such confidence that buried facts will be uncovered. Nonetheless, physically distant facts seem just as possible as historically lost facts and would seem to pose just as much of a problem.

Finally, there seems to be a potential problem with facts or circumstances of inquiry that are, by definition, uninquireable or uncompletable. Christopher Hookway gives one such example:

> Suppose that one of the branches of [a] tree is contained within a protective box which would have to be opened before [a] count [of its leaves] could be completed. And suppose that this box is designed so that opening it will trigger a bomb that destroys the entire earth. In that case, nobody could inquire long enough and well enough: trying to inquire well enough would disastrously prevent the inquiry continuing for long enough. (Hookway 2000, 54–55)

The possibility of inquiring fully into some fact or feature of the world seems to be ruled out by the very nature of the inquiry. Similarly, if we are interested in the state of the world prior to a time when any possible inquiry could have taken place, or we are interested in the state of the world after inquiry becomes impossible, there seems to be a straightforward definitional block on the inquiry itself. The very possibility of inquiry into these kinds of questions seems to be curtailed by the questions themselves. We cannot make the inquiry without contravening a condition of the question and thus derailing the inquiry. Similarly, suppose we are interested in discovering the state of some array of subatomic particles which interest us because they are affected by observation. In such a case, how can we find out what the unobserved state of these particles is without observing them? Our very attempt to ascertain an answer to our question seems to push the answer forever beyond our reach. These kinds of facts seem to be part of the way the world is, if our naive commitment to realism is anything to go by, but our inability to frame a final opinion on them means Peirce's account must judge us to be in error: no final opinion on a matter means there is no truth about it and no portion of reality that it represents.

Between them, the lost, distant and uninquireable facts seem to pose a significant problem for Peirce. He has to be committed to the view that such buried facts either do not exist and we could settle an inquiry into them, or that they are not part a of reality at all. We cannot settle opinion on them, so there is no truth about them and they do not feature in the description of reality represented by the final, settled body of belief and opinion. This is all counter-intuitive at best.

The later account of inquiry

Important developments

As we saw when examining Peirce's work on pragmatism, the ideas that emerged from the *Popular Science Monthly* papers of the 1870s were to undergo changes in light of crucial developments in his philosophical thinking. Indeed, the theories of truth and inquiry were affected at least as radically as the account of pragmatism, and Peirce's later views on inquiry, truth and reality are strikingly more subtle than their earlier counterparts. In what follows, we shall look at three important philosophical developments in Peirce's broader work before tracing out the account of truth and inquiry that emerges from them. As we shall see, Peirce's more sophisticated view of the architectonic and his growing anti-nominalism, a separation of the concepts of truth and reality, and new thoughts about the nature of inquiry and the role of science lead to a nuanced and subtle later theory. That later theory, at its clearest after the turn of the century, treats truth as a principle for guiding inquiry, places hope for a convergence of opinions at the centre of scientific endeavours, and recognises that not all inquiries can be modelled after an idealised picture of theoretical science. We shall then conclude this chapter by looking at how this later theory deals with problems facing the earlier account.

The effect of the architectonic

We have frequently mentioned Peirce's commitment to treating his philosophy architectonically, and the crystallisation of his views in this area around the turn of the century influenced the changes he made to earlier theories. In the case of inquiry, as we mentioned in our examination of his pragmatism, he sees a whole sub-branch of the normative science of logic dedicated to its study: the methodeutic.[9] We are familiar by now with the idea that Peirce thinks philosophy is subordinate to mathematics but super-ordinate to the special sciences. We have also seen that he thinks philosophy is divisible into phenomenology, the normative sciences and metaphysics, and that the normative sciences are divisible into aesthetics, or the study of what is 'objectively admirable' (EP2. 260 (1903)); ethics, or the study of 'self-controlled or deliberate conduct' (EP2. 260 (1903)); and logic, or the study of 'self-controlled, or deliberate, thought' (EP2. 260 (1903)). For our concerns here, though, the further division of logic is most important.

We noted in Chapter 2 that Peirce divides logic into speculative grammar, or the study of signs; critical logic, which examines the structure and forms of argument; and methodeutic, which he claims 'studies the methods that ought to be pursued in the investigation, in the exposition, and in the application of truth' (EP2. 260 (1903)). This third branch is where he places his pragmatic maxim, and it is also the place where his account of inquiry is properly located. The methodeutic, as the study of best methods pertaining to truth, is more or less the study of how best to conduct inquiry. Of course, this only tells us where Peirce places his more developed view of inquiry, not what that more developed view is. Nonetheless, a couple of interesting points emerge from placing the account of inquiry into a broader architectonic picture.

First, the normative elements of Peirce's account are brought to the fore by placing inquiry into the methodeutic branch of logic. Not only are we looking at a normative science, but the prescriptive nature of Peirce's account of inquiry becomes explicit here; he is concerned with the methods that *ought* to be pursued when we are investigating the truth of some matter. Arguably, Peirce's earlier account of inquiry has some prescriptive elements too, since we are asked to judge the effectiveness of different methods of inquiry, but the normativity is readily apparent in the later view of inquiry as methodeutic. This also draws upon the growing anti-nominalism in Peirce's later work. The ready acceptance of the reality of possibilities makes it much more tolerable to ask what the final conclusion *would* be if we were to follow the prescribed methods of the methodeutic.

The second important point to notice here is that by placing the account of inquiry into the methodeutic, Peirce is not merely interested in how different methods solve our problems or answer our questions, but also in how the understanding of how different methods solve our problems helps us to attain the truth. As he puts it:

> Many persons will think that there are other ways of acquiring skill in the art of inquiry which will be more instructive than the logical study of the theory of inquiry. That may be; I shall not dispute it; [...] I only claim that however much one may learn in other ways of the method of attacking an unfamiliar problem, something may be added to that knowledge by considering the general theory of how research must be performed. (CP2. 106 (1902))

The upshot of this is that Peirce sees that different inquiries may utilise and make progress through many different methods, but by understanding that there may be some 'purely logical doctrine of how discovery must take place' (CP2. 107 (1902)), we see how those inquiries can eventually attain truth.

The separation of truth and reality

In the early account of inquiry, we saw that truth and reality are explicitly linked. A pragmatic explication of truth and reality simply tells us that at the end of inquiry we will find a stable, doubt-proof body of belief which expresses truth and represents a body of facts as reality. In later work, however, Peirce begins to think of our contact with reality in different terms. In his account of the 1870s, he sees that in terms of the three grades of clearness, we have both clear and distinct ideas of reality:

> Every child uses [the concept of reality] with perfect confidence, never dreaming that he does not understand it. As for clearness in its second grade [. . .] a definition may perhaps be reached by considering the points of difference between reality and its opposite, fiction. A figment is a product of somebody's imagination; it has such characters as thought impresses upon it. That those characters are independent of how you or I think is an external reality. (EP1. 136 (1878))

The attempt to explain the third grade of clarity – understanding the practical bearings of holding some belief to be true – is what leads Peirce to draw his early accounts of truth and reality so close together. Whilst in later work Peirce still tends to define reality much as he does here, with the second grade of clarity, his accounts of how we make cognitive contact with reality change quite markedly, especially during the 1880s and beyond. Particular pressing was work by Josiah Royce[10] which suggested that the possibility of false beliefs about external objects led to difficulties for accounts of truth similar to that given by Peirce.[11] Peirce responds to this problem by suggesting that our contact with external realities is more direct and less mediated by thought than he had previously supposed. As we shall see in Chapter 4, this shift had especially important ramifications for his theories of signs, and his later account of how we come to have direct contact with reality is usually expressed in terms of indexical signs. Here, though, we need only note that in response to Royce's work Peirce began to emphasise that our cognitive contact with mind-independent reality comes not at the end of a long process of inquiry but directly through indexical or demonstrative concepts. The upshot is that the concepts of truth and reality are not nearly so intimately connected after 1885 as they were in his early statements of inquiry, and we very often find him suggesting that they can be separated entirely:

> Truth is a character which attaches to an abstract proposition, such as a person might utter. It essentially depends upon that proposition's not professing to be exactly true. But we hope that in the progress of science its error will indefinitely diminish. [. . .] If our hope is vain [. . .] no matter how scientific our methods may become, there never will be a time when we can fully satisfy ourselves either that the question has no meaning, or that one answer or the other explains the facts, then in regard to that question there certainly is no truth. But whether or not there would be perhaps any *reality* is a question for the metaphysician, not the logician. (CP5. 565 (1902))

Here, truth and reality are seen as distinct, and Peirce seems to suggest that we might well have a case where there is reality but no truth. Indeed, he also allows that in cases such as in pure mathematics we may well find instances of truth for which there is no corresponding reality:

> The pure mathematician deals exclusively with hypotheses. Whether or not there is any corresponding real thing, he does not care. His hypotheses are creatures of his own imagination [. . .]. But whether there is any reality or not, the truth of the pure mathematical proposition is constituted by the impossibility of ever finding a case in which it fails. (CP5. 567 (1902))

This separation of truth and reality and the corresponding notion that our inquiries may (or may not) happen upon truths without any need to settle matters of reality is an important development to Peirce's post-1870s account of inquiry.

New thoughts about inquiry and science

The third area of Peirce's philosophy where important developments took place was in his views about the nature of science and inquiry itself. We cannot detail all of Peirce's more mature views about the nature of science or scientific inquiry, but we can mention three especially important later developments here: his view that scientific inquiry is a form of self-controlled and deliberate conduct; his view that science and inquiry are guided by principles; and his view that the point, purpose and ambition of different domains of inquiry may vary. We shall look at these three points briefly, but it will be quite obvious that although we have treated these three developments to Peirce views of inquiry and science as separate, they are deeply connected to his ideas about the architectonic.

The first point, that science and inquiry is a matter of self-controlled and deliberate conduct, is a simple idea given the later placing of inquiry within the methodeutic sub-branch of logic. As we know, the architectonic structure of the normative sciences means that aesthetics gives guiding principles to ethics, primarily the guiding principle of pursuing the growth of reason. Ethics, as the 'theory of self-controlled, or deliberate, conduct' (EP2. 260 (1903)) aimed at securing the growth of concrete reasonableness, provides principles for logic, which becomes the science of how self-controlled and deliberate *reasoning* secures the growth of concrete reasonableness. Inquiry, as the study of best methods, is simply part of this self-controlled pursuit of the growth of concrete reasonableness.

The second point, that Peirce began to see science and inquiry as guided by assumed principles, is again made clearer by appeal to his architectonic developments around the turn of the century. In Chapter 2 we saw that Peirce emphasised the difference between his pragmaticism and the pragmatism of James and Schiller by clarifying that he took his 'pragmatism to be a mere maxim of logic instead of a sublime speculative philosophy' (EP2. 134 (1903)). The pragmatic maxim, as Peirce sees it in his later work, is simply a principle for use in logical investigations, and Peirce emphasises that inquiry and science have to start from a whole body of assumed principles:

> [I]nquiry must proceed upon the virtual assumption of sun-
> dry logical and metaphysical beliefs; and it is rational to settle
> the validity of those before undertaking an operation that sup-
> poses their truth. Now whether the truth of them be explicitly
> laid down on critical grounds, or the doctrine of Common-
> Sense prevent our pretending to doubt it, along with all these
> other sound first principles will be admitted, and so the whole
> inquiry will be concluded before the first outward experiment
> is made. (CP5. 521 (1905))

Amongst such underlying principles are that we are pursuing an
inquiry which will indeed admit of an answer, that there is only one
answer we can arrive at, that there is an external reality and so on.
We shall see the importance of this shortly, but it is worth emphasising a key part of this appeal to science and inquiry as underpinned
by such first principles. Although it looks as though Peirce is appeal-
ing to transcendental presuppositions for inquiry – how can we
engage in inquiry without these preconditions in place? – he is not,
in fact, committed to any of these principles being true. Just because
inquiry must be guided by these principles, it is not thereby prede-
termined that those principles encapsulate true beliefs:

> [A]ll that logic warrants is a *hope*, and not a belief. It must be
> admitted, however, that such hopes play a considerable part
> in logic. For example, when we discuss a vexed question, we
> *hope* that there is some ascertainable truth about it, and that the
> discussion is not to go on forever and to no purpose. A transcen-
> dentalist would claim that it is an indispensable 'presupposition'
> that there is an ascertainable true answer to every intelligible
> question. I used to talk like that, myself; for when I was a babe
> in philosophy my bottle was filled from the udders of Kant. But
> by this time I have come to want something more substantial.
> (CP2. 113 (1902))

Scientific inquiry, then, is underpinned by what Peirce often calls
'regulative principles'[12] or 'intellectual hopes'.

The third and final development to Peirce's thoughts about inquiry and science is that the needs and ambitions of an inquiry will vary depending on its domain of inquiry and what kind of question it seeks to answer. In a series of lectures delivered in 1898 at a private home in Cambridge, Massachusetts, Peirce suggested that we can see particular domains of science as growing and developing into more abstract sciences and tending gradually towards something like pure mathematics (EP2. 38–39 (1898)). Peirce sees what he calls 'descriptive sciences' such as history engaged simply in describing phenomena, but through inquiry and progress they develop into 'classificatory sciences' and endeavour to classify the previously described phenomena. Similarly, a classificatory science will develop into a 'nomological science', that is a science concerned with the laws that concern its phenomena. He then sees nomological sciences tending towards pure science and becoming metaphysics and logic, developing finally into mathematics.

The importance of this view of different sciences connected along a developmental continuum is that it leads Peirce to recognise that an inquiry will be driven by very different aims depending on what kind of inquiry it is. The aim of inquiry within a classificatory science is to understand that classification up to the point where the underlying laws of classification become fit for discovery. The aim of an inquiry in descriptive science is to give an accurate description of some phenomenon up to the point where we have sufficient understanding of these descriptions to begin classificatory studies; any nomological impulse is either unimportant or not pressing. The idea that we can describe all inquiry as simply aiming at the truth, then, is given over to a much more nuanced view whereby the exact needs and ends of an inquiry are explained in terms of what that type of inquiry needs to achieve. This also leads Peirce to make some very important claims about belief, doubt and action in relation to inquiry.

In this same series of lectures, Peirce drew a distinction between 'full belief' and what we might call 'scientific belief'. A full belief is the kind of strong belief upon which we are prepared to act. Scientific belief is a much weaker matter and is much closer to the kind of conjecture or hypothesis we use in our scientific endeavours. In what Peirce calls 'vital matters', questions which need an immediate response, we need to arrive quickly at an answer that allows us to obtain a full belief in order to act. Peirce thinks the manner of progress in inquiries of pure science, say, is quite unsuitable to the questions posed by 'vital matters'. However, by employing what he calls 'instinct' we can still obtain an answer that will give us a belief and enable us to act.[13]

The later view of truth and inquiry

Unlike Peirce's later account of pragmatism, we never find a well-contained single account of his later theory of inquiry. There are many reasons for this, but a significant one is that, where the later account of pragmatism emerged quite starkly from Peirce's need to differentiate his views from those of James and Schiller, no such imperative is present in the case of inquiry. Indeed, most of the criticisms we have raised against it were not developed until after Peirce's death. Nonetheless, from the three major developments we have just examined, we can give a fairly clear account of just what the later account of truth and inquiry is and what is distinctive about it in comparison to the account of the 1870s.

The introduction of hope

Many of the fundamental parts of Peirce's early picture of inquiry are retained in the later account. Indeed, around 1893 and 1894, Peirce intended to incorporate his early work from *Popular Science Monthly* into a longer manuscript called *How to Reason: Critick of Arguments*. Although important changes were made to the earlier papers in this work, they remained in very large part true to the early account. What we find is that inquiry is still a matter of attaining belief and avoiding doubt, and the idea that multiple investigations into a question might converge on a single and final answer is retained. However, Peirce now makes *hope* central to the notion of inquiry. In later amendments to his early papers on inquiry, he no longer describes 'the followers of science' as

> fully persuaded that the processes of investigation, if only pushed far enough, will give one certain solution to every question to which they can be applied. (EP2. 138 (1878))

Instead, they are described as being

> animated by a cheerful hope that the process of investigation, if only pushed far enough, will give one certain solution to each question to which they apply it. (MS 422 (1894))

As we have already mentioned, Peirce began to see science and inquiry as guided by principles and 'intellectual hopes', but what we are seeing here is the use of hope to temper one of the central claims of his early account. The scientific method is no longer claimed as a guarantee that all investigations making use of it will alight upon a single truth at the end point of inquiry. Instead, Peirce claims that inquirers engage in the scientific method armed with the intellectual hope that such inquiries will converge upon a final answer.

Peirce puts this point even more clearly in work for an 1896 review of Schröder's *Algebra und Logik der Relative*:

> [A]s to an inquiry presupposing that there is some one truth, what can this possibly mean except that there is one destined upshot to inquiry with reference to the question in hand – one result, which when reached will never be overthrown? Undoubtedly, we hope that this, or *something approximating to this*, is so, or we should not trouble ourselves to make the inquiry. But we do not necessarily have much confidence that it *is* so. (CP3. 432 (1896))

This use of regulative principles, or intellectual hopes, in the later account is not restricted to hopes about the efficacy of the scientific method. There is also a clear sense in which truth itself takes on the role of regulative principle.

Truth as a regulative principle

Just as we must engage in inquiry in the hope that the scientific method is effective enough to deliver a single answer to our guiding questions, we also have to begin in the hope that there is truth to be had at all:

> Logic requires us, with reference to each question we have in
> hand, to hope some definite answer to it may be true. That *hope*
> with reference to each case as it comes up is, by a *saltus* stated by
> logicians as a *law* concerning *all cases*, namely the law of excluded
> middle. (NEM4. xiii (Undated))

It seems, then, that we must start with the assumption that each
question fit for inquiry is either true or false and hope that this
assumption is a good one. This is in stark contrast to the apparent
confidence of the earlier statements whereby no one can 'escape the
predestinate opinion [. . .][,] [t]he opinion which is fated to be ultimately agreed upon' (EP1. 138–139 (1878)). Indeed, not only have
we relinquished the notion that truth is a guaranteed end point of
any well-conducted inquiry in favour of a hope that truth is to be
had, but Peirce also requires of us that we accept that some truths or
facts may never be uncovered:

> Despair is insanity. True, there may be facts that will never get
> explained; but that any given fact is of the number, is what expe-
> rience can never give us reason to think; far less can it show that
> any fact is of its own nature unintelligible. We must therefore be
> guided by the rule of hope[.] (EP1. 275 (1890))

The idea that our inquiry into some proposition or question must
begin with the intellectual hope that we can reach a final determinate answer is clearly no simple demand for naivety. Instead, we
acknowledge the possibility that some facts may never be explained,
but we assume as a regulative principle of inquiry that the propositions under investigation have a determinate truth value and go
about our investigations in good faith.

Selective inquiries

One final shift in Peirce's view seems to be that he no longer thinks
every question or inquiry is fit for, or subject to, the demands of a
long-run scientific investigation. This is already apparent in the 1894
restatement of the account from 'How to make our ideas clear' given

above. The early account states that a fully conducted inquiry can be had for 'every question'; the later restatement amends this to 'each question to which they apply it'. Similarly, we saw the law of excluded middle assumed as a regulative principle of inquiry 'with reference to each question we have in hand' (NEM4. xiii (Undated)).[14] One reason for this is simply a result of introducing intellectual hopes into the account of scientific inquiry. It makes sense to inquire only after questions for which the assumption of regulative principles of inquiry is well motivated. Christopher Hookway quotes the following passage from Peirce which makes this thinking clear:

> It is rational to make some question the object of an inquiry only if we can (at least) rationally hope that we will reach a solution that would also be reached by anyone who inquired into the same manner (and whose inquiry was not hampered by perversity or by unpropitious 'accidental circumstances'). (Hookway 2004b, 135)

It is not obvious that we can or must engage in the requisite intellectual hopes for every potential inquiry, so it seems clear that not every question is fit for such investigation. Such a shift in emphasis is also related to Peirce's growing sense that different sciences, different questions and different matters have different needs. A vital matter, some lived dilemma, does not need either the slow progress of long-run scientific investigation or the cool fallibilist detachment of scientific belief in order for us to arrive at the kind of answer that would underpin action. Similarly, the needs of, say, an inquiry that remains clearly within the remit of a descriptive science does not need the kind of final settled inquiry of a pure science such as mathematics. All we might need is a description adequate enough to allow us to move our science forwards. Settling the final truth on such matters of description may seem neither necessary nor possible nor even pressing.

The original problems for inquiry and truth

So far, we have seen a series of important developments to Peirce's thinking after he made his original statements on truth and inquiry in the late 1870s. In particular, we noted that his growing realisation of the architectonic structure of his philosophy led him to emphasise the normative dimensions of inquiry, with inquiry properly thought of as integral to the methodeutic branch of the normative science of logic. Similarly, his awareness of and reaction to the nominalism of the *Popular Science Monthly* accounts of truth, inquiry and pragmatism came to the fore with his increased commitment to the reality of 'would-bes'. Further, we noted that Peirce began to treat truth and reality separately, and as a consequence the notion of inquiry as giving a pragmatic explication of reality dropped out of the later accounts altogether. Finally, we saw that Peirce began to view inquiry and science in very distinct terms. In line with his architectonic, science and inquiry become simply self-controlled and deliberate reasoning geared towards the growth of concrete reasonableness; science and inquiry become principle-guided action underpinned by the assumption of regulative principles and intellectual hopes; and the needs of inquiry and scientific investigation vary depending on the type of inquiry, the purpose any answer would serve, and what kind of actions an answer would need to motivate.

As we have seen, this gives a later account of inquiry which looks quite different to the account of the late 1870s. We still see science as the model for inquiry, belief and doubt at the core of the account and truth as given in the final opinion at the end of inquiry. However, the view of science is more sophisticated; it is principle guided, self-controlled and deliberative, taking on different needs and questions at different developmental stages. Similarly, inquiry is a more subtle concept: it rests on intellectual hopes, its purest *scientific* form isn't the panacea to all of our questions and concerns, it may not be able to guarantee a final answer, but it is our best hope. Truth remains as the end point of inquiry, but it is now a regulative ideal, something we have to assume we can achieve to even get started. Moreover, it is something we might settle upon without being able to say anything decisive about reality at all, and we might find we have an account of some underlying reality without having settled any related truths.

All of these developments are interesting in showing just how complex, interconnected and subtle Peirce's later philosophy becomes, but the real nature of these developments is sharply brought out by looking at how they disarm the problems facing the earlier account of inquiry. It is important to bear in mind that none of Peirce's developments are deeply motivated by the need to respond to any of these problems, but looking at how we might answer such problems with the later theory is still instructive.

The scientific method doesn't give us belief

As we noted earlier, Peirce's belief/doubt model of inquiry seems to have the unwelcome consequence that we are driven to inquiry by the compulsion to remove doubt, but the scientific method he endorses requires that we embrace doubt in favour of a permanently settled belief at the end of inquiry. We are compelled to pursue belief by adopting a methodology which postpones the attainment of belief to some far off point at the inquiry's end. Whilst the complaint may well hold for the account of the late 1870s, there is less cause to be concerned about the later theory.

In Peirce's later account, we saw that different inquiries will have different needs for an answer or investigation, and that, correspondingly, we should think that there is a distinction between full belief and scientific belief. The kind of inquiry that will demand an immediate or urgent answer – the kind of compelling need for belief which seems to underpin the early account of inquiry – is what Peirce determines to be a 'vital matter'. It is indeed true that vital matters or questions will compel us to settle quickly and efficiently upon some belief, but Peirce's later view also suggests that the kind of detached long-run methods of the pure sciences are unsuitable for such questions:

> The scientific man is not in the least wedded to his conclusions. He risks nothing upon them. Some of them, I grant, he is in the habit of calling *established truths*; [. . .] It seems probable that any given proposition of that sort will remain for a long time upon the list of propositions to be admitted. Still, it may be refuted tomorrow [. . .]

But in vital matters, it is quite otherwise. We must act in such matters; and the principle upon which we are willing to act is a *belief*.

Thus, pure theoretical knowledge, or science, has nothing directly to say concerning practical matters, and nothing even applicable at all to vital crises. Theory is applicable to minor practical affairs; but matters of vital importance must be left to sentiment, that is, to instinct. (EP2. 33 (1898))

Where the scientific method is most at home is in the pure sciences, where we can accept scientific beliefs and make steady progress towards the end of inquiry. In matters where the need for full belief is urgent and compelling, we need not adopt the method of science. This clearly sidesteps the earlier problem, but it poses problems of its own. What is the relationship between full belief and scientific belief? Why should a method fit for settling the latter tell us anything interesting about the former? What are we to make of Peirce's related claim that belief has no place in science? What about 'vital matters' and their reliance on sentiment? Does this mean that domains such as ethics or moral reasoning are not fit for 'scientific' or theoretical investigation? We cannot explore these issues here, but needless to say they are of interest to Peirce scholars.[15]

Not all inquiry is 'problem solving'

The answer to the concern that not all inquiry is problem solving, that not all of our beliefs emerge from attempts to overcome real dilemmas, is handled in much the same way as the issue we have just discussed. Peirce's distinctions between different kinds of belief – full belief and scientific belief – and their fitness for different kinds of inquiry allows that we might also employ doubt in various ways. Indeed, we find that when Peirce returned to his 1878 paper 'The fixation of belief' to amend and use it in an 1893 manuscript, *Search For a Method*,[16] he no longer saw doubt as an overwhelming state of irritation but as something we may well choose to explore:

It is true that just as men may, for the sake of the pleasures of the table, like to be hungry and take means to make themselves so, although hunger always involves a desire to fill the stomach, so for the sake of the pleasures of inquiry, men may like to seek out doubts. (CP3. 372. n 2 (1893))

Put like this, then, we may actively pursue doubts. Or, to paraphrase, we may seek out problems to solve rather than waiting for our problems to impose themselves on us. Just as we can mark differences between the kind of full belief that we seek and need in vital matters and the scientific belief employed in the absence of any pressing need for an answer, we can see doubt as coming in both *assumed* and *imposed* types. In vital matters, for instance, doubt will *impose* itself forcefully upon us, and the need for full belief is compelling. In matters of pure science or mathematics, however, we might very easily *assume* some doubt in the interest of seeing what kind of scientific belief emerges.

This kind of acceptance of the broader role that doubt might play, especially in connection with the claims about full and scientific belief, again allows the later account to sidestep the issue. And, again, it also raises problems of its own. In particular, what does such a move do to Peirce's earlier anti-Cartesianism? Are we now to assume that Peirce will tolerate the method of doubt? Other amendments from around 1893 suggest that the assumption of doubt may well have its limits:

Doubt [. . .] is [. . .] usually [. . .] anticipated hesitancy about what I shall do hereafter, or a feigned hesitancy about a fictitious state of things. It is the power of making believe we hesitate, together with the pregnant fact that the decision upon the merely make-believe dilemma goes toward forming a bona fide habit that will be operative in a real emergency. (CP5. 373. n 1 (1893))

For Peirce, then, assumed doubts, or the problems we have sought out, are common enough, but it is their role in anticipating genuine problems and providing real solutions when a 'real emergency' occurs that gives them their value. Presumably, Peirce would take the Cartesian's methodological doubt to have none of these pre-emptive and preparatory virtues.

Issues with fated or final opinions

As we saw, two related objections to the early account of truth and inquiry came from Josiah Royce and Bertrand Russell. The Roycian worry, put simply, is what we are to make of truth if inquiry never reaches an end. If truth is the end of inquiry, then an inquiry without end means there are no truths. The Russellian worry, again put simply, is what happens if inquiry comes to a premature end. If truth is the end of inquiry, then a cataclysmic end to inquiry gives us a body of beliefs that Peirce would have to call truth, even though it would hardly be appropriate to think such beliefs necessarily had any resemblance to the truth at all.

The objections were always rather dubious complaints, but with an uncharitable reading of the early account we can see why one might worry. Tying truth to actual inquiries means truth must live and die with the fate of real inquiries; it would be naive to think inquiries cannot or do not go astray. However, in his later work Peirce manages to make it clearer that he does not need an actual inquiry to run its course in order to say something about belief, truth and inquiry. As we've frequently noted, Peirce's later work is deeply critical of the nominalism of his early accounts and takes the reality of possibility very seriously. Moreover, it treats inquiry as governed by regulative hopes about the possibility of arriving at a final answer. What this means is that we identify the truth with what would be believed in the final opinion if inquiry were carried satisfactorily to its end point, and accepting that inquiry can be derailed, we note that we set about an inquiry in the hope that the end point will, in fact, be attained:

> We do not aim at anything quite beyond experience, but only at the limiting result toward which all experience will approximate, – or, at any rate, would approximate, were the inquiry to be prosecuted without cessation. [. . .]

Prof. Royce seems to think that this doctrine is unsatisfactory because it talks about what would be, although the event may never come to pass. It may be he is right in this criticism; yet to our apprehension this 'would be' is readily resolved into a hope for *will be*. (CP8. 112–113 (1900))

Although Peirce is responding to Royce here, his answer holds for both problems. An inquiry may be of the type that we fail to complete or which ends prematurely, but, proceeding in the hope that it is not endlessly derailed or catastrophically curtailed, we can state that the truth is to be identified with what we *would* believe at the end of an inquiry if that inquiry *were* conducted sufficiently well and carried to its conclusion. We can see that neither Royce's nor Russell's case represents such a set of beliefs.

The problem of buried facts

As we noted earlier, the problem of buried facts can be divided into three related problems: the problem of lost facts, the problem of distant facts and the problem of uninquireable facts. All three types are instances in which it seems that we should have no real expectation that an inquiry could reach a satisfactory conclusion, either because facts seem irretrievably lost to history, separated from us by an unbridgeable distance or blocked by some definitional condition on inquiry. The worry is simply that Peirce's early account committed him to the view that there is no truth in such matters and that there is no corresponding feature of reality either. This seems counter-intuitive since our inability to discover a long-lost historical event doesn't obviously preclude that historical event from being real. As we pointed out earlier, this cluster of problems is widely seen as being fatal to Peirce's account. Interestingly, however, the later account that we have been detailing here seems to have ready answers to these concerns.

With regard to both the problem of lost facts and the problem of distant facts, we can see that Peirce has a set of responses available to him. First, we certainly do not have to claim that because an inquiry couldn't actually turn up a satisfactory final opinion about some dim fact of the past or distant feature of the universe that no truth is to be had in such matters. Just as we have seen with previous problems, we can identify the truth with what we *would* believe *were* we to take inquiry to a final and satisfactory end point, and we embark or address such questions with all the intellectual hopes and regulative ideals that one applies to every inquiry. Treating truth in these subjunctive terms certainly leaves us free to think there are truths here, even if we never actually attain them.

Second, we don't have to be concerned that any failure to arrive at a final belief will mean there is no underlying reality to these lost or distant facts. As we saw, Peirce is no longer committed to the idea that reality is given at, and by, the final opinion, so he can maintain that some purported historical fact either is or isn't part of reality, even if we cannot uncover the truth of the matter. Similarly, the physical remoteness of some feature of the universe may push truth through inquiry beyond our actual capabilities, but Peirce can maintain that such distant features are still part of reality.

It also seems that a further response is open to Peirce in his later account concerning these problems. Peirce makes it clear in his later work that we need not engage in every possible inquiry, especially if it seems that we cannot make a good-faith assumption of the regulative principles of inquiry in some case. It seems open whether questions about genuinely lost and distant facts are even the type of inquiry we would properly elect to undertake. Suppose it is the case that there are facts so lost in history that we are hard pushed to motivate our intellectual hopes for an inquiry at all. Why think that such an inquiry is worth undertaking? I would suggest that we perhaps would not. The kind of fact so lost to history that we couldn't turn up any truths about it at all would also seem to be causally remote from our current mental lives. What kind of questions or purpose could we have for such a fact? It is hard to imagine that it would concern any kind of vital matter, and such a question seems much more likely to arise, if at all, from the vaguest kinds of 'feigned hesitancy'. Indeed, the more remote the chance of settling an opinion, the less likely are its questions to motivate an inquiry. This is not to say, of course, that we would never choose to investigate such a matter. We are merely saying that on the later view, inquiries into lost and distant facts seem unmotivated enough that we simply wouldn't choose to engage in them at all. Inquiries will, we hope, turn up truths for questions worth investigating. But for empty or unmotivated questions, what concern or purpose can we have with truth? Peirce is, after all, giving us a pragmatic explication of truth, and where there can be no pragmatic outcome to an inquiry it is hard to see what work there can be for the pragmatist's concept.

In terms of what we have called uninquireable facts, however, the response from the later account cannot be quite the same as for the issue of lost and distant facts. This is primarily because we cannot make any appeal to regulative hopes and the reality of 'would-bes' in such cases. Recall the example we gave from Hookway (2000, 54–55) of the tree branch contained within a protective box that would destroy the earth if opened. In such a case, we cannot complete an inquiry into how many leaves there are on the branch without terminating that same inquiry. The problem is that it makes no sense to adopt an intellectual hope that we can complete such an inquiry since by definition we cannot. Similarly, it makes no sense to talk about what *would* be the case *were* we to take a well-conducted inquiry to its final state. A well-conducted inquiry would involve opening the box and curtailing the investigation before we had an answer to our question. Neither subjunctives nor intellectual hopes are of any help here. All the same, the later account can bypass these buried facts too.

The response open to Peirce is simply to assert that there is no truth of the matter in the case of uninquireable facts. This is not to deny that the number of leaves on the branch is a determinate part of reality, of the world external to whatever you or I may think of it, especially now that Peirce sees truth and reality as separable. But it is quite clear that by framing our questions in such a way that inquiry can provide no final answers for them, we have fenced off such facts from our pragmatic interest in them. What purpose could we have in investigating a question which we cannot answer? What traction could a question beyond answering have in our lives and interaction with the world? In terms of the third grade of clarity, such questions look to be empty. They are the kind of question that serious investigation would bypass, and it seems to be of no detriment to declare them unfit for inquiry and unsuitable for yielding truth.

Conclusion

The contrast between the earlier and later accounts, then, is quite marked. Peirce retains the fundamental treatment of belief and doubt and the mechanism of inquiry, and he still sees inquiry as converging upon a final state with a doubt-proof belief which gives us the truth. However, belief and doubt are treated much more subtly, inquiry treated in subjunctive terms need not *actually* be completed, we are no longer given a pragmatic explication of reality, and all inquiries are grounded in regulative assumptions and intellectual hopes. Not every question will motivate an inquiry, and even when it does, the needs of that inquiry may rest heavily on the field of investigation to which the question belongs. These changes – the anti-nominalist 'would-bes', the intellectual hopes, and the ability to judge whether questions are even suitable for inquiry at all – give clear answers to the problems which beset the earlier account. Other problems emerge, as we have noted, but in terms of making the developmental picture clear, the way in which the later account handles the problems which beset the earlier theory shows just how interesting Peirce's views of truth and inquiry become around the turn of the century.

Summary

As part of his *Popular Science Monthly* papers of the 1870s, Peirce gave a pragmatic elucidation of the concept of reality. That elucidation led to his belief/doubt model of inquiry, his account of truth as what is believed at the end of inquiry, and reality as the body of facts represented by the beliefs in that final state.

- Peirce offered four methods of inquiry, of which science is the only one that will ensure that our beliefs become properly resistant to doubt.

- A series of problems with this early account focuses on the identification of truth and reality with inquiry. What happens if our inquiries are ended prematurely or fixed artificially? Does that give us a body of truth and representation of reality?
- A more serious body of problems focuses on the possibility that there are facts and features of the world that it is implausible to expect we can ever complete an inquiry into. These problems together are known as the 'the problem of buried facts'.
- In later work, Peirce came to revise and develop many of the views in his early account of truth and inquiry. These revisions prove important in counteracting the various problems facing the earlier account.
- Peirce's increased sense of his architectonic, his separation of his accounts of truth and reality, and changes in his views about the nature of science and inquiry from the mid-1880s mean that many of the earlier concerns no longer apply to his accounts of truth, reality and inquiry.
- Key to Peirce's later view is that inquiry into every possible question is no longer considered essential; not every problem is suitable for inquiry. Further, inquiry is governed by intellectual hopes that the questions into which we inquire will admit of an answer, and truth becomes a regulative ideal, a principle we cannot engage in inquiry without.

Further reading

Although it is not solely about Peirce's accounts of truth and inquiry, I would recommend that newcomers to the area read Susan Haack's 'The pragmatist theory of truth' (1976). A genuine problem for any pragmatist account of truth is the often lazy 'strawman' treatment it receives in mainstream philosophy. Haack's paper goes a long way to clearing up these issues and disentangling Peirce's account from those of other pragmatists.

More specifically on Peirce's accounts of truth and inquiry, everyone should read the first four chapters of Christopher Hookway's *Truth, Rationality and Pragmatism* (2000), which gives a deep and subtle treatment of Peirce's views on truth. Of equal importance, and also absolutely essential reading, is Cheryl Misak's *Truth and the End of Inquiry: A Peircean Account of Truth* (1991). This book-length treatment of Peirce's account of truth and inquiry will give an excellent introduction not only to these areas of Peirce's work, but it will also prove enlightening on Peirce's pragmatism, logic and semiotic. These two texts represent a genuinely important contribution to understanding Peirce's work on truth, and if you read nothing else on this topic, read these.

If you do want to read more than Hookway and Misak, however, I would recommend Mark Migotti's 1998 paper 'Peirce's double-aspect theory of truth', which offers a novel defence of Peirce against the buried secrets argument. Also, David Wiggins' 2004 'Reflections on inquiry and truth arising from Peirce's method for the fixation of belief' offers an examination of some of Peirce's later responses to his original *Popular Science Monthly* statements of truth and inquiry in the 1870s.

Notes

1 Concerns with scepticism and sceptical arguments are often treated seriously, of course. Nonetheless, there is always a concern with the nature of the argument rather than with its impact upon our lived experiences, and there is always an air of the academic parlour game about such debates.
2 Such beliefs have spawned books and newspaper articles, but all are without an ounce of scientific credibility.
3 For example, the discovery of the electron by J.J. Thomson in 1897 using cathode ray tube experiments converged on the same theoretical entity suggested by Pieter Zeeman's use of magnetic fields to split spectral lines in 1896. Zeeman's work was recognised by Hendrik Lorentz as indicating a negatively charged subatomic particle. Indeed, even Peirce and Frege arriving independently at accounts of quantificational logic represents an interesting case of convergence.
4 As Peirce notes, 'however satisfactory such a definition may be found, it would be a great mistake to suppose that it makes the idea of reality perfectly clear' (EP1. 127 (1878)). As we have noted, giving a definition of some concept is to contribute towards giving only a 'distinct' understanding, but this is never enough to give us a complete understanding.
5 See Haack (1976) for a worthwhile account of the various pragmatist accounts of truth.

6 See Wright (2001) for a clearer expression of this worry.

7 For some details of this intriguing story, see Gu *et al.* (2012).

8 Indeed, see Lenzen (1965) for a summary of Peirce's work in the area, or even Kragh (2009) for a brief comment on the role of Peirce's spectroscopic work in our understanding of auroral phenomena.

9 Peirce also used the term 'speculative rhetoric' to refer to this branch of logic (for instance, CP2. 105–110), but we shall persist with the term 'methodeutic'.

10 See Royce (1885/1965).

11 Chapter 4 of Hookway (2000) gives a full exposition of Peirce's reaction to Royce's arguments and their importance in how he thought about reference, truth and inquiry after 1880.

12 See, for example, CP1. 405 (1891) or CP8. 44 (1885).

13 The whole question of 'vital matters' and 'scientific belief' is actually rather fraught. Peirce says in the same lectures of 1898 that 'what is usually and properly called belief [. . .] has no place in science at all' (EP2. 33 (1898)). This seems to pose all kinds of worrying consequences given Peirce's view of truth and inquiry.

14 We also find Peirce suggesting that

> we have no reason to think the unanimity will be quite complete, nor can we rationally presume any overwhelming *consensus* of opinion will be reached upon every question. All that we are entitled to assume is in the form of a *hope* that such conclusion may be substantially reached concerning **the particular questions with which our inquiries are busied**.' (CP6. 610 (1891), *bold italics added*).

15 On the matter of 'scientific belief', for instance, Chapter 1 of Hookway (2000) is an excellent treatment, as is Migotti (2005). On the questions surrounding 'vital matters', Misak (2004) gives the clearest discussion of the issues.

16 Like most of Peirce's book-length projects of this time, *Search For a Method* was never completed.

Four
Sign theory

Introduction

Beyond the confines of philosophy and in the broader academic world, Peirce is most famous for his theory of signs. As philosophers, we tend to think of him primarily for his pragmatism or for his theory of truth. In other arenas, though, his theory of signs and signification is what marks his most lasting contribution. What is more, Peirce's work on signs is central to much of the rest of his philosophical endeavour. As we examine his work in this chapter, we shall see that the development of his semiotic is deeply tied to his philosophical endeavours elsewhere. If it isn't some insight in his account of signs leading directly to changes in the rest of his work, then the ramifications for semiotic of some new development are one of the very first things he turns to. We find that his earliest anti-Cartesian statements of the 1860s are couched in semiotic terms, that he sees semiotic as underpinning his broader view of logic, that he attempts to provide a proof of his pragmatist principle in terms of signs, and that he draws important connections between the process of representation and the process of inquiry. In short, he sees the relevance of semiotic everywhere. In an important correspondence with the English philosopher and semiotician Victoria Lady Welby, Peirce states the centrality of semiotic thus:

> [I]t has never been in my power to study anything, – mathematics, ethics, metaphysics, gravitation, thermodynamics, optics, chemistry,

comparative anatomy, astronomy, psychology, phonetics, economics, the history of science, whist, men and women, wine, metrology, except as a study of semiotic. (SS 85–86)

Given the strength of Peirce's views about semiotic and its importance to philosophy, it is regrettable that philosophers have tended to pay Peirce's sign theory scant attention. Indeed, to say that the interest in Peirce's semiotics outside of philosophy far outstrips the interest shown by contemporary philosophers is something of an understatement. In some respects, this is unsurprising since the breadth and complexity of Peirce's semiotic make it difficult to see its applicability to the concerns of contemporary philosophy. Analytic philosophers' interest in sign theory extends about as far as its overlap with the philosophy of language, but given the origins and assumptions of that discipline, semiotic can look archaic and unattractive. For example, a common assumption is that Peirce incorrectly assumes too much common ground between linguistic and non-linguistic signs[1] and so is starting from questionable assumptions. More importantly, though, the representationalist and formalist drive of much twentieth-century philosophy of language, coupled with what was for a long time its privileged position of 'first philosophy', have meant that analytic philosophers often see their work as having superseded anything that Peirce was actually doing with his sign theory. Peirce may have had very similar interests to contemporary philosophers of language and his work may have similar or even greater explanatory power,[2] but the complex and difficult theories Peirce developed look positively Ptolemaic in comparison to the Copernican elegance of analytic philosophy of language. None of these assumptions are really true of course, but they go some way towards explaining the lack of attention Peirce's semiotic receives from much contemporary philosophy. All the same, a greater appreciation of Peirce's semiotic would be of benefit.

Interest is much livelier outside of philosophy, but a similar problem lurks nearby. One finds interest in and mention of Peirce's sign theories in such wide-ranging disciplines as art history,[3] literary theory, psychology and linguistics. There are even entire disciplinary approaches and sub-fields – semiotics, bio-semiotics, cognitive semiotics – which rest squarely on Peirce's work. Whilst this greater appreciation of Peirce's semiotic marks a happier state of affairs than that which we find in philosophy, there is still a worry that, as the leading scholar of Peirce's sign theory, T.L. Short, puts it, 'Peirce's semiotics has gotten in amongst the wrong crowd'.[4] Short's complaint may be a little hyperbolic, but his concern is well founded considering the piecemeal and selective use of Peirce's ideas in certain areas. From a cursory reading of much work in these areas, one might think Peirce had only ever identified his early tripartite division of signs into *icons*, *indices* and *symbols*. There is much more to the theory of signs than this, and a richer and deeper understanding of Peirce's developed accounts of semiotic would be valuable.

The first account we shall look at is his early 1860s theory of signs as 'thought-signs'. As we shall see, these early attempts offer a relatively simple account of signs and sign action and are motivated by the anti-Cartesian sentiment of Peirce's early writing. Of particular interest is the introduction of two long-standing features of Peirce's semiotic. First, we see Peirce's famous icon/index/symbol distinction introduced here for the first time, and second, we see the issue of infinite chains of signs. This latter point, as we shall see, proves to be something of a persistent problem.

The second account that we shall examine is given around 1903 and coincides with a series of lectures and grants that Peirce was making around this time. As we shall see, it extends far beyond the earliest accounts of the 1860s and gives us what is perhaps Peirce's most complete and fully worked out account of signs. It contains an extended class of sign types and incorporates many of Peirce's philosophical developments from his accounts of pragmatism and truth, but intriguingly, it still contains a problematic notion of infinite sign chains.

The final account that we shall look at comes from the later, more academically isolated period of Peirce's life. From around 1906 onwards, Peirce extends his account of signs to expand the basic structure of signification, allowing an increased number of ways in which the sign represented its object and in how we might come to understand that representational connection between sign and object. As we shall see, this development in Peirce's account has none of the neatness of the earlier accounts and is at times wild and conjectural. It is, however, ripe with insight and ideas that in many respects are yet to be fully explored.

Before we introduce these accounts, though, a few words of caution are in order. First, as presented it may seem that we are dealing with very discrete or distinct accounts when we look at the early, middle and final theories. To call these distinct accounts, however, is in a sense inaccurate. Rather, they are connected and we can trace the steady development of one to the other. Second, and related, despite the quantity of work on Peirce's semiotic, there is still much in our understanding of his work that is incomplete and speculative, especially when it comes to the final account, and interpretation of the work can vary.[5] Divisions and outlines of the semiotic are, then, to some degree contentious and even artificial. Finally, perhaps more than in any other area of his work, Peirce's penchant for neologisms and dense difficult terminology runs wild in his work on signs. There are interpretative points where this causes considerable problems and serious bones of contention in the scholarship, especially in the later work where it is obvious Peirce is experimenting with the best terminology.

In what follows, we shall endeavour to cut through these difficulties and artificial divisions, but it is important to be aware of them. It is all too easy to assume that work on Peirce's semiotic is a done deal, but this is far from the case.

The basic structure of signs

Peirce gives many definitions of signs throughout his writing. For example:

> A sign has, as such, three references: 1st, it is a sign to some thought which interprets it; 2d, it is a sign for some object to which in that thought it is equivalent; 3d, it is a sign, in some respect of quality. (EP1. 38 (1868))

> A *Sign*, or *Representamen*, is a First which stands in such genuine triadic relation to a Second, called its *Object*, as to be capable of determining a Third, called its *Interpretant*, to assume the same triadic relation to its object in which it stands itself to the same Object. (EP2. 272–273 (1903))

> I define a Sign as anything which is so determined by something else, called its Object, and so determines an effect upon a person, which effect I call its Interpretant, that the later is thereby mediately determined by the former. (EP2. 478 (1908))

Allowing for variation in terminology across the fifty-year gap that separates these passages, what we see is Peirce's consistent and basic claim that signs are composed of three interrelated parts: a *sign*, an *object* and an *interpretant*. We will say more about these three components in a moment, but at its simplest, this picture requires us to see the *sign* element as the representing or signifying component; for example, a rash as a sign of disease. The *object* element is simply whatever the *sign* represents or signifies; for example, the disease which causes the rash. Finally, there is the *interpretant* element of the sign. This is the most innovative and distinctive feature of Peirce's account and is thought of, initially at least, as the understanding that we have of the sign/object relation. The importance of the interpretant for Peirce is that signification is not a simple dyadic relationship between sign and object, as it is for someone like Saussure.[6] Rather, a sign signifies an object only in the course of being interpreted. This makes the interpretant central to the content of the sign in that the meaning of a sign is manifest in the interpretation that it generates in sign users. Things are, however, more complex than this, and we shall look at these three elements in more detail.

Sign-vehicles

In many ways, the sign element is a simple concept to grasp. There are, however, some potential hazards with the terminology at use here since we are talking of the three elements of *a* sign, one of which is the sign. As it stands, this can be confusing and does not fully capture Peirce's ideas about the sign element. Strictly speaking, we are interested in the *signifying element*, since it is not the sign as a whole that signifies. This is why we find Peirce talking of a sign's signifying 'in some respect of quality' or as a 'First'[7] in the definitions given above. By treating the sign as the signifying element, then, Peirce is more properly speaking of the sign refined to those elements most crucial to its functioning as a signifier. Peirce uses numerous terms for the signifying element, including 'sign', 'representamen', 'representation' and 'ground', for instance. These terms are often attached to different periods of his writing or are sometimes theory-laden. Here we shall refer to that element of the sign responsible for representing or signifying an object as the 'sign-vehicle'.[8]

This notion that a sign does not signify in all respects and has some particular signifying element is perhaps best made clear with an example. Consider a molehill in my lawn taken as a sign that moles are present. Not every characteristic of the molehill plays a part in its signifying the presence of moles. The exact colour of the molehill is secondary since molehills vary according to the soil from which they are composed. Similarly, the sizes of molehills vary according to the size of the mole that makes them, so again this feature is secondary in the molehill's ability to signify. What is central here is the causal connection that exists between the type of dirt-mound in my lawn and moles: since moles make molehills, molehills signify moles. Consequently, primary to the molehill's ability to signify the mole is the brute physical connection between it and a mole. This, then, is the sign-vehicle of the sign – its brute physical presence. For Peirce, it is only some element of a sign that enables it to signify its object, and when speaking of the signifying element of the sign, or rather the sign-vehicle, it is this qualified sign that he means.

Objects

Objects, like sign-vehicles, are a simple concept. At its simplest, the object of a sign is the thing that the sign-vehicle refers to or signifies. However, just as with the sign-vehicle, not every characteristic of the object is relevant to signification: only certain features of an object enable a sign to signify it. For Peirce, the relationship between the object of a sign and the sign-vehicle that represents it is one of determination: the object determines the sign. Peirce's notion of determination is by no means clear and is open to interpretation, but for our purposes, we can treat it as the *placing of constraints* or conditions on successful signification by the object, rather than as the object *causing* or *generating* the sign. The idea is that the object imposes certain parameters that a sign must fall within if it is to represent that object. However, only certain characteristics of an object are relevant to this process of determination. To see this in terms of an example, consider again the case of the molehill.

The sign is the molehill and the object is the mole. The mole determines the sign in as much as if the molehill is to succeed in signifying the mole it must show the physical presence or causal impact of the mole. If it fails to do this it fails to be a sign of that object. Other signs for this object, apart from the molehill, might include the presence of mole droppings or a particular pattern of ground subsidence on my lawn, but all such signs are constrained by the need to show the physical presence of the mole. Clearly, not everything about the mole is relevant to this constraining process: the colour of moles might vary, they might be male or female, young or old. None of these features, however, are essential to the constraints placed upon the sign. Rather, the causal connection between it and the mole is the characteristic that it imposes upon its sign, and it is this connection that the sign must represent if it is to succeed in signifying the mole.

Interpretants

Interpretants are the most interesting element of Peirce's sign. Put simply, a sign's interpretant is the understanding of, or response to, the sign-vehicle/object relation generated by the sign. But as one would expect with Peirce, there are many more complex features of the interpretant, and although several bear further comment, we shall mention just two for the time being.

First, although we have characterised the interpretant as simply the understanding we reach of some sign-vehicle/object relation, there is a crucial translational or developmental feature too; the interpretant acts as a further sign of the object, and so as a development of the 'original' sign. The idea is that the interpretant provides a translation of the sign, allowing us a more complex understanding of the sign's object. Indeed, two of the leading scholars of Peirce's semiotic, James Liszka (1996) and David Savan (1988), both emphasise the need to treat interpretants as translations, with Savan even suggesting Peirce should have called the interpretant the translatant (Savan 1988, 41).

Second, just as with the sign/object relation, Peirce believes the sign/interpretant relation to be one of determination: the sign determines an interpretant. Further, this determination is not determination in any causal sense. Rather, the sign determines an interpretant by using certain features of the way the sign signifies its object to generate and shape our understanding. So the way that smoke generates or determines an interpretant sign of its object, fire, is by focusing our attention upon the physical connection between smoke and fire.

For Peirce, then, a sign (or perhaps, an instance of signification) contains a *sign-vehicle*, an *object* and an *interpretant*. Moreover, the object determines the sign by placing constraints which any sign must meet if it is to signify the object. Consequently, the sign signifies its object only in virtue of some of its features. Additionally, the sign determines an interpretant by focusing our understanding on certain features of the signifying relation between sign and object. This enables us to understand the object of the sign more fully.

Semiosis and semiotic process

A final and important feature of Peirce's basic sign structure is that it comes from viewing the sign as, fundamentally, a process concept. The clearest way of seeing this is that Peirce treats the three elements of a sign — *sign-vehicle, object, interpretant* — as essentially connected. If we take away any one of the three elements, whatever we are left with is no longer a sign. A sign-vehicle without an object or an interpretant is simply not functioning as a sign.[9] When we take account of one of the important features of the interpretant mentioned above – its translational or developmental aspects – we can see that signs and signification are processive. The interpretant of a sign acts as a further, more developed sign of the original object. Of course, given the essential triadic nature of signs that we have just mentioned, this 'further sign' of the original object must have an interpretant in order to be a sign. Take a contrived and fairly contained example described 'semiotically'. An intruder makes a noise which starts my dog barking, alerting me to the presence of the intruder. The intruder is the object, the particular noise is the sign-vehicle, my dog's barking is the interpretant. But notice, my dog's barking functions as a further sign of the intruder, my response to the dog's barking, as an interpretant. And we could continue.

What we are looking at here is a crucial part of Peirce's sign theory, that signs are part of a developing process of information and understanding attached to particular objects. Considered in and of itself, a sign is a static picture of some part of this process. Within the process itself, a triadic sign is connected to other triadic signs, both generating and being generated by other such *sign-vehicle/object/interpretant* triads. This semiotic process of signs in action is simply called semiosis, and, as we shall see, it is crucial part of Peirce's theory of signs.

The early typology

Peirce wrote about signs as early as 1865 in a paper on Kant, written for a lecture series intended for delivery at Harvard.[10] However, the clearest and most significant early attempt at an account of signs comes in his 1867 paper 'On a new list of categories' (EP1. 1–10 (1867)) and the important three-paper *Journal of Speculative Philosophy* series from 1868 and 1869. In this early account, we find the same basic sign structure outlined above: any sign, or 'representation' as Peirce calls it at this early stage, will have a sign-vehicle, an object and an interpretant. Similarly, Peirce's notion of sign process or semiosis is also present, and interpretants are treated as further signs of the object. Peirce's own rather dense way of putting it is:

Besides the related thing, the ground, and the correlate, a mediating representation which represents the relate to be a representation of the same correlate which this mediating representation itself represents. Such a mediating representation may be termed an interpretant. (EP1. 5 (1867))

Importantly, though, Peirce describes signs as generating further interpretants in one of three possible ways. First, signs can generate further interpretants via 'a mere community in some quality' (EP1. 7 (1867)). These he calls *likenesses*, but they are more familiarly known as *icons*. Second, those 'whose relation to their objects consists in a correspondence in fact' (EP1. 7 (1867)) are termed *indices*. And finally, those 'whose relation to their objects is an imputed character' (EP1. 7 1867) are called *symbols*.

Put simply, if we come to interpret a sign as standing for its object in virtue of some shared quality between the two, then the sign is an icon. Peirce's early examples of icons are portraits and noted similarities between the letters *p* and *b* (EP1. 5 (1867)). On the other hand, if our interpretation comes in virtue of some brute, existential fact – a causal connection between sign and object, for instance – then the sign is an index. Early examples include the weathercock and the relationship between the murderer and his victim (EP1. 5 (1867)). And finally, if we generate an interpretant in virtue of some observed general or conventional connection between sign and object, then the sign is a symbol. Early examples include the words 'homme' and 'man' sharing a reference (EP1. 5 (1867)). This gives us the earliest, and perhaps most persistent, of Peirce's sign typologies – his famous division of signs into icons, indices and symbols. Although Peirce's precise thoughts about the nature of this division were to change throughout the philosophical development of sign theory, it nonetheless remains throughout his work and is also the division most frequently adopted by those looking to use his semiotic.

Although rather cursory, this description gives a clear sense of Peirce's earliest and most basic account of signs. Whilst there are many subtleties to the account that we might draw out, three important features are worth paying close attention to. The first concerns its motivation and connection to Peirce's other philosophical work, the second concerns the scope of signs in this early account, and the third pertains to the infinite nature of semiosis on this picture.

The anti-Cartesian motivation of the early account

Peirce's early account of sign theory is importantly connected to the anti-Cartesianism of his early philosophy. Although we have paid limited attention to Peirce's early anti-Cartesian statements in previous chapters, it is worth noting that in his three-paper *Journal of Speculative Philosophy* series of 1868 and 1869, he is at pains to argue against what he sees as key tenets of the Cartesian position. Peirce is especially troubled by the apparent use of intuition, introspection, internalism and incognisable concepts in the Cartesian method, and he argues against these. Key to his argument is the use of signs and semiotic.

To put the argument rather roughly, Peirce takes all thinking to be through signs – there can be no thought without signs – but since signs must be preceded and followed by further signs, there can be no first or last sign or thought. For Peirce, this means there can be no such thing as an *intuition*, that is, no such thing as a 'cognition not determined by a previous cognition of the same object' (EP1. 11 1868). Similarly, there can be no such thing as introspection or a purely internalistic picture of cognition, since signs contain an external component, their object. And finally, for something to be incognisable, that is, beyond inclusion in a chain of semiotic inference, we would have to curtail the semiotic process by positing a sign without an interpretant; something incognisable would have no interpretant. But by definition, every sign has an interpretant, so the incognisable makes no sense according to this semiotic picture. With thought and knowledge construed as an inferential semiotic process, the premises of Cartesian methodology are simply untenable on Peirce's view.

The detail of the arguments across these papers is naturally much more involved than this. But, importantly, we can see that Peirce's early sign theory is motivated by his anti-Cartesian account of thought and knowledge and is instrumental in his denial of intuition, introspection, internalism and incognisable concepts. In his later work, this prominent anti-Cartesian element gives way to a realisation that signs are a central feature of all philosophy and important in their own right.

The symbolic focus of thought-signs

Related to the anti-Cartesian motivation of this first account, the second important feature of Peirce's early work is his close association of signs with cognition. As we noted, Peirce states quite clearly that all thought is in signs (EP1. 24 (1868)). Crucial to this view is Peirce's early idea that every interpretant is itself a further sign of the signified object. Since interpretants are the interpreting thoughts we have of signifying relations, and these interpreting thoughts are themselves signs, it seems to be a straightforward consequence that all thoughts are signs, or as Peirce calls them, 'thought-signs'. The most important consequence of this for us is that Peirce is less concerned with the relevance of icons and indices in the sign typology of his early account than he is with symbols:

> The objects of the understanding, considered as representations, are symbols, that is, signs which are at least potentially general. But the rules of logic hold good of any symbols, of those which are written or spoken as well as those which are thought. They have no immediate application to likeness [icons] or indices, because no arguments can be constructed of these alone, but do apply to all symbols. (EP1. 7–8 (1867))

This gives Peirce's early account of signs a rather narrow scope; it is concerned primarily with the general and conventional signs of which our language and cognition consist. The reason for this narrow focus is simple: for Peirce, since symbols are 'potentially general' and fall under the remit of general rules, they are a fit subject of study for his primary focus, logic. This early account, then, focuses mainly on general and conventional signs, those signs identified by Peirce as symbols. Icons and indices, although noted at this early stage, are considered of secondary philosophical importance. As we shall see later, this narrow focus is something that Peirce was to revise.

Infinite semiosis

Although obvious from what we have already said, it is worth emphasising a third important feature of this early account. Given the anti-Cartesian drive of his account, and the centrality of thought-signs within it, Peirce's first theory of signs seems necessarily committed to the claim that an infinity of further signs must both *proceed* from and *precede* any given sign. We already understand the picture of semiosis or sign action central to Peirce's semiotic: interpretants count as additional signs; signs are themselves interpretants of earlier signs. The notion of infinite semiosis follows quite naturally from this, and the idea that a given sign might be part of a potentially infinite process is not troubling in and of itself. However, the definition of signs as essentially triadic that we find in the early account has the consequence that infinite chains of signs are conceptually necessary.

To see this, imagine a chain of signs with a last or final sign. The final sign that terminates the semiotic process, in order to be the last sign, will have no interpretant. If it did determine an interpretant, that interpretant would function as a further sign and generate a further interpretant, and so the final sign would not, in fact, terminate the chain. However, since any sign must determine an interpretant to count as a sign, the final sign would not be a sign unless it had an interpretant. In short, if the final sign determines an interpretant it is not the final sign, but if it fails to determine an interpretant it is not a sign at all.

Similarly, imagine a chain of signs with a first sign. The same argument, *mutatis mutandis*, holds here. This first sign could not be the interpretant of a preceding sign. If it were, that previous sign would be the first sign. However, since any sign must be the interpretant of a previous sign, a first sign would not be a sign unless it was also an interpretant of some previous sign. In short, it cannot be a first sign if it is determined by a previous sign, but if it fails to be determined by a previous sign, it is not a sign at all. The problem is that if we allow a final sign with no interpretant, or a first sign which is not the interpretant or some earlier sign, then we have failed signs in the semiotic process.

This may seem initially like a simple bind for first and last signs, but the definitional breach required to make a sign chain finite is, in fact, infectious. A failed sign at the start or end of a chain affects the rest of the semiotic chain, causing something like a collapse of dominoes. For example, if the final sign fails to be a sign in virtue of generating no interpretant, then since that failed sign is supposed to act as the interpretant of the previous sign and function as a further sign in its own right, it has also failed to be an interpretant. The consequence of this is that the previous sign has failed to generate a proper interpretant and so failed to be a sign. The consequence of this is that . . . and so on. The alternative is not to countenance terminating sign chains. Obviously, if we cannot end the semiotic process, then signs continue generating signs *ad infinitum*.

Peirce was both aware of and untroubled by infinite semiosis. In part, this is due to the anti-Cartesian context in which the early account arises, since any exceptions to the standard thought-sign in Peirce's work allow space for intuitions and incognisables to be re-instated. Indeed, a first sign in a sign chain would explicitly meet Peirce's definition of an intuition: 'a cognition not determined by a previous cognition of the same object' (EP1. 11 1868). Similarly, a final sign would seem to meet Peirce's definition of the incognisable: 'the meaning of a word is the conception it conveys, the absolutely incognizable has no meaning because no conception attaches to it' (EP1. 51–52 1868). A final sign has no interpretant attached to it; it is beyond our understanding. Infinite semiosis, then, plays a clear role in Peirce's early account.

Despite never explicitly relinquishing infinite semiosis, many of the concepts that lead to it are replaced or revised and the concept becomes less prominent in Peirce's later work, where the anti-Cartesian drive of the early semiotic is dropped and the treatment of signs as thought-signs gives way to a broader view. Just how much weaker the presence of infinite semiosis becomes as a result of these changes is open for debate. Some scholars, T.L. Short for example (Short 2004, 2007), think that infinite semiosis is a characteristic only of Peirce's earlier accounts, whilst others such as James Liszka (1996) or David Savan (1988) treat infinite semiosis as present in all of Peirce's accounts. One thing is clear, however. The prominence of infinite semiosis in the early theory suggests some serious difficulties for Peirce's account of semiotics in the 1860s.

The problems posed by infinite semiosis

Arguably, the idea that infinite chains of signs must, on pain of definitional collapse, both precede and follow any given instance of a sign is troubling, but even if we were to grant Peirce's confident assurances that the presence of an infinite regress should not deter us here,[11] there are still problems with the theory of how the infinite chains are formed. In particular, two clear problems arise because of the structurally undifferentiated nature of any given point in the semiotic chain; that is, no sign is really very different to the next. Consequently, without a clear end or beginning to the semiotic chain, it becomes hard to see how any particular sign could really *mean* anything or be *about* anything. We'll elaborate on these two problems, but it is noteworthy that even early commentators on Peirce's 1860s account found such difficulties in his theory.[12]

The first worry is this: since the interpretant gives us the meaning of a sign in terms of understanding or translation into a further sign, which is itself understood or translated into a further sign, and so on, it becomes hard to see exactly where the meaning of a sign is actually given. It is perhaps most useful to see this problem by leaning on the notion that an interpretant is a translation of the original sign. If in order to understand a word, we must find a suitable translation for it, but our translation must itself be translated, and so on for any further translation we find, then it seems as though we will never arrive at an understanding of the word. Instead, we are caught in an infinite process of translation. Intriguingly, Peirce was aware of this concern too:

[N]o present actual thought [. . .] has any meaning, any intellectual value; for this lies not in what is actually thought, but in
what this thought may be connected with in representation by
subsequent thoughts. So that the meaning of a thought is altogether something virtual. It may be objected, that if no thought
has any meaning, all thought is without meaning. (EP1. 42 1868)

His response to the problem is, again, to suggest that we are being
too troubled by an infinite series[13] and to invoke a processive
answer:

[T]his is a fallacy similar to saying that, if in no one of the successive spaces which a body fills there is room for motion, there
is no room for motion throughout the whole. At no one instant
in my state of mind is there cognition or representation, but in
the relation of my states of mind at different instants there is.
(EP1. 42 1868)

For Peirce, it is the semiotic process, the movement from one sign
to another, that gives signs their meaning. Translatability, rather than
the individual translations, are where we must look for meaning.
However, as T.L. Short notes,[14] this is an unsatisfactory answer whose
deficiencies are shown by its tolerance of 'nonsense' signs. We can
easily imagine a nonsense sentence or concept which is nonetheless
translatable into other languages or words, but it seems a stretch
to think that translatability confers meaningfulness in such cases.
However, Peirce seems to be committed to the view that it is. This is
a troubling consequence.

The second worry comes at the other end of the semiotic chain,
so to speak. Just as the lack of a final interpretant makes it hard to
see how any sign can ever mean anything – it is trapped in interminable translation – the lack of a first sign makes it hard to see
how any object external to the sign chain can ever enter into it. The
concern is perhaps made clearer by contrasting a sign chain with
a first sign against an infinite sign chain of the type Peirce insists
upon. Imagine that we happen across a sign, the word 'apple', say.

We know that this sign is an interpretant of a previous sign, which is itself an interpretant of a previous sign and so on. In the case of a finite chain, it seems we can trace back through the signs until we reach the object which gives rise to this sign, perhaps a wonderfully ripe Cortland apple. In such a case it is clear how the external object enters into the chain. It causes the first sign, which is then translated and developed in further signs and interpretants. In the case of infinite sign chains, it is harder to see how this might work. Tracing back 'apple', we would find signs of the very same object, but this would just continue in an infinite chain where every sign is a sign for some earlier sign. What confidence could we have that an object really lay at the heart of this semiotic chain? All we have are thought-signs and an idealist picture of meaning.

There are lots of reasons why this might be troubling, not least that it seems to run counter to a common-sense picture of how a sign and a corresponding sign chain get to be about something. The more important reason, though, is that it also seems to run counter to Peirce's anti-Cartesian concerns here. In short, if we have no direct cognition of an external object – if our cognitions, or thought-signs, are always translations or developments of some earlier thought-sign – then the object itself remains forever outside of cognition. As such, the object in and of itself remains incognisable. This is, of course, a simple upshot of the Kantian idealism apparent in Peirce's notion of thought-signs, but it certainly leaves him as committed to objects beyond cognition as the Cartesian methodology he was arguing against.

The two concerns raised here against the early account are problematic. However, they are put to rest by various developments in Peirce's later work. Interestingly, the worries themselves don't seem to motivate the changes we find in his later work, but changes in his broader ideas about inquiry, pragmatism and signs in general mean the ideas that lead to these problems recede. The problems are still worth paying attention to, however, since their lack of prominence in later accounts of signs, and the reasons for this, are a useful barometer for just how deep the changes to Peirce's semiotic are.

The middle typology of 1903

In 1903, some thirty-five years after his earliest account of signs, Peirce gave two series of lectures: one on pragmatism at Harvard and another called *Some Topics of Logic* at the Lowell Institute. Part of these lectures, and the supplementary material Peirce produced for the audiences, include an account of signs that goes far beyond the early account of the 1860s. In it Peirce retains the basic sign structure we outlined above and, by paying close attention to those elements of signs and the various interactions between them, gives what seems to be an extensive account of signification, along with an exhaustive typology of signs far beyond the range of his early account of the 1860s.

We shall look at the details of that account shortly, but it is worth noting three important things about the 1903 account in comparison to his earlier theory of signs. First, where the early account suggests three classes of sign, this 1903 account suggests ten classes. Second, where the account of the 1860s treats the general sign, or *symbol*, as the main focus of sign theory, the 1903 account takes many more sign types to be crucial to philosophy and logic, and so within the remit of semiotic. Third, Peirce's view of infinite semiosis seems to have changed, due in no small part to some significant changes in his work in other areas of philosophy. Indeed, the changes which seem to affect his early view of infinite semiosis are the very grounds which give rise to this much-extended and developed 1903 typology and are worth looking at more closely.

Of the important changes to Peirce's broader philosophy, two are crucial to the developments in his semiotic. The first comes from developments we have already noted in our earlier discussion of the account of inquiry, truth and reality in Chapter 3. As we saw, in the 1880s Peirce came to see the index as much more important than he had previously believed. In terms of his account of inquiry, his growing awareness of the role that indexicality and direct demonstrative reference play in our contact with the external world was responsible for his separation of truth and reality. We saw the importance of this change in his views for the development of his later accounts of inquiry. And in other areas such as logic, this growing awareness of indexicality led to important developments. As we shall see in Chapter 5, developments in symbolic logic made by Peirce and his Johns Hopkins student Oscar Mitchell in the early 1880s led directly to his discovery of quantification theory.[15] An essential part of this development was the inclusion of singular propositions and individual variables for objects that cannot be picked out by definite descriptions. Peirce treated these non-general signs as indices, which in turn led him to identify the index as an essential part of logic.

Especially important for our current concerns, though, is that this growing appreciation of different sign types and the connection between semiotic and his broader philosophy seems to have led Peirce to take signs other than the symbol more seriously. In particular, it led Peirce to realise that some symbolic signs have distinctly indexical or non-general features.[16] We've already noted the limited scope of Peirce's early theory of signs, and these developments to his accounts of inquiry and logic in the 1880s make one thing clear: non-symbolic signs, especially indices, are a crucial part of semiotic. As it stood, then, the semiotic of the 1860s was woefully inadequate to the task of capturing the range of signs and signification that Peirce now thought important for philosophy and logic.

The second philosophical development worth noting, albeit briefly, is Peirce's increased commitment to the reality of 'possibilities'. As we noted in Chapter 2 when we examined the pragmatic maxim, Peirce considered much of his earlier work in philosophy to be too nominalistic. This nominalism affected the manner in which he expressed the pragmatic maxim, implying that only *actual* rather than *potential* practical effects could count towards the pragmatic explication of a concept. And as we noted in Chapter 3, this apparent nominalism underpinned a certain body of complaints against his early account of truth and reality: only an *actual* inquiry suitably completed gives us a pragmatic explication of truth and reality. There is also a sense that this nominalism affects his early account of semiotics, and a sign seems to be meaningful only in so far as it is actually interpreted. By 1903, of course, Peirce is firmly committed to the reality of what he calls 'would-bes' – possibility or potential is to be taken just as seriously as any actual or concrete instances – and this solves various problems with his pragmatic maxim and his account of inquiry and truth. Moreover, we find this shift present in his talk of interpretants too, where an interpretants' *capability* for determination is emphasised.[17] The immediate impact on his 1903 account of signs is, as we shall see, subtle, but it is a development especially worth noting because it marks a beginning to a series of important changes in his views of interpretants.

The 1903 account of signs, then, as a result of these changes in his wider philosophy, marks a highly significant stage in Peirce's development of semiotic. When compared to the account of the 1860s, it has a much broader scope and is motivated by his increased sense of the connections between the different elements of his philosophy. When compared to the later, final account, as we shall see, it is also notable for its relative neatness and apparent completeness. It is time, then, to examine the details of Peirce's 1903 account and return to the three elements of signification – namely, the sign-vehicle, the object and the interpretant – and see how Peirce thinks their function in the process of signification leads to an extended classification of sign types.

Sign-vehicles

Recall that each sign has a sign-vehicle; that is, a sign signifies its objects not through all its features, but in virtue of some particular feature. By 1903, Peirce believes the central features or functioning of sign-vehicles can be divided into three broad types and, consequently, that signs can be classified accordingly. This division depends upon whether sign-vehicles signify in virtue of qualities, existential facts or conventions and laws. Further, signs with these sign-vehicles are classified as *qualisigns*, *sinsigns* and *legisigns*, respectively.

Examples of signs whose sign-vehicle relies upon a quality are difficult to imagine, but an example used by David Savan is instructive:

[. . .] I use a color chip to identify the color of some paint I want to buy. The color chip is perhaps made of cardboard, rectangular, resting on a wooden table etc., etc. But it is only the color of the chip that is essential to it as a sign of the color of the paint. (Savan 1988, 20)

There are many elements to the coloured chip as a sign – its shape, its material composition and so on – but it is only its colour that matters to its ability to signify. Any sign whose sign-vehicle relies, as with this example, on simple abstracted qualities is called a *qualisign*.

An example of a sign whose sign-vehicle uses existential facts is smoke as a sign for fire; the causal relation between the fire and smoke allows the smoke to act as a signifier. Other cases are the molehill example used earlier and temperature as a sign for a fever. Any sign whose sign-vehicle relies upon existential connections with its object is named by Peirce a *sinsign*.

Finally, the third kind of sign is one whose sign-vehicle functions primarily through convention, habit or law. Typical examples would be traffic lights as a sign of priority and the signifying capability of words. These sign-vehicles signify in virtue of the conventions surrounding their use. Peirce calls signs whose sign-vehicles function in this way *legisigns*.

Objects

Just as Peirce believes signs can be classified according to whether their sign-vehicles function in virtue of qualities, existential facts or conventions and laws, he believes signs are similarly classifiable according to how their object functions in signification. Recall that, for Peirce, objects 'determine' their signs. That is to say, the nature of the object constrains the nature of the sign in terms of what successful signification requires. Again, for Peirce, the nature of these constraints falls into three broad classes: qualitative, existential or physical, and conventional and law-like. If the constraints of successful signification require that the sign reflect qualitative features of the object, then the sign is an *icon*. If the constraints of successful signification require that the sign utilise some existential or physical connection between it and its object, then the sign is an *index*.

And finally, if successful signification of the object requires that the sign utilise some convention, habit or social rule or law that connects it with its object, then the sign is a *symbol*.

This is a trichotomy with which we are already familiar from the early account, and indeed, the examples of icons, indices and symbols are largely the same as before: icons are portraits and paintings, indices are natural and causal signs, symbols are words, and so on. There are, however, additional instances. For example, icons include diagrams used in geometrical reasoning, indices include pointing fingers and proper names, and symbols include broad classes of speech act like assertion and judgment, all of which suggests a considerable broadening of this trichotomy. There are subtleties to Peirce's view of objects here, and he is not convinced these categories can be kept entirely discrete.[18] We shall not explore this work here except to note his opinion that icons and indices are likely to retain a strong 'symbolic' element. How far this marks a further development of his views from the 1860s, rather than showing some residual commitment to his earlier symbol-centric semiotic, is unclear.

Interpretants

As with the sign-vehicle and the object, Peirce holds that we can classify signs in terms of their relation with their interpretant. Again, he identifies three categories according to which feature of the relationship with its object a sign uses in generating an interpretant. Further, as with the classification of the sign in terms of the sign-vehicle and the object, Peirce identifies qualities, existential facts or conventional features as the basis for classifying the sign in terms of its interpretant.

If the sign is fit to determine an interpretant by focusing our understanding of the sign upon the qualitative features it employs in signifying its object, then the sign is classified as a *rheme*. Examples are not straightforward, but one way of understanding rhemes is to think of them as unsaturated predicates like '— is a dog', '— is happy', '— loves —' or '— gives — to —', and so on. Whenever we understand a sign in terms of the qualities it suggests its object may have, we generate an interpretant that qualifies its sign as a rheme.

If, on the other hand, a sign is fit to determine an interpretant by focusing our understanding of the sign upon the existential features it employs in signifying an object, then the sign is a *dicent*. We can think of dicents as saturated predicates, or propositions, like 'Fido is a dog', 'Larry is happy', 'Fido loves Larry', 'Larry gives food to Fido', and so on.

Finally, if a sign determines an interpretant by focusing our understanding on some conventional or law-like features employed in signifying the object, then the sign is a *delome*, or as Peirce most frequently, but confusingly, calls them, *arguments*. Further, just as we can think of a rheme as an unsaturated predicate and a dicent as a proposition, we can think of the delome as an argument or rule of inference. Our ability to understand a sign in terms of its place in some pattern of reasoning and system of signs enables us to derive information from it (by deductive reasoning) or make conjectures about it (by inductive and abductive reasoning). So, whenever we come to understand a sign as focusing our attention upon some conventional feature of its relationship with an object, that is, enabling us to understand the sign as part of a rule-governed system of knowledge and signs, we have an interpretant that qualifies a sign as a delome (or argument).

The 1903 typology: ten classes of sign

Peirce believed that the three elements and the respective classifications they imposed upon signs could be combined to give a complete list of sign types. That is, since a sign has a sign-vehicle, it can be classified as either a qualisign, a sinsign or a legisign. Additionally, since that sign has an object, it can be classified as either an icon, an index or a symbol. And finally, since that sign will also determine an interpretant, it can be classified as either a rheme, a dicent or a delome. Each sign is then classifiable as some combination of each of its three elements, that is, as either one of the three types of sign-vehicle, plus one of the three types of object, plus one of the three types of interpretant. Initially, this seems to yield twenty-seven possible classificatory combinations, but because of certain of Peirce's phenomenological theories,[19] restrictions on how we can combine the different elements mean there are in fact only ten types of sign.

The rules for the permissible combinations in Peirce's 1903 account are actually quite simple so long as we bear two things in mind. First, types of each element are classifiable as either a *quality*, an *existential fact* or a *convention*. That is, across the three elements of a sign, there are three types deriving from qualities (the qualisign, the icon and the rheme), three deriving from existential facts (the sinsign, the index and the dicent) and three deriving from conventions (the legisign, the symbol and the delome). Second, the classification of the interpretant depends upon the classification of the object, which in turn depends upon the classification of the sign-vehicle. The rules that determine permissible classifications, then, are that if an element is classified as a quality, its dependent element may only be classified as a quality. If an element is classified as an existential fact, its dependent element may be classified as either an existential fact or a quality. And if an element is classified as a convention, its dependent element may be classified as a convention, an existential fact or a quality. This leaves us with ten permissible combinations among sign-vehicle, object and interpretant and, so, ten possible kinds of signs. They look something like this:

Table 4.1

INTERPRETANT	OBJECT	SIGN-VEHICLE	EXAMPLES (from CP2. 254–263 (1903))
Rheme	Icon	Qualisign	'A feeling of "red"'
Rheme	Icon	Sinsign	'An individual diagram'
Rheme	Index	Sinsign	'A spontaneous cry'
Dicent	Index	Sinsign	'A weathercock'
Rheme	Icon	Legisign	'A diagram' [type]
Rheme	Index	Legisign	'A demonstrative pronoun'
Dicent	Index	Legisign	'A street cry'
Rheme	Symbol	Legisign	'A common noun'
Dicent	Symbol	Legisign	'An ordinary proposition'
Delome	Symbol	Legisign	'An argument'

These ten types of sign are simply called after the combination of their elements: an ordinary proposition is a *dicentic-symbolic-legisign*; a spontaneous cry, a *rhematic-indexical-sinsign*; and so on.

How useful such a typology might prove to be is rather an open question, and even Peirce shows a tendency to treat it as a matter of simply tracing out the full implications of his account of signs. For example, whilst he explores the roles of rhematic, dicentic and delomic symbolic-legisigns in abductive, inductive and deductive argument forms (EP2. 297–299 (1903)), he is also open to the idea that one need not use the typology very precisely:

> It is a nice problem to say to what class a given sign belongs; since all the circumstances of the case have to be considered. But it is seldom requisite to be very accurate; for if one does not locate the sign precisely, one will easily come near enough to its character for any ordinary purposes of logic. (EP2. 297 (1903))

All the same, the clear increase in scope, sophistication and integration with his wider philosophy is made especially clear by comparing this typology with the simple icon/index/symbol division of the early account.

Infinite semiosis in the 1903 account

The 1903 account is a clear advance and development on the theory of the 1860s. However, it does not advance so far away from some of the features of the early account as it might initially seem. In particular, the issue of semiosis and the problems it poses to the early account are still lurking in some respect in the 1903 theory. Recall that we suggested Peirce's commitment to infinite semiosis posed two problems for his early theory of signs. First, it was hard to see how any particular sign could *mean* anything since there was no final sign in which meaning was given. And second, it was hard to see how any particular sign could be *about* anything since there was no first sign where an external object was interpreted directly, instead of mediately via an earlier sign. Although the 1903 account is no longer troubled by the second of these two problems, the first problem still remains as an issue.

As we pointed out, the 1903 account emerges, in part, from Peirce's growing realisation that the index as a sign for particular individuals is a crucial part of any sign theory and cannot be passed over. Moreover, Peirce sees the indexical sign as serving a very particular indicative purpose, that of creating a direct connection with its object. In an extended example, Peirce states this view of the indexical sign quite clearly:

> When a driver, to attract the attention of a foot-passenger and cause him to save himself, calls out 'Hi!', so far as this is a significant word, it is, as will be seen below, something more than an index; but so far as it is simply intended to act upon the hearer's nervous system and to rouse him to get out of the way, it is an index, because it is meant to put him in real connection with the object, which is his situation relative to the approaching horse. (EP2. 14 (1895))

An index, then, is a sign that is meant to connect our understanding directly with external objects, even though it is not intended to give us any deeper information about that object. In the same passage just quoted, Peirce goes on to say that the point of certain indices is to enable a hearer or interpreter to 'establish a real connection between his mind and the object' (EP2. 14 (1895)). What Peirce has here, then, is a sign which provides a way of introducing external objects directly into a sign chain without the mediation of other signs; the index functions as a demonstrative concept.[20] This in effect solves one issue of infinite semiosis – signs can be about external objects through the use or presence of an indexical sign in the sign chain.

With regard to the other issue, that sign chains continue into chains of interminable translation, Peirce still seems to be committed to the kind of problematic view of semiosis that leaves him subject to this worry. In the supplementary material produced for his 1903 Lowell Institute lectures, for example, he says:

> The triadic relation is *genuine*, that is, its three members are bound together by it in a way that does not consist in any complexes of dyadic relations. [. . .] The [interpretant] must indeed stand in such a relation, and thus be capable of determining [an interpretant] of its own; but besides that, it must have a second triadic relation in which the [sign-vehicle], or rather the relation thereof to its Object shall be its own (the [interpretant's]) Object, and must be capable of determining [an interpretant] to this relation. All this must be true of the [interpretant's interpretant] and so on endlessly. (EP2. 273 (1903))

Peirce, at his prosaic best, is reconfirming his commitment to infinite chains of interpretants generating further interpretants. The strength of the claim is mitigated somewhat by the presence of his anti-nominalism, as an interpretant need only be *capable* of participating in this interminable process of translation. All the same, the original concern that the meaning of a sign is never found once one is committed to chase on continually through successive interpretants seems as pertinent to the 1903 account as it was to the early sign theory of the 1860s.

The final typology

The final account of semiotics that we shall examine was developed in the last decade of Peirce's life, perhaps concentrated most in the years 1906–1910. In many respects, the seeds for this last account of signs were already sown in 1903. There are a host of reasons why Peirce produced so much work on semiotic in the final years of his life, some personal and some philosophical. In purely personal terms, the reception of his public lectures of 1903 was not as successful as he might have hoped. James thought them obscure and was against their publication, whilst Peirce seemed to have made a questionable impression upon his audience.[21] Subsequently, Peirce began of necessity to retreat into a life of geographical and intellectual isolation. However, in the spring of 1903, Peirce began a correspondence with the English aristocrat Victoria Lady Welby. Welby was an autodidact whose book *What is Meaning?* had been reviewed by Peirce for *The Nation* magazine. Their shared interest in signs and meaning gave Peirce an outlet for expressing the ideas about semiotics developed towards the end of his life. Their correspondence continued for eight or so years, and it provides a rich resource for our understanding of his final accounts of semiotics. Indeed, Lady Welby introduced Peirce's work to the linguist and writer Charles K. Ogden, who, in an appendix to the seminal 1923 book written with I.A. Richards, *The Meaning of Meaning*, offers one of the earliest resources on Peirce's later account of signs.

In philosophical terms, however, by 1903 Peirce had started to see the broader connections amongst the different branches of his philosophy much more clearly. In the build-up to the 1903 lectures, Peirce had submitted an application for a grant to the Carnegie Institute, hoping to secure money to enable him to write a full statement of his philosophy and logic. Part of that application was spent tracing out the philosophical and architectonic connections that lie at the heart of much of his later philosophical work. As we know, the application failed, but it helped to draw Peirce's attention to the place of sign theory within his broader body of philosophical theory and to see the centrality of sign theory to his views on the logic of scientific progress and the process of inquiry. If we are to conduct self-controlled, principle-guided inquiry in the hope of tending towards an end point and answer – thereby contributing to the growth of concrete reasonableness – then sign theory has to be the conduit for this process. As we mentioned previously, after Peirce's views on the architectonic structure of philosophy became clearer around the turn of the century, and at the time of the Carnegie Institute application, he saw logic as divided into three branches: speculative grammar, critical logic and methodeutic.

Speculative grammar gives the theoretical explanation of the nature and structure of signs, critical logic studies the nature and form of arguments, and methodeutic shows how signs and arguments generate the habits and actions that lead to the growth of concrete reasonableness. The proper place for the accounts of pragmatism and inquiry, then, is in the methodeutic, whilst the proper place for the theory of signs, sign structure and sign action is in the speculative grammar. The connection between the two in the architectonic is clear, and the end-directed nature of inquiry becomes something an account of signs must accommodate.

The developments to the later account of semiotics are deeply interesting, but they are also speculative and incomplete and our understanding of them has to fill in many blanks. There is nothing like universal agreement on what is going on, and the questions of just how we should interpret what Peirce has to say in the later accounts is made more fraught by Peirce's experimental terminology. Nonetheless, there is much in the final accounts that we can be confident about, not least that Peirce's growing sense that semiotic chains are end directed and deeply connected to his account of inquiry leads him to see signs as having multiple objects and multiple interpretants.

Changes to the object

The dynamic object

The dynamic object is, in some senses, the object that generates a chain of signs. The aim of a sign chain is to arrive at a full understanding of an object and so assimilate that object into the system of signs. Using slightly more simplistic terms, Joseph Ransdell (1977, 169) describes the dynamic object as the 'object as it really is', and Christopher Hookway (1985, 139) describes it as 'the object as it is known to be [at the end of inquiry]'. Indeed, Hookway's description shows an acute awareness of the connection between the dynamic object and the process of inquiry in Peirce's later sign theory. An example from James Liszka (1996, 23) captures Peirce's idea quite clearly. Consider a petroleum tank half full with fuel. Various signs for this half-full state are available: perhaps there is a fuel gauge attached to the tank, or perhaps the tank makes a distinctive sound when we strike it, and so on. But despite these various signs, the object underlying them all is the *actual* level of fuel in the petroleum tank; this is the dynamic object.

The immediate object

Ransdell (1977, 169) describes the immediate object as 'what we, at any time, suppose the object to be', and Hookway (1985, 139) describes it as 'the object at the time it is first used and interpreted'. The immediate object, then, is not some additional object distinct from the dynamic object but is merely some informationally incomplete facsimile of the dynamic object generated at some interim stage in a chain of signs. Returning to the petroleum tank example, when we strike the tank the tone that it emits (which functions as the sign-vehicle) represents to us that the tank is not full (but it does not tell us the precise level of fuel). The immediate object, then, is a less-than-full tank.

Clearly, the immediate and dynamic objects of a sign are intimately linked, and Peirce consistently describes and introduces the two together (see CP4. 536 (1896)). However, the connection between the two is most clear when we consider the connections between sign chains and inquiry. The dynamic object is, as we have suggested, the goal and end point that drives the semiotic process, and the immediate object is our grasp of that object at any point in that process. Ransdell, for instance, says:

> [T]he immediate object is the object as it appears at any point in the inquiry or semiotic process. The [dynamic] object, however, is the object as it really is. These must be distinguished, first, because the immediate object may involve some erroneous interpretation and thus be to that extent falsely representative of the object as it really is, and, second, because it may fail to include something that is true of the real object. In other words, the immediate object is simply what we at any time suppose the real object to be. (Ransdell 1977, 169)

Put this way, it is clear how Peirce's growing concern to capture the parallels between semiosis and the process of inquiry leads him to identify two objects for the sign.

Changes to the interpretant

The immediate interpretant

As its identification with the second grade of clarity suggests, the immediate interpretant is a general definitional understanding of the relationship between the sign and the dynamic object. In an extended example where the dynamic object is the weather on a stormy day, Peirce describes the immediate interpretant as 'the schema in [our] imagination, i.e. the vague Image of what there is in common to the different images of a stormy day' (CP8. 314 (1907)). The immediate interpretant, then, is something like recognition of the syntax of the sign and the more general features of its meaning. Indeed, Peirce seems to take the immediate interpretant to be 'all that is explicit in the sign apart from its context and circumstances of utterance' (CP5. 473 (1907)). Also instructive is David Savan's description of the immediate interpretant as the

> explicit content of the sign which would enable a person to say whether or not the sign was applicable to anything concerning which that person had sufficient acquaintance. It is the total unanalyzed impression which the sign might be expected to produce, prior to any critical reflection upon it. (Savan 1988, 53)

In terms of an example where ordinary sentences are the signs, the immediate interpretant will involve something like our recognition of grammatical categories, syntactic structures and conventional rules of use. For instance, without knowing anything about its context of utterance, we can surmise certain things about the sentence, 'We don't want to hurt him, do we?' We know it is a question, we know it concerns doing harm to some person, the person is male, and so on. These things are part of the immediate interpretant of the sign.

The dynamic interpretant

The second type of interpretant that any sign must have is the dynamic interpretant. This is our understanding of the sign/dynamic object relationship at some actual instance in the chain of signs. Peirce describes the dynamic interpretant as the 'effect actually produced on the mind' (CP8. 343 (1908)) or as the 'actual effect which the sign, as a sign, really determines' (CP4. 536 (1906)). The dynamic interpretant, then, is the understanding we reach, or which the sign determines, at any particular semiotic stage.

To continue with linguistic examples, we know that the dynamic interpretant is the actual interpretation we make or understanding we reach in the first instance of interpretation. For instance, when you say to me whilst pointing at some cowardly woman we know, 'I saw her duck under the table', the dynamic interpretant is my understanding that you are the utterer, that I am the addressee, and that you saw our cowardly acquaintance hide beneath a table.

There is also an interesting connection between the dynamic interpretant and the immediate object. As the understanding we actually reach at any particular point in the sign chain, the dynamic interpretant represents an incomplete understanding, or interpretation, of the dynamic object. More important, though, is that the immediate object of some sign in a sign chain consists of the actual interpretations made previously; that is, it consists of the dynamic interpretants from earlier stages in the sign chain. As Ransdell (1977, 169) puts it, the 'immediate object is, in other words, the funded result of all interpretation prior to the interpretation of the given sign'. The dynamic interpretant, then, is the actual interpretation or understanding we make at some point in the semiotic process, and it also constitutes, along with previous dynamic interpretants, the immediate object, or the partial understanding we have of the dynamic object at any particular point in the semiotic process.

The final interpretant

Peirce describes the final interpretant as 'that which would finally be decided to be the true interpretation if consideration of the matter were carried so far that an ultimate opinion were reached' (CP8. 184 (1909)). Elsewhere he describes it as the 'effect that would be produced on the mind by the sign after sufficient development of thought' (CP8. 343 (1908)). The final interpretant, then, seems to be what our understanding of the dynamic object would be at the end of inquiry, that is, if we had reached a true understanding of the dynamic object. Peirce's notion of inquiry is clearly central here. As Hookway points out, we might best define the final interpretant as the understanding

> which would be reached if a process of enriching the interpretant through scientific enquiry were to proceed indefinitely. It incorporates a complete and true conception of the objects of

the sign; it is the interpretant we should all agree on in the long run. (Hookway 1985, 139)

As an example, consider again the kinds of utterance that we have already looked at. In such a case as your uttering, 'I saw her duck under the table', the final interpretant would be the understanding where there is 'no latitude of interpretation at all' (CP5. 447 (1905)), that is, where the meanings of the words, the identity of the agents involved and so on are absolutely determinate. So, the final interpretant of your utterance of 'I saw her duck under the table' is my coming to a determinate understanding of what you mean. We can envisage how this would come about by my asking a variety of questions, like 'are you using "duck" as a verb or a noun?', or even 'are you talking to me?', and developing a series of dynamic interpretants that get us closer and closer to the final interpretant.

Just as the dynamic interpretant has clear connections with other elements of Peirce's semiotic, so too does the final interpretant. As should be clear from the connections that emerge from the notion of inquiry, the final interpretant interacts strongly with the dynamic object. The final interpretant, then, is important to our understanding of the dynamic object in a couple of ways. First, it is the point where our grasp of the dynamic object would be complete, and, according to Ransdell (1977, 169–170), it is where the immediate object and the dynamic object coincide. This represents the full assimilation or integration of the dynamic object into our system of signs. Second, the final interpretant functions as an exemplar or normative standard by which we can judge our actual interpretative responses to the sign. As David Savan puts it, 'Peirce's intention was to identify the third type of interpretant as providing a norm or standard by which particular stages (Dynamical Interpretants) of an historical process may be judged' (Savan 1988, 62).

The final typology classification

Just as the early and interim accounts include a corresponding classification of sign types, Peirce's final account holds similar typological ambitions. Peirce states explicitly that there are sixty-six classes of sign in his final typology (See EP2. 481 (1908)). Strictly speaking, the six elements that we have detailed yield only twenty-eight sign types, but we are interested in Peirce's very final typology. He believes that we can obtain these sixty-six classes, rather in the manner of the 1903 typology, by identifying ten elements of signs and signification, each of which has three qualifying classes, and then working out their permissible combinations. These ten elements include the six sign elements identified above plus four other elements that focus on the relation between signs, objects and interpretants. The ten elements and their respective sign types, taken from Peirce's 1908 letters to Lady Welby (EP2. 483–491), are as follows:

1 In respect of the sign itself (what we have been calling the sign-vehicle), a sign may be either (i) a *potisign*, (ii) an *actisign* or (iii) a *famisign*.[22]
2 In respect of the immediate object, a sign may be either (i) *descriptive*, (ii) *designative* or (iii) *copulant*.
3 In respect of the dynamic object, a sign may be either (i) *abstractive*, (ii) *concretive* or (iii) *collective*.
4 In respect of the relation between the sign and the dynamic object, a sign may be either (i) an *icon*, (ii) an *index* or (iii) a *symbol*.
5 In respect of the immediate interpretant, a sign may be either (i) *ejaculative*, (ii) *imperative* or (iii) *significative*.
6 In respect of the dynamic interpretant, a sign may be either (i) *sympathetic*, (ii) *shocking* or (iii) *usual*.
7 In respect of the relationship between the sign and the dynamic interpretant, a sign may be either (i) *suggestive*, (ii) *imperative* or (iii) *indicative*.
8 In respect of the final interpretant, a sign may be either (i) *gratiffic*, (ii) *action producing* or (iii) *self-control producing*.
9 In respect of the relation between the sign and the final interpretant, a sign may be either a (i) *seme*, (ii) *pheme* or (iii) *delome*.
10 In respect of the relation between the sign, the dynamic object and the final interpretant, a sign may be either (i) an *assurance of instinct*, (ii) an *assurance of experience* or (iii) an *assurance of form*.

The reason that Peirce believes these ten elements will yield sixty-six classes is clear enough. The same combinatorial considerations given for the 1903 account apply here: a *conventional* element can qualify its following elements as *conventional, existential* or *qualitative; existential* elements can only qualify following elements as *existential* or *qualitative;* and *qualitative* elements may only qualify following elements as *qualitative.* However, the precise manner and order in which these elements interact will determine what the sixty-six classes of signs will look like in the final typology. Unfortunately, these ten divisions and their classes represent a baffling array of under-explained terminology, and there is little to indicate precisely how we should set about the task of combining them. Even though we may be confident about the number of signs in the final typology, other details are sketchy and underdeveloped, and there still exists no fully satisfactory account of the sixty-six classes. As Nathan Houser points out, 'a sound and detailed extension of Peirce's analysis of signs to his full set of ten divisions and sixty-six classes is perhaps the most pressing problem for Peircian semiotics' (Houser 1992, 502).

There is lots of good work on the typology,[23] but ultimately it is not clear that any account will overcome the problems posed by the incomplete and cursory nature of the final account. Indeed, it is not clear that Peirce himself was fully at ease with his final typology and how its elements should hang together. As he himself said:

> The ten divisions appear to me to be all Trichotomies; but it is possible that none of them are properly so. Of these ten Trichotomies, I have a clear apprehension of some, an unsatisfactory and doubtful notion of others, and a tolerable but not thoroughly tried conception of others. (EP2. 483 (1908))

This final account of signs, then, extends far beyond the early and middle accounts. And whilst it outstrips both, it has none of the neatness or manageability of the 1903 theory. What is notable, though, is that whilst the basic structure is retained and semiosis is still clearly in evidence from the definition of signs, the problems of infinite semiosis are bypassed.

Of the two problems previously mentioned – how a sign comes to mean anything without an end to interpretation and how a sign can be about anything without a first immediate sign of an external object – neither has any traction within this final account. The problem of first signs, solved by taking indexical signs more seriously in the 1903 account, is here solved by the notion of the dynamic object. Peirce's division of the object is, as he says, 'to distinguish two Objects of a Sign, the Mediate without, and the Immediate within the Sign' (EP2. 480 (1908)). The dynamic object is that first, indexically connected object, and the immediate object, from within the sign, is what Peirce calls 'a hint' at the external object. This is more or less the same resolution of the problem as in 1903, except here we find the mediate contact between signs and external objects built directly into the sign.

The issue of a final sign, on the other hand, is resolved by the presence of the final interpretant. The meaning of the sign is given at this semiotic end point, the true interpretation and ultimate opinion. Along with Peirce's anti-nominalism and realism about 'would-bes', we can see that the meaning – in one sense anyway – of any sign is simply its final interpretant, the interpretation that we would arrive at after sufficient semiotic development or translation. The parallels with inquiry are already noted, but it is also clear that worries of infinite semiosis are of no concern here.

Summary

An ever-present feature in Peirce's philosophy is his account of semiotics, or sign theory. There are at least three quite distinct accounts of semiotic in his work: an early account from the late 1860s, a middle account from around 1903, and a later account from 1906–1910.

- The early account treated signs almost exclusively in terms of thought. These thought-signs are composed of a sign-vehicle, an object and an interpretant (although Peirce does not use these terms early on), and there are three distinct types of sign: the icon, the index and the symbol.

- In the middle account, Peirce treated signs as extending beyond simple thought-signs and accepted that signs encompass a much broader range of phenomena. His 1903 account retained the basic sign structure of sign-vehicle/object/interpretant, but it included a much wider range of signs. In this typology, Peirce took there to be ten sign types.

- In the later account, Peirce extended his account of signs even further, drawing much closer parallels with his concepts of inquiry and final causation. He also developed the basic sign structure, noting one type of sign-vehicle, two types of object (the dynamic and the immediate) and three types of interpretant (the immediate, the dynamic and the final). This typology included sixty-six classes of sign.

- A common feature throughout Peirce's various accounts of signs is the sign process itself, or semiosis. Semiosis is the system by which signs develop and change and by which information about the object of the sign grows. One consequence of this is that there are infinite chains of signs leading to and from any given sign. Exactly how strong the commitment to an infinite semiotic process is tends to be a key difference between the various systems. The early account has infinite chains leading both to and from any given sign; the middle account has infinite sign chains leading from, but not to, any given sign; and the final account does not necessarily have infinite chains following either to or from any given sign.

Further reading

Peirce's semiotics is an area where the use and proliferation of the secondary literature is at its largest. Much of this is an attempt to apply some portion of Peirce's writing on signs to another discipline or subject matter. However, just how one should view Peirce's theory of signs and the various stages of its development is itself a broad area of interest. I shall leave the interested reader to pursue the application of Peirce's semiotic for themselves and instead point out the most important works to introduce and develop Peirce's sign theory.

A good introduction to Peirce's semiotic, and especially clear on what we have here called the middle or 1903 typology, is James

Liszka's *A General Introduction to the Semiotic of Charles Sanders Peirce* (1996). Liszka's approach to Peirce's semiotic places special emphasis on the role of the categories and the triadic nature of signs and semiotic. In a similar vein is David Savan's *An Introduction to C.S. Peirce's Full System of Semiotic* (1988). This is an important monograph with a very similar approach to Liszka's, but its focus is more fully on Peirce's final typology. Between them, Savan (1988) and Liszka (1996) offer a fairly complete view of the triadic approach to Peirce's semiotic.

A recent and important monograph which represents the main alternative to the triadic approach is T.L. Short's *Peirce's Theory of Signs* (2007). Short emphasises the developmental pressures on Peirce's account and develops a view of Peirce's semiotic in terms of teleology, final causation and symbolic growth. This is a wide-ranging monograph, and careful reading pays dividends. I take a related view to Short's to be given in Joseph Ransdell's 1977 'Some leading ideas in Peirce's semiotic'. Although Ransdell and Short have recently taken their views to be at odds in various ways, this paper by Ransdell is particularly insightful in its discussion of the later developments in sign structure in terms of inquiry and the growth of information.

A final approach is also worth mentioning, although it is perhaps less widespread than the approaches of Liszka and Savan or Short and Ransdell. This is the view found amongst Peirce scholars such as Mats Bergman in his *Peirce's Philosophy of Communication* (2009) and Ahti-Veikko Pietarinen in *Signs of Logic: Peircean Themes on the Philosophy of Language, Games, and Communication* (2006b). The latter is much more complicated and extends far beyond a simple account of semiotic, but both are notable for their treatment of Peirce's semiotic in game-theoretic and dialogic terms. This reading of the sign theory focuses squarely on the role of semiotics in communication.

Notes

1 See, for instance, Burks (1949).
2 See, for example, Atkin (2005, 2008a, 2008b), Boersema (2002, 2009) and Agler (2011) for accounts of how Peircian semiotic might meet some of the various concerns of twentieth-century philosophy of language.
3 See, for example, Elkins (2003).
4 See Short (2007, ix).

5 There is variation even on matters as simple as how to describe the different developmental stages. For instance, Liszka (1996) identifies four typologies instead of three. Short (2007) identifies three central problems, but perhaps seven separate accounts. There is less disagreement than this might suggest, but all the same there is variation.

6 See, for instance, Saussure (1916/1974).

7 This is an allusion to Peirce's theory of phenomenological categories and his view that the sign elements are classifiable in terms of these categories. Firsts in such a context are thought of as qualities. We shall look at the categories in detail in Chapter 6, but it is worth commenting here that we find the theory deeply embedded in his semiotic.

8 So far as I am aware, 'sign-vehicle' is not a term Peirce uses directly. We find him describing the sign as 'a vehicle conveying into the mind something from without' (CP1. 339 (1903)), but the exact term is perhaps more closely associated with Charles Morris (1938).

9 Without delving into other accounts of signs too deeply, we can see that Saussure's notion of a sign as being composed of a sign and an object (signifier and signified) would not qualify as a sign on Peirce's view since there is no interpretant. Similarly, Locke's signs as words signifying ideas or 'internal conceptions' (Locke 1975, Book III, Chapters 1 and 2) would not qualify as Peircian signs because there is no object.

10 The eleven-paper Harvard lecture series, *On the Logic of Science* (W1. 162–302), was in fact never delivered, apparently for lack of audience interest.

11 For instance, we find him assuring us that any fears we have that an infinite series is impossible are unfounded since 'Achilles, as a fact, will overtake the tortoise' (EP1. 23–24 (1868)).

12 See, for example, Leonard (1937) or Gentry (1952).

13 Intriguingly, Peirce makes frequent allusion to worries in the style of Zeno's paradox when defending the infinite semiosis of his early account of signs. His solution here is reminiscent of the usual 'at-at' solutions to such worries as the arrow paradox: there may be no motion at an instant, but across an interval which includes the instant, 'the arrow moves'. Peirce's claims about 'thought' look similar.

14 See Short (2004, 217–218).

15 See Peirce (1883).

16 A similar realisation for Peirce at this time was that symbols with heavily iconic features played a very important role in mathematics and mathematical reasoning (see Hookway 1985, Chapter 6).

17 See, for example, his fifth Harvard lecture of 1903 (EP2. 202), where a sign's *capability* for repetition is emphasised as a key characteristic.

18 By 1903, for example, Peirce is explicitly of the view that it would be hard, if not impossible, to find any pure instances of icons and indices. Rather, he begins to suspect that icons and indices were always partly symbolic

or conventional. Peirce experiments with some additional terminology and types of icon and index. These he calls the hypo-icon (see CP2. 276 (1903)) and the sub-index (see CP2. 330 (1903)), respectively. We shall not explore these signs further here (see Goudge (1965) and Atkin (2005) for more on Peirce's view of indices and Legg (2008a) for more on icons), but it is worth noting that by 1903, the simple icon/index/symbol trichotomy is something of an abstraction, and Peirce suspects that any single sign may display some combination of iconic, indexical and symbolic characteristics.

19 We shall look more closely at Peirce's phenomenology in Chapter 6, but, in short, he took there to be three phenomenological categories – firstness, secondness and thirdness. Given how we are classifying signs here, we can think of these as corresponding to qualities, brute facts, and laws or conventions.

20 As it happens, Peirce had introduced the concept of sign's 'pure demonstrative application' in his *Journal of Speculative Philosophy* papers of the 1860s (see EP1. 40 (1868), for instance). However, this was a feature that sat outside of the semiotic chain and was not a sign in and of itself. It is only after the work of the 1880s that the concept Peirce is groping for in the 1860s becomes a sign and so part of the semiotic process.

21 In a letter sent to Justus Buchler (Buchler 1954, 54), for instance, George Santayana, who attended the 1903 Harvard lectures, described Peirce as 'red-nosed' and 'dishevelled' and his lecture as '*ex-tempore* and whimsical'.

22 By the time of the final accounts, Peirce was experimenting with terminology, so these types are perhaps more familiar as the qualisigns, sinsigns and legisigns of the 1903 account.

23 See, for example, Weiss and Burks (1945), Sanders (1970), Savan (1988), Jappy (1989), Müller (1994) and Farias and Queiroz (2003).

Five
Logic

Introduction

Peirce was deeply committed to the study of logic. He came across it early, first reading his older brother's copy of Richard Whately's *Elements of Logic* when he was twelve, and he remained a devoted logician throughout his life. As we previously noted, he was the first person to be identified as a logician in *Who's Who*, and even in times of near penury he remained dedicated to working on his logic. Even in his own lifetime, where Peirce's academic genius was known it was as a logician. During his employment at Johns Hopkins University in the early 1880s, his contributions to and standing in the field were frequently noted by the celebrated figures of what was then the dominant approach to logic. W.S. Jevons (1881) pointed to Peirce's work as greatly advancing the field, and in his review of the Peirce-edited *Studies in Logic* (Peirce 1883), English mathematician John Venn stated:

> Mr C.S. Peirce's name is so well known to those who take an interest in the development of the Boolean or symbolic treatment of Logic that the knowledge that he was engaged in lecturing upon the subject to advanced classes at the Johns Hopkins University will have been assurance that some interesting contributions to the subject might soon be looked for [.] [. . .] [T]he volume under notice [. . .] seems to me to contain [a] greater quantity of novel and suggestive matter than any other recent work on

the same or allied subjects which has happened to come under my notice. (Venn 1883, 594)

Given the kind of work that Peirce was producing on logic, not only at the time of his Johns Hopkins appointment but throughout his life, it is unsurprising that leading contemporaries knew of his work and placed a high value on it. We know that with the increased isolation that Peirce experienced after the termination of his Johns Hopkins post, his logical work drew less attention, and, as we shall see in a moment, his *precise* place in the history of logic is still contentious. Nonetheless, we now know that Peirce was responsible for all manner of firsts and innovations. He developed complex functional treatments of the logical proposition; made key developments in the notion of logical relations; developed a theory of quantifiers roughly contemporaneous with Frege but more directly influential on the development of modern mathematical logic; originated much of the quantifier notation that we currently use; developed truth-functional treatments of logical connectives; introduced truth tables; developed triadic logics; and generated an intriguing diagrammatic logic that encompassed much that we now recognise as first-order logic, second-order logic and complex modal logics, with prototype 'possible-worlds' semantics.

This is certainly an impressive list of accomplishments, and for anyone who knows anything about the official history of modern mathematical logic, these are big claims, but the list above actually offers a relatively modest account of Peirce's achievements. Other commentators on Peirce's work claim even more for his list of firsts. Jaako Hintikka (1997) places him at the heart of the model-theoretic tradition, as a forebear of Tarski's work in logic, and names him as an early proponent of game-theoretical semantics. Randall Dipert (1984) identifies early meta-logical speculation on decidability in Peirce's work and, along with Christopher Hookway (1985, 199–200), identifies an early anticipation of Peano's postulates for natural numbers. To be clear, when judged against Peirce's writings, none of these claims is the least bit laboured or far-fetched. Peirce's published contributions to the development of logic are mighty, and the depth and range of his overall body of work on logic, most of it under-appreciated or unrecognised, is simply staggering – even more so when one considers the relative isolation he experienced through much of his intellectual life. Arguably, though, Peirce is still under-appreciated in the history of logic.

How one understands Peirce's place in the history of logic depends very much on how one places his work in relation to the mathematical development of modern logic that characterises much of the twentieth and twenty-first centuries. According to the official story, modern logic begins with Frege's *Begriffsschrift* in 1879, where we find the first theory of modern quantification. Jean van Heijenoort's influential book *From Frege to Gödel* (1967) places Peirce's early work in algebraic logic as part of an interesting dead end, seeing it as having no real historical impact and as part of the lumbering Aristotelian dinosaur swept away by the powerful new quantifier logic of Frege and Russell. Others see the history differently:

> So what is Peirce's place in the history of logical theory? He was a working member of a tradition which was largely suppressed in his own time and in the next couple of decades. Because of this suppression, few if any of his most interesting ideas were developed by others. By the time the model-theoretical tradition was revitalised again among logicians and philosophers, some of Peirce's problems and ideas had been superseded or even forgotten. (Hintikka 1997, 32)

However, even this is not quite true. Important work by Dipert (1989) and Putnam (1982) makes it abundantly clear that Peirce exercised incredible influence over the development and dawning of modern logic, markedly more so than Frege, in fact. The key to the rise of modern logic is undoubtedly the development of quantification, but the factors which bring quantification to the forefront of modern logic at the dawning of the twentieth century stem from Peirce's work, not Frege's. To quote Putnam at length:

> When I started to trace the later development of logic, the first thing I did was to look at Schröder's [*Vorlesungen über die Algebra der Logik*]. I simply wished to see how Schröder presented the quantifier.

Well, Schröder does mention Frege's discovery, though just barely; but he does not explain Frege's notation at all. The notation he both explains and adopts [. . .] is Peirce's. [. . .] [M]any famous logicians adopted Peirce-Schröder notation, and famous results and systems were published in it. Lowenheim stated and proved the Lowenheim theorem (later reproved and strengthened by Skolem, whose name became attached to it together with Lowenheim's) in Peircian notation. In fact, there is no reference in Lowenheim's paper to any logic other than Peirce's. (Putnam 1982, 295–297)

What this tells us is that whilst in the official retelling Peirce's early influence was sidelined and Frege given credit for inventing a system of quantification, Peirce's work and influence were hardly suppressed. He was instrumental in establishing modern logic by lying at the root of a chain of influential work that goes from Peirce to Schröder to Peano and on to Whitehead and Russell and the dawn of modern mathematical logic. We shall unpack this more in what follows, but if the historical origin of modern logic should focus on the quantifier, then Peirce is there at the very heart of it. To paraphrase Putnam (1982, 301), the discovery of quantification may be Frege's, but Peirce discovered quantifiers so that they stayed discovered.[1] And whilst this is still an under-appreciated fact, it is no longer the well-kept secret it once was.

It is time, then, that we examined some of Peirce's logical work in a little more detail. We shall begin by looking at some general characterisations of Peirce's view of logic. This is worthwhile because, as influential as much of his work was, his published papers especially, Peirce was still working in a logical tradition that can look strange to us. We shall then examine his work in developing Boolean or algebraic logic. This is often seen as his 'early' period of work and certainly covers the period of his life up to and beyond his Johns Hopkins appointment. It also represents that portion of Peirce's logical work which is most well known and which has the broadest influence over the rise of modern mathematical logic. Finally, we shall look at Peirce's later work on diagrammatic logic. This work was produced when Peirce was more isolated from the academic world and so is less well known and less understood than his earlier algebraic work on logic, but as we shall see, it is a rich and interesting area of his philosophical output.

Peirce's view of logic

To the modern eye, Peirce's work on logic can look confused, under-explained and difficult to place in line with our current understanding of the discipline. This is partly due, as we've mentioned, to his early work developing the approach to logic used by Boole, Jevons, Clifford and others of the algebraic tradition, an approach mostly unfamiliar to us today. An additional obscuring factor is the kind of language Peirce uses and his need to mark distinctions wherever he sees them. As Quine notes in regard to Peirce's early work on relatives:

> [H]e made a hobby early and late of taxonomic terminology. We have self relatives, aliorelatives, cyclic relatives, equiparents, disquiparents, concurrents, opponents, and copulatives. (Quine 1995, 25)

This modern under-appreciation is also due to Peirce's deep understanding and awareness of the history of logical thought. In the modern mind, logic begins with Frege, and before him there is only 'the dark ages'. Peirce, however, saw himself as part of a continuum of concerns stretching from Aristotle through medieval logicians and beyond to Leibniz, and at times his work reflects this conception of the field. However, when we look closely at how Peirce saw logic, and especially when we clarify certain points in his work, we can see that his view resonates strongly with many of our current ideas.

In what follows, we shall look at a variety of themes or views that are readily apparent in Peirce's take on logic. We shall start with some very simple and general definitions before turning to a distinction we mentioned in Chapter 1, namely the distinction between Peirce's broad view of logic and the more narrow concern with 'deductive' logic that interests us here. For Peirce, as we shall see, this is not

an entirely neat or natural division, and this can help us to understand his work more clearly. Next we shall look at how Peirce views
logic as a combination of normative and descriptive elements. We
shall then look at a clear anti-psychologist strain in his work before
finally turning to what seems to be a clear anti-logicist element to
his work. That is, there seems to be a denial of the claim, familiar to
us from Frege and Russell, that logic is, in some sense, foundational
for mathematics.

Peirce's general approach to logic

Peirce spent much of his life trying to publish a complete and
lengthy treatment on logic, and he gave numerous definitions of
its study. These definitions tend to shift and change depending on
just what else was driving his philosophical interest at a given time.
When he is developing his accounts of inquiry, we find reference to
doubt and belief in his definitions,[2] and when he is developing his
middle typology of signs or the ten-fold sign distinction around the
turn of the century, we find a strong semiotic element in his definitions.[3] This serves to emphasise just how crucial a role Peirce sees
logic playing within the broad scope of philosophy, but regardless,
there are some very straightforward definitions of logic in his work
that give a good simple sense of his view:

> Whatever opinion be entertained in regard to the scope of logic,
> it will be generally agreed that the heart of it lies in the classifi-
> cation and critic of arguments. (EP2. 200 (1903))

And further still:

> Logic in the narrower sense is that science which concerns itself
> primarily with distinguishing reasonings into good and bad, and
> with distinguishing probable reasonings into strong and weak
> reasonings. Secondarily, logic concerns itself with all that it must
> study in order to make those distinctions about reasoning, and
> with nothing else. (*Reasoning and the Logic of Things*, 143 (1898))

This all seems quite familiar to us. Many simple, modern logic text-books will introduce the topic in exactly this way. 'Logic is the theory of *good reasoning*. Studying logic not only helps you to reason well, but helps you *understand* how reasoning works' (Restall 2006, 1). When we gloss Peirce's interest in classifying reasoning and argument into good and bad in terms of validity, this is simply logic more or less as we understand it.

The scope of logic: broad vs narrow

Another important feature of Peirce's approach to logic that we must note is that we can divide his concerns between broader and nar-rower conceptions of the discipline. We mentioned in Chapter 1 that Peirce saw himself as a logician, but also that, for him, logic is a very broad discipline incorporating much of what we would now think of as epistemology, the philosophy of language and the phi-losophy of science. However, our interests in this chapter are with Peirce's work in the much narrower domain of deductive logic. Most important for us here, though, is understanding that these two construals of logic – broad and narrow – are well accounted for in Peirce's architectonic view of philosophy. Moreover, the way they are related to each other tells us something very interesting about his view of logic.

To begin with, we can very briefly touch upon how Peirce sees the relationship between broad logic and narrow logic in architectonic terms. As we noted in Chapter 1, the Peircian view of philosophy is that it is divided into three broad classes of study: phenomenology, normative science and metaphysics. Further, the normative sciences divide into ethics, aesthetics and logic. It is here that the discipline of logic is given its broadest construal in Peirce's philosophy; this is where we find his views on sign theory; his pragmatism; his theories of truth, inquiry and science; and so on. But as we also noted, logic, as a normative science, is also divisible into the three sub-disciplines of speculative rhetoric, critical logic and methodeutic. Speculative rhetoric is where we find much of the sign theory that we examined in Chapter 4, and methodeutic concerns itself with 'the methods that ought to be pursued in the investigation, in the exposition, and in the application of truth' (EP2. 260 (1903)). Critical logic, however, is concerned with the classification of arguments and the means by which we determine 'the validity and degree of force of each kind' (EP2. 260 (1903)). Again, critical logic can be divided into deductive, abductive and inductive arguments, and it is here, in this particular sub-division of the normative science of logic, that we find Peirce's narrow view of the discipline.

The upshot of this architectonic relationship between the broad and narrow construals of logic is that, for Peirce, all elements of the discipline are deeply interconnected and entangled. Semiotics, as a part of speculative rhetoric, provides many of the principles and materials for exploring deductive logic; this is why we find Peirce defining 'narrow' logic as 'the science of the necessary laws of Signs and especially Symbols' (CP2. 93 (1902)). As sub-fields of methodeutic, pragmatism, inquiry and the pursuit of truth all proceed because of what logic provides: 'logic may be defined as the science of the laws of the stable establishment of beliefs' (CP3. 429 (1896)). Indeed, as we shall see in the next chapter, even *cosmological metaphysics* can be seen as the proper scientific explanation of the *logical* structure of the universe for Peirce.

On the one hand, then, it is possible to dive down into Peirce's architectonic and finger just a small part of it that looks exactly like our contemporary view of logic – it is the *deductive* component of the *critical logic* portion of the *normative science* of logic. But to think we might profitably slice off the narrow logic of Peirce's work in this way is to miss something deeply instructive and crucial to understanding his philosophy. Narrow logic is crucial to much of his view both in relying on the disciplines that are super-ordinate to it and in informing and being enriched by its subordinate fields of study.

The normativity of logic

A further feature of Peirce's view of logic is that he takes it be a *normative*, or prescriptive, discipline.

> [At] the heart of [Logic] lies the classification and critic of argu-
> ments. [...] This classification is not a mere qualification of
> the argument. It essentially involves an *approval* of it – a *qualitative*
> *approval*. (EP2. 200 (1903))

On this view, logic is not simply a matter of describing or discovering the laws and rules of proper reasoning. Rather, logic also contains
a normative or prescriptive element that compels us to reason in this
way. Peirce is not alone in this view of logic as a normative discipline, of course. Frege held similar views: 'like ethics, logic can also
be called a normative science. How must I think in order to reach
the goal, truth?' (1979, 128). Similar views were held by Ramsey
and Wittgenstein.[4] Interestingly, though, Peirce's normative view
comes coupled with a strong 'descriptive' view of logic:

> If we wish to be able to test arguments, what we have to do, is to
> take all the arguments that we can find, scrutinize them and put
> those which are alike in a class by themselves and then examine
> all these different kinds and learn their properties. Now the clas-
> sificatory science of reasons so produced is the science of Logic.
> (W1. 359 (1866))

Logic, for Peirce, whilst deeply normative, is also a descriptive
discipline on par with such 'classificatory sciences' as physics or
chemistry. Again, Peirce is not alone in this. Frege treats the 'laws
of logic' as both descriptive and prescriptive too, but the source
of Peirce's view of the normativity of logic is again interesting and
shows the rich intertwining of his philosophical ideas.

We already know that within Peirce's broader architectonic view
of philosophy, logic, on both its broad and narrow construals, is a
normative science. But more interesting is that the prescriptive drive
of logic does not come from anything essential about logic on this
view. At its base level, logic is the scientific study and classification of
arguments. This is overwhelmingly descriptive. However, by using
those arguments and methods which are classified as 'good' within
the science of logic, we can help to secure the 'growth of concrete

reasonableness'. Recall that within the normative sciences, aesthetics is super-ordinate to ethics, which is in turn super-ordinate to logic. The ultimate aesthetic ideal, that which is unconditionally admirable, is to see the growth of reason or order in the universe. The discipline of ethics gives the study of what is unconditionally admirable in the way of action, and logic, in the way of reason or thought (as a species of action). An unconditionally admirable logical action, then, is whatever reasoning, thought or argument secures the growth of concrete reasonableness. Since we *should* strive for the growth of concrete reasonableness, and the proper study and classification of logical arguments shows us how to achieve that through reasoning, logic is something that we *should* use and follow. The science of logic looks *descriptive* – it is classificatory – but using this science and following its laws allows us meet a broader *prescriptive* requirement to contribute to attaining the ultimate aesthetic ideal.

Peirce's anti-psychologism

During the nineteenth century, the study of psychology held considerable influence and prestige. For many, the new science had enough explanatory power to mean that other disciplines might be reducible to it. This kind of psychologism was especially prevalent in mid-nineteenth-century logic and mathematics, where it was frequently suggested that logical and mathematical laws could be explained by the laws of psychology. J.S. Mill's psychologism about number was the target of Frege's famous anti-psychologism is his *Foundations of Arithmetic*, usually credited with being the decisive refutation of psychologism. Peirce was similarly anti-psychologistic, frequently turning his ire on the theories of German logician Christoph von Sigwart, but also seeing a tendency to be impressed by psychological reductionism across philosophy more broadly:

> Philosophers have always been very loose and inaccurate thinkers; [. . .] their minds have been so turned in the direction of

psychology that when they have once found how any given element of thought affects the human consciousness, they feel as if they had touched bedrock and got to the bottom of that element. [. . .]

It may be said that logic is the theory of reasoning and reasoning can only be performed by a mind. That is certainly true [. . .] [b]ut it does not follow that the phenomena psychologists discover have any bearing upon the theory of reasoning. (EP2. 385 (1906))

For Peirce, the study of psychology can never tell us anything of importance about the study of logic for the reasons familiar to us from most anti-psychologistic arguments. As Peirce puts it, 'Logic is the science of truth and falsity [. . .][;] the fact that a proposition is conscious or unconscious does not affect its truth or falsity' (EP2. 385 (1906)). But there is more to Peirce's anti-psychologism than this, and again, it stems from his architectonic view of philosophy. For Peirce, psychology is subordinate to philosophy; it takes the principles and methods of its super-ordinate disciplines and offers concrete realisations of them. To make psychology foundational for philosophy is to reverse the explanatory direction of the architectonic. As Peirce puts it, 'psychology is as special a science as physics is. [. . .] Now to found the science of the general upon the science of the special is absurd' (EP2. 385 (1906)).

Before moving on, there are a couple of things worth noting about this anti-psychologism. First, whilst Peirce is aware of the tendency towards reductionism in psychologism – even logic or maths are reduced to psychology – his own denial is not a reversal or alternative reductive thesis. Psychology is not meant to be reduced to logic or mathematics. His claim is simply that psychology must draw upon philosophy, including and especially logic, and whilst psychology can tell us interesting things about the processes of reasoning, it can tell us nothing about logic. Second, logic, for Peirce, is a general or formal science in a sense that we would currently take it to be. It is the study of logical forms in and of themselves; our grasp of those forms is irrelevant.[5]

Peirce's anti-logicism

The final feature of Peirce's general view of logic that we shall note is his anti-logicism. This is an interesting feature of his work in logic, especially given the context of the rise of modern mathematical logic. It is a notable feature of the work of the orthodox founding figures of modern logic – Frege, Russell and even Dedekind – that their work emerges from a growing concern with the foundations of mathematics. The response of Frege or Dedekind, for instance, was to place logic in a foundational role for mathematics, or, to be more precise about early logicist views, to see arithmetic as a part of logic.[6] For Peirce, this doesn't make sense of the relationship between the two disciplines:

> Logic can be of no avail to mathematics; but mathematics lays the foundation on which logic builds. (CP2. 197)

We might think that this comes simply from what we know about Peirce's architectonic view of philosophy and its relation to other disciplines. In the straightforward sense of sub- and super-ordinacy that governs the structure of Peirce's theory here, we know that mathematics is foundational for everything, so it must also be foundational for logic – the dependence claim of the logicist looks to be reversed in Peirce's account. True as this is, however, the priority of mathematics for logic is stronger for Peirce than even this broader structural relationship suggests:

> I hold that logic is guided by mathematics in a sense which is not true of any other science. Every science has its mathematical part, in which certain results of the special sciences are assumed as mathematical hypotheses. But it is not merely in this way that logic is mathematical. It is mathematical in that way, and to a far greater extent than any other science; but besides that it takes the proceedings of mathematics in all their generality and founds upon them logical principles. (EP2. 36 (1898))

In many ways, this is a difficult complication to grasp clearly, but it is crucial to understanding Peirce's anti-logicist position fully.

Besides the structural priority of mathematics over logic, the idea is that there is a sense in which the entire content of logic is also given by mathematics. In the normative sciences, for example, aesthetics is super-ordinate to ethics and so gives principles and laws which ethics realises, but the content of ethics is particular to it. Aesthetics gives us the quest for the unconditionally admirable, but ethics brings with it the study of unconditionally admirable *action* or *conduct*. The relationship between mathematics and logic, however, is not quite like this in Peirce's view. Mathematics gives logic, much like every discipline, a body of organising principles, but the task of logic is to construct logical principles from the body of necessary reasoning that constitutes mathematics. It is as though mathematics gives logic both its content and its guiding principles.

Clearly, then, Peirce is not a logicist in any conventional sense of that label. Before concluding, however, it is worth noting an interesting notion in Peirce's view of the relationship between logic and mathematics that adds something of a wrinkle. Even within the architectonic structure of philosophy and the sciences, the very tool we've used here to say something about his anti-logicism, Peirce sees change, growth and convergence occurring. Indeed, he expresses the view that 'logic seems destined to become more and more converted into mathematics' (EP2. 39 (1898)). For Peirce, mathematics lies at the heart of everything, including logic, but he doesn't see so large a gap between them, and indeed, in the process of convergence, logic may just be or become mathematics. To call Peirce an anti-logicist, then, is perhaps to downplay the strength of the deep connection he sees between mathematics and logic.

Summary of Peirce's view of logic

Peirce's view of logic in the most general terms looks quite familiar to us. He has a distinction between logic construed broadly and narrowly, and his narrower conception looks very like our own view of the scope of deductive logic. He sees logic as a normative science, a view not very different from Frege or Wittgenstein. He is staunchly anti-psychologist, a view that is almost beyond question in the

age of modern logic. And whilst he is anti-logicist in an important sense, he also sees a necessarily close relationship between the
study of logic and the study of mathematics. This makes his view of
logic sit comfortably alongside our own, familiar and easy to compare. However, there is another way in which all of this is framed
by some bigger and deeper differences. The broader conception
of logic means that deductive logic relies on signs and semiotics,
and metaphysics must draw on and realise the general principles
that logic of all kinds gives it. In some moods, it seems that Peirce
thinks that the content of metaphysics must eventually develop into
a logic and that logic must eventually develop into mathematics.
Similarly, the normativity of logic comes from the need for logic
to function properly within its architectonic setting and make its
own contributions to the aesthetic ideal and to the growth of concrete reasonableness. Moreover, the architectonic drives much of his
anti-psychologism and underpins his anti-logicism. So whilst many
of the central themes of Peirce's view of logic make it seem like a
familiar and friendly beast, beneath all that there are some dazzling
differences and a temperament we may not know nearly so well as
we think.

Peirce's algebraic logic

Peirce's best-known work in logic is concentrated in an earlier period
of his academic life when most of what he produced extended the
algebraic work of George Boole and William Stanley Jevons. It is
instructive, then, to have some sense of the tradition and body of
research that Peirce was most closely engaged with during this earlier period of work on logic.

The primary figure in this tradition is George Boole (1815–1864).
Boole was a notable British mathematician in his day; there is even a
stained glass window dedicated to his memory in Lincoln Cathedral
in the town of his birth. He was self-taught, respected, accomplished
and, for the last fifteen years of his life, a professor of mathematics at Queens College, Cork. His main contribution to the history
and development of logic was that he saw the possibility of treating

much of the familiar categorical logic of Aristotle in terms of classes and class membership. The upshot, as Boole saw it, was that logic could then be treated algebraically. To give a cursory example, take two well-known Aristotelian categorical statements, A and E:

A: All y are z (universal affirmative)

E: No y are z (universal negative)

For Boole, such statements (and any logical operations on them) may be translated into rather straightforward algebraic equations. Where 1 is simply the class of all things and 0 is the empty class, we find the following algebraic translations of A and E:[7]

A: $y(1 - z) = 0$

E: $yz = 0$

The Aristotelian form A is simply translated as 'the class of y and All-with-z-subtracted (i.e. not z), is empty'. Similarly, form E is trans- lated as 'the class of y and z is empty'. But these are simply instructive instances of how Boole read the algebraic translation of logical state- ments. His work in algebraic logic actually extends far beyond this, giving us a well-developed calculus for transforming his algebraic statements in line with syllogistic reasoning. Indeed, especially interesting is that we even find an algebraic reading of sentential connectives in his work. To give the simplest of examples, $y + z = 1$ (meaning y or z is true (but not both)), and $y \times z = 0$ (meaning y and z are false). This marks a genuinely important advance in logic, and Boole's idea that one might give a logical analysis of statement connectives with more or less the same mathematical machinery that one uses to express logical statements was novel.

All of this work was something of a (albeit under-appreciated) milestone in the development of mathematical logic, and it was this tradition and the problems within it that occupied Peirce's early work. Boole's work was, as stated, an algebra of logic or reason- ing, and it certainly raised enough questions for fruitful work by other logicians. For instance, how was this logical algebra connected to algebra conceived more generally? It is obvious that the two are different: $y \times y = y$ in the algebra of logic but not in more familiar algebras for numbers, for instance, so how are the two connected?[8] Peirce's interest, however, focused on a different set of problems, mostly concerning how one should extend this kind of algebraic treatment of sentential connectives and how one might add some complexity to the treatment of classes that one finds in Boole's logic. These concerns led to some fruitful developments not just for Peirce, but for logic, mathematics and philosophy as a whole. In coming to grips with these problems, Peirce developed a truth-functional treatment of propositional logic which gives us the basis of his various truth-table definitions of logical connectives, and he also developed a Boolean algebra for relatives which leads to his account of quantification. We shall look at these two broad developments in turn.

Peirce's truth-functional treatment of propositional logic

In an interesting paper, 'Description of a notation for the logic of relatives, resulting from an amplification of the conceptions of Boole's calculus of logic', written in 1870 and published in the *Memoirs of the American Academy of Arts and Sciences* in 1873, Peirce introduces two interesting forms of notational development for Boolean logic. The first is the use of a logical summation function with indices attached to it, Σ_p. As Dipert (2004, 290) notes, this is the first clear use of quantifier-like variable binding, and this proto-quantifier proves to be important in developing the later more conventional quantifier system which we shall examine in a moment. The second and more immediately interesting development for us is Peirce's use of a new notation for class inclusion, $\prec$. A statement such as 'S $\prec$ P' would simply mean that 'S is included in P' or 'all members of S are members of P'.

Peirce is initially concerned with making the notation of Boole's algebra easier and more in line with logical notions, but two things are important here. First, Peirce's aim in this 1870/1873 paper is (in part) to show that logical algebra could 'be extended over the whole realm of formal logic, instead of being restricted to that simplest and least useful part, the logic of absolute terms' (Peirce 1870/1873, 44). His notation for class inclusion here allows him to move away from simple Aristotelian categorical logic and syllogisms and look towards a clear analysis of propositions and propositional logic. Second, his development of this symbol over the next fifteen years or so allows him to treat propositions and connectives in truth-functional terms and develop what we now think of as truth tables.

Within ten years of introducing his 'claw' symbol for class inclusion, $\prec$, Peirce begins to make explicit connections between it and truth-functional analyses of logic. In both his 1879 paper 'On the algebraic principles of formal logic' (W4. 21–73 (1879)) and his 1880 paper 'On the algebra of logic', we find Peirce talking of '$\prec$' in terms of truth, but, even more interesting, we find him placing it at the centre of a propositional analysis of logic. Indeed, he is unequivocal in his claim that a propositional analysis of $\prec$ is strong enough to capture anything we might want to know about *subject/predicate* statements or the inference from conclusion to premise. As he notes:

> In consequence of the identification in question, in S $\prec$ P, I speak of S indifferently as subject, antecedent, or premise, and of P as predicate, consequent, or conclusion. (Peirce 1880, 22 fn *)

This in an intriguing claim on Peirce's part, since it shows clearly his concern to place an analysis of conditional statements at the core of logic and an eschewing of the term-focused, syllogistic logic that had previously predominated. Peirce has by this point come to see the analysis of propositional structure in terms of truth as key to his aim of broadening the scope of algebraic logic.

Over the next five years, Peirce develops these ideas in various ways, and in a series of drafts and notes leading up his 1885 paper, 'On the algebra of logic: a contribution to the philosophy of notation', we see some of the most interesting developments of his work in algebraic logic. First of all, his most explicit analysis of $\prec$ in truth-functional terms can be found with his description of propositions in terms of truth values (CP3. 366 (1885)) and his description of '$x \prec y$' as being identical to the Boolean claim that $(x = \text{false})(y = \text{true}) = 0$ (i.e. $x \prec y$

is false whenever x is false and y true). This is simply a truth-functional definition of the material conditional; whenever the antecedent is false and the consequent true, the whole proposition is false.

The second interesting thing to note about this body of work is that as Peirce expands upon the basic claims about a truth-functional treatment of ≺, he sets out what appears to be the earliest known work on the truth-table proof methods which are now an integral part of the propositional calculus in logic. For instance, in the same 1885 paper, 'On the algebra of logic: a contribution to the philosophy of notation', we find a verbal description of a now common truth-table technique called *the method of assigning variables*. In order to show that an argument form is valid or that a statement is a tautology, one simply assigns 'falsity' to the conclusion or, in the case of a tautology, to the main connective. One then attempts to assign truth values to the remaining connectives and variables in a way that retains consistency. If this can be done, if there is a way in which values can be assigned consistently to the remaining variables, then the argument is not valid or the statement is not a tautology. Peirce's description of the proof of what is now known as 'Peirce's law' uses exactly this method:

> A fifth icon is required for the principle of excluded middle and other propositions connected with it. One of the simplest formulae of this kind is
>
> $\{(x \prec y) \prec x\} \prec x.$
>
> This is hardly axiomatical. That it is true appears as follows. It can only be false by the final consequent x being false whilst its antecedent $(x \prec y) \prec x$ is true. If this is true, either its consequent, x, is true, when the whole formula would be true, or its antecedent $x \prec y$ is false. But in the last case the antecedent of $x \prec y$, that is x, must be true. (CP3. 384 (1885))

There are many instances of Peirce beginning to produce what we would clearly recognise as truth tables or truth-table matrices,[9] including a 1902 manuscript which gives simple, and now recognisable, instructions for constructing tables for propositions with increasing numbers of variables, along with what looks like a truth-table example for the bi-conditional (CP4. 260–262 (1902)).[10] Most striking, however, is a three-page manuscript from 1909[11] in which Peirce gives clear truth-table definitions for a triadic logic with six binary sentential connectives and four monadic sentential connectives.

Peirce's work on triadic logic is remarkable and interesting for a few reasons. First, it presents an account of three-valued logics at least eleven years earlier than they had ordinarily been thought to originate:

> Lukasiewicz was also the first to define by means of a matrix a system of sentential calculus different from the usual one, namely his three-valued system. This he did in the year 1920. Many valued systems, defined by matrices, were also known to [Emil] Post. (Tarski 1956, 40 n 2)

Second, its three values, V (*verum* or true), F (*falsum* or false), and L (limit), show the usual connectedness with Peirce's broader philosophy, and the L value in particular suggests connections to his work in semiotics and inquiry. Thirdly, and most important here, we see a compellingly clear use of truth tables and truth-functionality in constructing and defining the extension of two-valued to three-valued logic.

Peirce's development of quantification

As we have just noted in looking at Peirce's development of a truth-functional treatment of propositional logic, his 1870 paper 'Description of a notation for the logic of relatives' introduced an interesting piece of notation for logical summation, Σ_p, where sigma represents a logical sum of variables which might take the place of the index, p. This looks to us very like contemporary notions of quantifiers with variables bound to them. Indeed, he also introduced a related notation for logical multiplication, Π'. Whilst there is a marked similarity to our current notions of existential and universal quantifiers, and this development to Boolean algebra was part of Peirce's progress towards a full and published account of quantification in 1885, it is still not quantification as we know it. Rather, these symbols are meant as mere notational shorthand for logical addition and summation in the various developments Peirce was making to Boolean algebra. All the same, they do mark a step on a series of developments that started for Peirce in 1867 and led to his accounts of quantification in 1883 and 1885.

The first step comes from Peirce's early additions and developments to Boole's logical algebra. Amongst the problems facing Boole's algebra, as far as Peirce was concerned, was that its means of expressing particular propositions was inadequate. Peirce thought his developments overcame this and related problems:

> The advantages obtained by the introduction of them are three, viz., they give unity to the system; they greatly abbreviate the labor of working with it; and they enable us to express *particular* propositions. This last point requires illustration. Let i be a class only determined to be such that only some one individual of the class a comes under it. Then a -, i, a is the expression for some a. Boole cannot properly express some a. (CP3. 18 (1867))

Obviously, this is the beginning of an attempt to give adequate expression to what we now think of in terms of existential quantification.

By the time of the 1870/1873 paper noted above, Peirce had begun to experiment with the notational variants mentioned and with indexing logical sums and products. Indeed, in that paper we see Peirce describing Π' in terms of logical multiplication and Σ' in terms of logical addition (CP3. 97 fn 1 (1870)). As we noted above, a Boolean reading of '×' and '+' as logical connectives gives us a form of logical conjunction and disjunction: '$y \times z$' simply means 'y and z'; $y + z$ simply means 'y or z'. Peirce's apparent intention in 1870, then, is to take Π' to mean something like '$y \times y' \times y'' \times y''' \times \ldots$' and Σ' to mean something like '$y + y' + y'' + y''' + \ldots$'

(CP3. 97 (1870)). This looks like one rather familiar account of the universal quantifier as a complex conjunction over all the objects in the domain and the existential quantifier as a complex disjunction over all the objects in the domain. Although this is not a theory or account of quantification, Peirce is clearly beginning to develop a logical notation and a set of apparatus that show many of the features of quantifiers.

Peirce returned to these problems and notations in various papers over the next ten years, but most notable are two papers from the early 1880s: first, his 1883 'Logic of relatives', published as an appendix to the Peirce-edited collection *Studies in Logic by Members of the Johns Hopkins University*, and second, his 1885 'On the algebra of logic: a contribution to the philosophy of notation' in the *American Journal of Mathematics*. In these papers we find Peirce's full account of quantification.

In *Studies in Logic* (1883), Peirce is concerned primarily with explaining the logic of relative terms and in attempting to explain how we might combine the relative terms, for example, '. . . is a lover of . . .' (l) and '. . . is a benefactor of . . .' (b). He introduces the following definitions of the combined relations 'i is a lover of a benefactor of j' (l b), and 'i is a lover of everything but benefactors' (l†b):

> The two combinations are defined by the equations
>
> $$(l\ b)[i\ j] = \Sigma[x](l)[i\ x](b)[x\ j]$$
>
> $$(l\dagger b)[i\ j] = \Pi[x]\ \{(l)[i\ x] + (b)[x\ j]\}$$
>
> The sign of addition in the last formula has the same signification as in the equation defining non-relative multiplication. (CP3. 333 (1883))

These can be rendered into a form which would be relatively familiar in contemporary quantifier logic – $(\exists x)(Lix\ \&\ Bxj)$ and $(\forall x)(Lix \oplus Bxj)$[12] – but what is clear is that Peirce sees these quantifier statements as a useful notational device for the expression of complex relative statements rather than as objects of study in their own right. Indeed, later in the paper he gives the quite familiar logical statements

Σ[i]Σ[j]l[i j] and Π[i]Σ[j]l[i j] as translations of the multiply quan-
tified statements 'somebody loves somebody' and 'everybody loves
somebody', but he makes it clear this system of referring to relations
is primarily there to help when the expressions of his relative logic
become complex.

Two years later, in the 1885 paper 'On the algebra of logic',
however, we find Peirce aiming to 'to develop an algebra adequate to the treatment of all problems of deductive logic' (CP3. 364
(1885)). There, Peirce offers what in many ways looks like a relatively systematic account of his Boolean logic, suggesting a syntax
and postulates (CP3. 385 (1885)). But more importantly for our
concern here, he gives a direct statement of intent with regard to
quantifiers and quantifier statements. Peirce dedicates a section of
his paper – §3 'First-intentional logic of relatives' (CP3. 392–397
(1885)) – to the discussion of 'some' and 'all' in Boolean logic, and
in it gives an account of quantification largely familiar to a modern
audience. He notes, for instance, the distinction between individual
variables and quantifiers and their dual role in quantifier statements
(CP3. 393 (1885)). He nominates the use of Σ for 'some' and Π for
'all', and he continues his identification of them in terms of logical
sum and logical product (CP3. 393 (1885)). He also shows how to
translate from ordinary language into quantifier statements (CP3.
394–395 (1885)) to give some rudimentary statements on what
looks like second-order logic, or the use of quantification over predicates and relative terms rather than just indices.[13]

The development of a theory of quantification in Peirce's early
algebraic logic, then, follows an interesting journey. He begins
in the 1860s with a concern for the lack of expressive power of
Boolean algebra – 'Boole cannot express some a' (CP3. 18 (1867)) –
and ends some eighteen years later with a well-developed and
nuanced account of quantification. As we've just seen, he developed the notation for and suggested a conceptual connection
between Σ and complex disjunction and between Π and complex
conjunction as early as 1870, and by the mid-1880s we have what
is seen by many as one of the great turning points in modern logic,
quantifier logic.

We have already mentioned that the significance of Peirce's discovery is not always given due credit. Modern logic is more or less born with quantification, and whilst there is recognition that Peirce had developed, independently, an account of quantification by no later than 1885, Frege's system of quantification given in his 1879 *Begriffsschrift* (Frege 1979) is credited with being the first and most important statement. Frege is, quite rightly, seen as a central figure in the founding of modern mathematical logic, but even setting aside the interesting uses of quantifiers in Peirce's work from 1870/1873, Peirce clearly has an equal claim to importance, primarily due to the immediate influence of his account. Peirce's treatment of quantifiers was taken up in 1891 by Ernst Schröder in the second volume of his *Lectures in the Algebra of Logic* (Schröder 1891), and he even retained Peirce's notation. Similarly, Giuseppe Peano, who had developed a system of quantification of his own in 1888, developed and used the Peirce-Schröder notation. Even Russell made use of Peirce-Schröder-Peano-style notation in his earlier work. Peirce's notation and views on quantifiers can even be found in C.I. Lewis' (1918) *Survey of Symbolic Logic*, where Σ and Π are used and defined in terms of logical sum and logical product, just as Peirce had done (Lewis 1918, 234–235). Frege's account, on the other hand, was not taken up with the same readiness, and only after the later championing of Frege's work by Russell was his seminal status established.

Such issues of priority, importance and recognition can become fraught at times, and this is especially true in the question of how to place Peirce's account of quantification in the history of logic. Setting those issues aside, though, we can see how interesting and fecund Peirce's research in algebraic logic proved to be, not only for him, but for modern logic more generally. The development of quantification was a truly remarkable achievement.

Peirce's graphical logic

The contributions to algebraic logic that we have just been examining were amongst Peirce's most significant achievements. However, this work was concentrated into the first fifty years of his life, and even though he continued to work 'algebraically' in the later part of his life, as we saw in his 1909 treatment of three-valued logics, his later work was essentially diagrammatic or graphical. This graphical logic, developed primarily from the mid-1890s onwards, represented a significant break from the standard modes of logical work, and even Peirce was aware that the more orthodox approach was algebraic:

> Algebraic reasoning involves intuition just as much as, though more insidiously than, does geometrical reasoning; and for the investigation of logic it is questionable whether the method of graphs is not superior. [. . .] In the opinion of some exact logicians, they lead more directly to the ultimate analysis of logical problems than any algebra yet devised. [. . .]

> It is logical algebra, however, which has chiefly been pursued. (CP3. 619–620 (1902))

In what follows, we shall look at just how Peirce came to develop such complex systems of graphical logic in the last twenty years of his life. We will then briefly introduce his three main systems of existential graphs, the alpha, beta and gamma systems.

The origins of Peirce's existential graphs

Given that the diagrammatic approach, both for Peirce and in contemporary logic, is in a sense a heterodox move, it is worth asking just why he shifted from a body of well-received and groundbreaking algebraic logic to developing what he came to call *existential graphs*. We shall look at some of the more direct influences on his development of diagrammatic logics in a moment, but it is worth pausing to make two observations about Peirce's personal views here. The first is that he often described himself as thinking not in language but in pictures,[14] and in a very important sense he took diagrammatic logic to be the best expression of our logical reasoning. Indeed, he very commonly described his existential graphs as 'moving pictures of thought, [. . .] thought in its essence free from physiological and other accidents' (CP4. 8 (1905)).

The second point is that the assumed stark contrast between algebraic and diagrammatic logics is, perhaps, something of a Whiggish imposition of ours. Peirce certainly did not see them as being fundamentally different parts of deductive logic.[15] Indeed, there is even good evidence of his talking of algebraic logic in terms of diagrams and 'movement of thought' as early as 1885:

> [The syllogistic formula 'All M is P, S is M, therefore S is P'] is really *a diagram* of the relations of S, M, and P. [. . .] As for algebra, the very idea of the art is that it presents formulae which *can be manipulated*, and that by observing the effects of such manipulation we find properties not to be otherwise discerned. [. . .] These are patterns which we have the right to imitate in our procedure, and are the icons par excellence of algebra. (EP1. 227–228 (1885), *italics added*)

It's not obvious that, except in matters of efficacy, Peirce took there to be such a huge difference in the motivations of the two approaches.

The influence of J.J. Sylvester and A.B. Kempe

Aside from some of his more personal opinions and characteristics, we can also see Peirce's shift towards diagrammatic logics as influenced by his contact with the work of the mathematicians James Joseph Sylvester and Alfred Bray Kempe. Sylvester, who was both a visitor at the Peirce's home when Charles was still a child and a colleague of Peirce's at Johns Hopkins University in the 1880s, published a paper in *Nature* exploring the connections between chemistry and algebra (Sylvester 1878). In this paper, Sylvester drew an analogy between the use of diagrams to represent chemical bonds and valency and their potential use in algebra. Sylvester is also credited with introducing the notion of a 'graph' into what became known in mathematics as graph theory. Peirce, as both a chemist and a colleague of Sylvester, knew about this work.

More influential, though, was work by Alfred Bray Kempe. Kempe had worked with Sylvester in the 1870s, although not on graph theory, but in 1886 he published a paper in the *Philosophical Transactions of the Royal Society of London* (Kempe 1886) exploring the use of graphs in visualising mathematical problems and as a tool for understanding the nature of mathematical knowledge. Peirce was deeply impressed with Kempe's paper and saw it as having the 'intrinsic value [. . .] of taking us out of the logician's rut, and showing us how the mathematician conceives of logical objects' (CP5. 505 (1905)). For Peirce, the graphical representation of mathematical problems was inspiring, and Peirce was quickly looking at ways to improve Kempe's ideas and combine them with his own on logic.[16]

The increased sense of semiotic

In addition to the role that developments in mathematical graph theory played in Peirce's move to diagrammatic logic, it is also worth noting the importance of his increased attention to semiotics. We saw in Chapter 4 that Peirce increasingly saw semiotics as central to his philosophy as a whole. Further, we have noted in this chapter that the architectonic relationship between the broad and narrow construal of logic is mediated by signs and semiotic, and this becomes especially apparent in Peirce's later diagrammatic logic. As we have mentioned, Peirce thought of diagrams as 'pictures of moving thought', and we can indeed see two influential semiotic elements in his thinking here. First, he saw diagrams in terms of icons and even indices:

> A diagram is a representamen which is predominantly an icon of relations and is aided to be so by conventions. Indices are also more or less used. (CP4. 418 (1903))

And second, he saw the dynamic element of graphical logic in terms of semiosis:

> There must be operations of transformation. In that way alone can the symbol be shown determining its interpretant. (CP4. 374 (1901))

The process from entitative to existential graphs

These influences – Peirce's personal views of thought and logic, the influence of developing mathematical work in graph theory making use of chemical diagrams, and the growing importance he placed on semiotics and its role in logic – combined to see Peirce develop what to many looks like a whole new approach to logic. Although we shall concentrate below on Peirce's system of existential graphs, developed from 1896 onwards, it is worth noting that in 1897 Peirce published an early attempt at diagrammatic logic in *The Monist* (Peirce 1897) outlining a system he later called 'entitative graphs'. We shall not explore the details here, but in that paper we see Peirce drawing direct analogies between chemical bonds and valencies, and relative propositions. Remarkably, he wrote a letter to the editor of *The Monist*, Paul Carus, before this 1897 paper was even published suggesting he had a better, much improved system. Carus declined to publish the second system, but this system was something that Peirce developed for the remainder of his life, giving us an alpha portion, which corresponds roughly to modern propositional logic; a beta portion, which corresponds roughly to modern predicate logic; and a gamma portion, which offers examples of second-order and modal logic. We shall now look at this work in more detail.

The alpha graphs

Peirce's existential graphs are all connected, so the gamma portion builds upon the beta, and the beta portion builds upon the alpha. We cannot really devote proper space to exploring them here, but we can give a programmatic outline at least, and we shall begin by looking at the alpha graphs, which deal with propositions. However, we will first look at Peirce's logical machinery and rules for actually constructing logical diagrams before moving on to how these diagrams can be transformed to represent the process of logical reasoning. In short, we are interested in two questions concerning logical graphs: how do we 'build' them, and how do they 'move'?

The sheet of assertion

The first element of Peirce's existential graphs that we must examine is what he calls *the sheet of assertion*. In constructing logical expressions diagrammatically, we need a surface to express that diagram upon. This surface is the sheet of assertion and for our purposes will be simply the page where we write our propositions. The sheet of assertion, however, functions as a graphical representation of the universe of discourse; it is the domain of objects that our logic models. The sheet of assertion with nothing on it is a graph; a sheet of assertion with a proposition on it is a graph which represents one of the objects in the universe of discourse.

Scribing

The next feature we need in order to understand how Peirce's alpha graphs are built is what is called *scribing*. This is a rather simple follow-on from the sheet of assertion and is merely the process of writing propositions on the sheet of assertion. However, whatever we write, or scribe, upon the sheet of assertion is something we assert, and something we assert to be true in the universe of discourse represented by the sheet of assertion. For me to scribe 'P' on a sheet is simply to assert that P is true in the domain given by that sheet. These assertions are themselves called *graphs*, but we shall try to bypass this in what follows.

Juxtaposition

We are not limited in the number of propositions we can scribe on a sheet of assertion – we can scribe whatever we want. However, unlike the kinds of propositional calculus we are used to, there are no symbols for logical operations such as conjunction or disjunction. Instead, to scribe two propositions on the sheet of assertion – to juxtapose them – is simply to assert that both exist. This is essentially conjunction. The following sheet of assertion simply says that both P and Q are true in this domain, or rather 'P & Q':

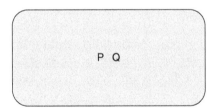

Cutting

The last element we will look at for building alpha graphs is cutting. Just as we can assert that a proposition is true in the domain given by the sheet of assertion by scribing it on that sheet, we can also assert that some proposition is false in the domain given by the sheet of assertion by placing it within a cut on that sheet. To cut a proposition is simply to enclose it. For instance,

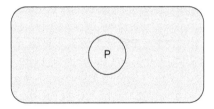

is simply to assert that P is false in the domain given by the sheet of assertion, or rather, ~P. Cuts can be nested, that is, we can place a cut around another cut:

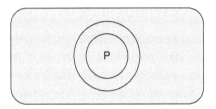

It is important to take note of how many cuts or enclosures sur-
round a given assertion when we nest such cuts, since in terms of
transformation rules for the alpha graphs, whether an assertion is
evenly or *oddly* enclosed is important. We need to know if there are an
odd or even number of cuts around a graph or assertion.

One final point to note about cutting is that, treated as negation
and combined with juxtaposition as conjunction, the alpha graphs

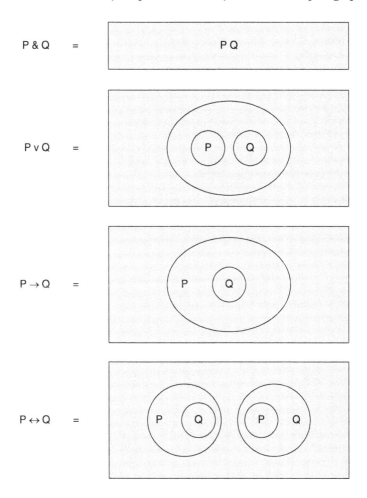

have the same expressive power as ordinary propositional logic through De Morgan equivalences.

Transformation in alpha graphs

We have seen, albeit in a very cursory way, how to build alpha graphs, but of course, since these are meant to give us moving pictures of thought, it is important that we also understand how these images 'move'. Peirce gives us various rules for transformations, or as he calls them, 'Codes of Permission' (CP4. 415 (1903)), but these are usually reduced to the following five rules for transforming any graphs on a sheet of assertion:

> Rule 1: The rule of erasure – Any evenly enclosed assertion[17] may be erased from the sheet of assertion.

> Rule 2: The rule of insertion – In any oddly enclosed area of a graph, any assertion may be scribed.

> Rule 3: The rule of iteration – If an assertion occurs on the sheet of assertion, in a cut, or in a nest of cuts, it may be scribed on any other area which is contained within the area in which the assertion is made.

> Rule 4: The rule of deiteration – If any assertion could be the result of iteration, it may be erased from the sheet of assertion.

> Rule 5: The rule of the double cut – A double cut may be removed from an assertion on any area of the sheet of assertion, or inserted around any assertion on any area of the sheet of assertion.

To show these rules of transformation in action, it is worth looking at an example. In what follows we shall see a transformation from a graph which represents an initial state of 'P or Q' and 'not P' to a graph which represents a final state of 'Q'. This will effectively give one possible alpha graph that shows the reasoning of the disjunctive syllogism.

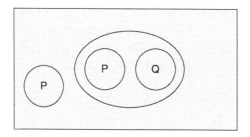

Figure 5.1

Here we have a sheet of assertion with the simple assertions ~P and P v Q scribed upon it. How, using the rules of transformation, can we turn these graphs into Q? Here's one way.

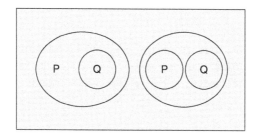

Figure 5.2

Rule 2 – the rule of insertion – allows us to scribe any assertion we like into an oddly enclosed area. Since the assertion expressed by placing a single cut around P gives us an oddly enclosed area, we scribed the assertion 'not Q' (i.e. a Q enclosed with a cut) inside that area.

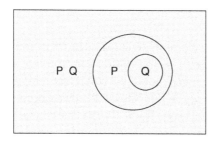

Figure 5.3

Rule 5 – the rule of the double cut – allows us to remove (or insert) double cuts from the sheet of assertion. Here, one part of the sheet of assertion contained a doubly enclosed P and doubly enclosed Q, so we removed those double cuts.

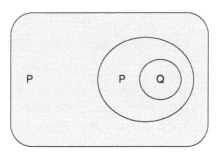

Figure 5.4

Rule 1 – the rule of erasure – allows us to remove any evenly enclosed assertion from the sheet of assertion. The assertion Q has zero cuts, so it is evenly enclosed and can be erased.

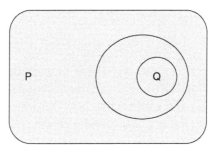

Figure 5.5

Rule 4 – the rule of deiteration – allows us to remove any assertion that could be the result of iteration from the sheet of assertion. In this case, the singly enclosed P could be the result of applying the rule of iteration to the unenclosed P, so we can remove it.

As we've already seen, Rule 1 – the rule of erasure – allows us to remove any evenly enclosed assertion from the sheet of assertion. The assertion P has zero cuts and so is evenly enclosed and can be

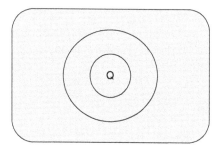

Figure 5.6

erased, leaving only the doubly enclosed Q on the sheet of assertion. This leaves us with the final step of applying Rule 5 – the rule of the double cut – to that doubly enclosed Q to arrive at:

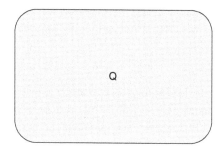

Figure 5.7

Thus, by applying the rules of transformation we can transform the graph on a sheet of assertion from our starting point in Figure 5.1 to our end point in Figure 5.7, thereby modelling the disjunctive syllogism.[18]

Although there is much more that we might say about the alpha graphs, we have seen enough to give at least some sense of how Peirce sees these existential graphs. One thing is worth emphasising since it is hard to capture in the example we have just given. Peirce sees these graph transformations as a dynamic, processive thing – the graph is literally changed. Construed in the manner just shown, it is too easy to think we are looking at something similar to a style of natural deduction where we see which propositions can be derived by which rules. However, as we have stated before, these graphs are iconic representations of the dynamic process of logical reasoning, and the transformations on graphs should be viewed in that light.

The beta graphs

Moving on to beta graphs, we find Peirce building upon the system given in the alpha graphs by introducing icons and graphical conventions for representing individuals and relations. What Peirce produces with this extension of existential graphs covers many areas that are familiar to us from quantifier logic with identity, and whilst drawing such parallels is useful, we have to be careful since Peirce's interests in developing the beta graphs vary from the interests of modern logicians. Again, we shall examine the materials for building beta graphs before examining which transformations are permissible within them.

Spots and lines

The primary materials added to the alpha graphs when building beta graphs are what we shall call 'spots' and 'lines', although strictly speaking there is little difference between them. A *spot*, as one may expect, is simply a heavy dot such as this, •, and when scribed on a sheet of assertion, it asserts that there is an individual in existence in the universe of discourse represented by the sheet of assertion.

In Peirce's beta graphs, a spot can be spread out, so to speak, to form a *line*. A line, scribed on a sheet of assertion thusly, –, would make the same assertion as •; namely, that there is an individual in existence in the universe of discourse. So why have spots *and* lines?

The reason is simply that we want to assert more than that an individual or individuals exist; we often want to say things about those individuals, and the line of the beta graph allows us to do this. For example, we are able to scribe monadic predicates at one end, or 'hook', of a line, so that

———— is thirsty

asserts that 'something is thirsty'. Through juxtaposition, from the alpha graphs we can also scribe such things as

in order to assert that 'something is hungry and something is thirsty'. However, we can also use the 'hooks' of a single line to scribe an identity relation such as

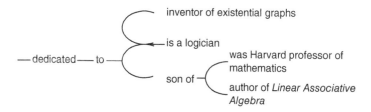

This simply asserts that 'something (the same thing) is hungry and thirsty'.

Lines can also branch in complex ways in order to predicate multiple properties of the same thing or to capture relations of multiple adicity, such as dyadic or triadic relations. For example:

This, scribed on a sheet of assertion would assert that there exists someone who dedicated something to someone who invented existential graphs, is a logician, and was the son of someone who was both a Harvard professor of mathematics and the author of *Linear Associative Algebra*.

As we can see, there are lines which represent monadic predicates: '— is a logician'; dyadic predicates: '— is the son of —'; and even triadic predicates: '—dedicates — to —'. And there are also assertions of identity: something (the same thing) *is* the Harvard professor of mathematics *and* the author of *Linear Associative Algebra*.

Cuts

The final thing to note is that just as we can 'cut' an assertion in alpha graphs, we can do the same with beta graphs. So to enclose our earlier assertion 'something is thirsty', like this:

is to assert 'nothing is thirsty'. However, we can also impose a cut upon an assertion that, so to speak, 'dissects' a line, like this:

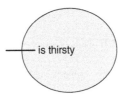

If we were to scribe this on the sheet of assertion, we would have asserted that 'there is something which is not thirsty'. We must be careful here, though, since we can also find juxtaposed assertions on a sheet which look very similar:

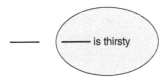

However, this graph asserts both that 'there is something' and 'nothing is thirsty'. The difference between the two, as we can see, is that in the first case the line makes contact with the negative or enclosed assertion. This tells us the line is making an assertion of identity. In the later case, the line makes no contact and so is an 'independent' assertion on the sheet.

The relationship to quantifiers

Before we move on and introduce the rules for transforming graphs in the beta portion by looking at an example, it is worth pausing to note something about the relationship between what we have just seen and quantifiers. Peirce's main concern in the beta graphs is to give us an iconic diagrammatic logic for relations. However, a corresponding treatment of the quantifiers falls out of this quite naturally. Clearly, the notion of existential quantification, ∃, is given in the simplest and most basic terms. To scribe a spot or line on the sheet of assertion is to make an existential claim. This makes for three interesting features of quantification in Peirce's beta graphs: existential quantifiers are 'basic', there are no variables or binding, and by extension there are no free variables and so no free logic. The last point is simple – since one cannot scribe an assertion upon the sheet of assertion without being committed to that thing existing in the domain of discourse, one cannot make any assertions free from existential import. The second feature is one of 'notation': there need be no variables to designate individuals with additional symbols to quantify over them, since a scribed or graphic presence on the sheet of assertion is enough to do both jobs. And the first feature is the simple observation that from the assertion of existence by scribing a spot or line, one could then form equivalent beta-graph versions of all the major quantifier expressions. For example, if we were insistent upon giving quantifier equivalences in beta graphs, we give the transformations seen in Figure 5.8.

Transformation in beta graphs

The rules for transformation in beta graphs are essentially the same as those in the alpha portion, except that they are updated to accommodate the elements introduced for building graphs in beta.

—— F	=	(∃x)(Fx)	=	~(∀x)(~Fx)
(— F)	=	~(∃x)(Fx)	=	(∀x)(~Fx)
—— F	=	(∃x)(~Fx)	=	~(∀x)(Fx)
—— F	=	~(∃x)(~Fx)	=	(∀x)(Fx)

Figure 5.8

Rule 1: *The rule of erasure* – Any evenly enclosed assertion and any evenly enclosed portion of a line may be erased from the sheet of assertion.

Rule 2: *The rule of insertion* – In any oddly enclosed area of a graph, any assertion may be scribed and two lines oddly enclosed in the same area may be joined.

Rule 3: *The rule of iteration* – If an assertion occurs on the sheet of assertion in a cut or in a nest of cuts, it may be scribed on any other area which is contained within the area in which the assertion is made. Further, (i) an additional branching line may be added to a line, provided it crosses no cuts; (ii) a line which 'terminates' at a cut may be extended into the cut; and (iii) any line extended into a cut, as by clause (ii), can be joined to any corresponding iterated assertion in that area.[19]

Rule 4: *The rule of deiteration* – If any assertion could be the result of iteration, it may be erased from the sheet of assertion. Further, (i) any 'loose' line of identity which could have been iterated under Rule 3 clause (i) can be retracted or removed from its 'original' line; and (ii) any 'loose' line which could have been iterated under Rule 3 clause (ii) can be retracted and removed back to the outside of the cut it extends across.[20]

Rule 5: *The rule of the double cut* – A double cut may be removed from an assertion on any area of the sheet of assertion or inserted around any assertion on any area of the sheet of assertion regardless of whether the cuts cross lines.

Again, the best way to see how these rules work is through some simple examples. First, let's look at an argument which in quantifier logic is a simple instance of *modus ponens* – $(\forall x)(Fx \rightarrow Gx)$, $(\exists x)(Fx)$ ⊢ $(\exists x)(Gx)$:

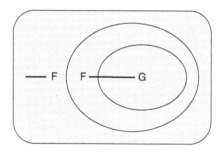

Here, our sheet of assertion simply gives the premises – $(\forall x)(Fx \rightarrow Gx)$, $(\exists x)(Fx)$ –which we are intending to transform into $(\exists x)(Gx)$. Our first transformation:

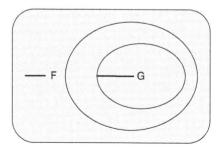

is had through Rule 4 – the rule of deiteration – which allows us to remove – F from the inner area of the sheet since it could be the result of iteration of the instance of – F from the outer part of the sheet. Next we have:

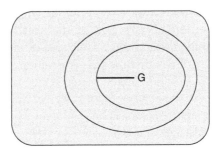

Here Rule 1 – the rule of erasure – allows us to remove any evenly enclosed assertion or line. The remaining instance of – F was unenclosed, that is, it had zero enclosures and so was removed. Finally we can make the following transformation:

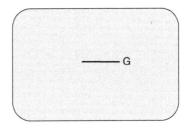

by using Rule 5 – the rule of the double cut. This leaves us with the assertion we were aiming for.

A more complex example using the Aristotelian syllogism Barbara – all M are P, all P are S, therefore all M are S – shows more of the rules in action as they apply to lines in the beta graphs. As should be familiar, we begin with our premises scribed on the sheet of assertion and aim to transform them into our conclusion. First we have:

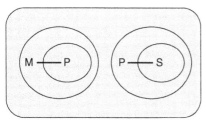

Our starting point

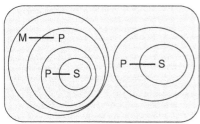

By Rule 3 – the rule of iteration

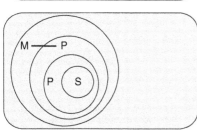

By Rule 1 – the rule of erasure

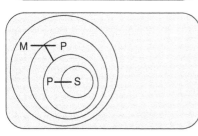

By Rule 3 – the rule of iteration, clause (i) – we have extended a line from the line connecting M and P but have crossed no cuts

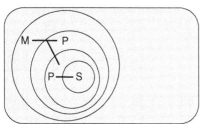

By Rule 3 – the rule of iteration, clause (ii) – we have extended a line introduced in the previous step into the cut at which it terminated

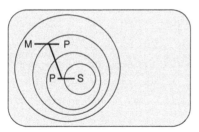

By Rule 2 – the rule of insertion – any two lines oddly enclosed may be joined

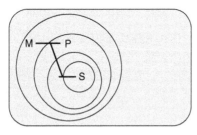

By Rule 4 – deiteration – the second more-enclosed P here could have been the result of iteration from the first less-enclosed P and so can be erased from the sheet

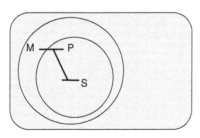

By Rule 5 – the rule of the double cut – we can remove the two inner cuts

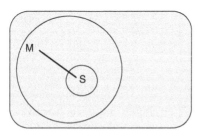

By Rule 1 – the rule of erasure – being surrounded by two cuts, P was evenly enclosed, and so we could remove it from the sheet

Again, there is much more that we could say about beta graphs, and the way they are presented here omits many details and nuances of Peirce's view. Nonetheless, it should at least be possible to see how Peirce sees this portion of his existential graphs working.

The gamma graphs

Our treatment of both the alpha and beta graphs has really only skimmed the surface of those portions. The final portion, the gamma graphs, will receive an even less satisfactory treatment, in part because there is much more to these graphs than could possibly be covered here. More importantly, though, the gamma graphs extend far beyond the alpha and beta portions and Peirce never managed to give a complete statement of them, returning and changing the system multiple times from his earliest statements in 1903 to more complex and nuanced views in the years immediately before his death in 1914. What we find is that Peirce believes he can use a system of graphs to explain the process of abstraction. Transforming assertions such as 'the grapes are sour' to 'the grapes have sourness' allows us to abstract the property of *sourness* from the original assertion and talk of sourness as though it were a thing or entity in and of itself. He is also interested in using a system of graphs to talk about the nature of the alpha and beta graphs themselves. This leads Peirce to make a range of developments to his notions of spots and lines and cuts. However, perhaps the clearest use to which Peirce puts his gamma graphs is in giving an explanation of modality, and it is his account of a graphical treatment for the logic of possibility and necessity that we shall briefly review here.

Multiple sheets of assertion

The first move that Peirce makes in giving an account of possibility and necessity in terms of graphical logic is to develop his notion of the sheet of assertion. Instead of thinking of our domain of discourse as ranging over the single sheet of assertion we use to scribe graphs on, we should instead think of our logical assertions as ranging over a collection of sheets of assertion which are tied to each other, so to speak, at different points (CP4. 512 (1903)). The very top sheet of assertion gives us the domain of discourse for our actual, or rather *an* actual, world. As Peirce puts it:

For our alpha sheet, as a whole, represents simply a universe of existent individuals, and the different parts of the sheet represent facts or true assertions made concerning that universe. (CP4. 512 (1903))

To use modern terminology, we can obviously think of these different sheets of assertion as representing different universes of discourse, or different *possible worlds*. These different possible worlds, or different sheets of assertion, are connected to each other at various points, but not every sheet will be connected to other sheets. Peirce describes the 'interaction' between these different sheets in terms of cuts or points of connection thusly:

At the cuts we pass into other areas, areas of conceived propositions which are not realized. In these areas there may be cuts where we pass into worlds which, in the imaginary worlds of the outer cuts, are themselves represented to be imaginary and false, but which may, for all that, be true, and therefore continuous with the sheet of assertion itself. (CP4. 512 (1903))

Peirce is not entirely certain about all of this, but the picture of different sheets of assertion, connected at different points either through assertions which run through all the sheets or through 'cuts' which allow us to pass into worlds, is quite evocative. An imaginary world, which at some outer point may be 'true' and continuous with the sheet of assertion itself, is enigmatically tentative but certainly hints at a kind of modal realism.

The broken cut

The next important development that Peirce makes is a means of scribing upon the sheets in these 'books'. What Peirce does is maintain the alpha and beta elements and introduce a new kind of cut which he calls the 'broken cut'. By enclosing an assertion upon the sheet with a cut composed of a broken or dotted line, thusly,

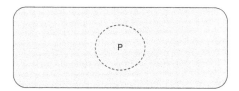

we are asserting that it is possible that P is not true. That is, the graph we have just drawn says ◊~P.

It is also possible to combine this new kind of assertion with the previous assertions of alpha and beta to build gamma graphs. So, for example, one may place alpha and beta cuts around broken cuts and vice versa. Interestingly, this allows us to make various assertions of possibility and necessity:

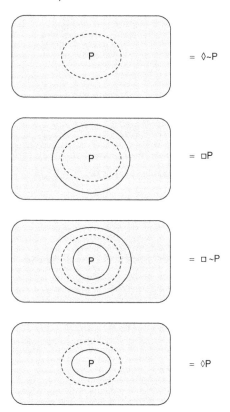

And we can, of course, even iterate the modal operators in the gamma graphs by more complicated nesting. For instance:

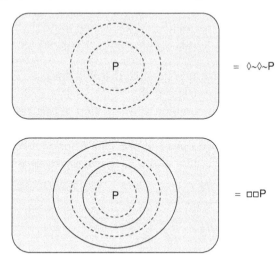

$= \Diamond{\sim}\Diamond{\sim}P$

$= \Box\Box P$

And so on.

The rules of transformation in gamma

Although there are other elements we might include here, the use of multiple sheets of assertion and broken cuts is enough to give us a sense of how Peirce takes gamma graphs to represent possibility and necessity. The next task is to say a little about how Peirce sees the transformation of gamma graphs taking place. The first thing to note is that he is cautious about which of the rules of transformation from the alpha and beta portions could be used on broken cuts in the gamma graphs. For instance, we find in 1903 (CP4. 516) a gamma version of the rule of insertion which can be given like this:

> Rule 6: *The rule of insertion for broken cuts* – In a broken cut already on the sheet of assertion, any assertion may be scribed.

But there are no rules relating to iteration, deiteration or double cuts[21] for the broken cuts. Interestingly, Peirce scholars such as

J.J. Zeman (1964) and Ahti-Veikko Pietarinen (2006a) have noted that by allowing more or less of the rules of iteration, deiteration and double cuts to apply to the gamma graphs, we can chart the various modal systems familiar to contemporary logicians. The only rules that seem to relate directly to the broken cuts themselves are the following two:

Rule 7: *The rule of cut conversion to broken* – Any evenly enclosed unbroken cut may be transformed into a broken cut.

Rule 8: *The rule of cut conversion to unbroken* – Any oddly enclosed broken cut may be transformed into an unbroken cut.

To see how these rules are supposed to govern the 'movement' of graphs concerning possibility and necessity, we can use some very simple examples which we would expect to hold for a modal system. For example, we would expect to find that P, therefore ◊P, holds. And it does:

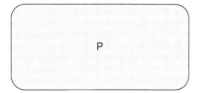
Premise, or starting point

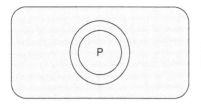
Rule 5 – the rule of the double cut (from alpha or beta)

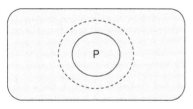
Rule 7 – the rule of cut conversion to broken – the outermost cut on the graph from stage two of the transformation has zero cuts around it and so is evenly enclosed, allowing us to transform that outermost cut to broken cut

Similarly, we would expect to be able to transform □P into P in the gamma graphs. And again, we can:

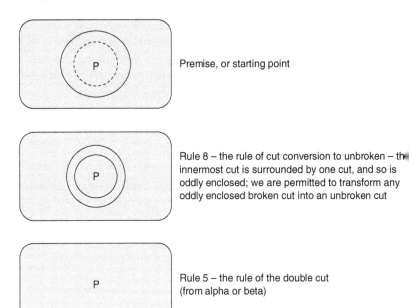

Premise, or starting point

Rule 8 – the rule of cut conversion to unbroken – the innermost cut is surrounded by one cut, and so is oddly enclosed; we are permitted to transform any oddly enclosed broken cut into an unbroken cut

Rule 5 – the rule of the double cut (from alpha or beta)

These are very simple examples, of course, and we have left out lots of details, some of which are rather important. All the same, we have at least a partial sense of what we might do with Peirce's gamma portion of his graphs. However, before moving on, it is worth mentioning a development that Peirce experimented with leading up to his 1906 paper for *The Monist*, 'Prolegomena to an apology for pragmaticism'.

Tinctures

By 1906, just three years after the account of gamma graphs outlined above, Peirce had developed the idea that by using different 'tinctures' on the sheets of assertion we could mark the difference between modalities. Peirce thought that the modalities could be divided into three classes – the actual, the possible and the destined – and he eventually settled on twelve different tinctures for graphs (four of each class). It is not important for us to spend time examining the divisions of the tinctures, how Peirce thought they could be used to build graphs, what the transformation rules would be and so on, but what is especially interesting is that as an extension of the modal logic we find in the gamma graphs outlined above, it shows that, for Peirce, the domain of gamma graphs included many of the wide applications of modal logic that we use today. For instance, one mode of tinctures applies to alethic modal logic, another looks as though it covers what we would think of as epistemic modal logics, others exist for erotetic modal logics, or deontic modal logics, and more besides.

In comparison to the alpha and beta graphs, the gamma portion of Peirce's diagrammatic logic is less clear and less complete, but it is a rich and promising area of investigation. All we have done here is gesture at it, but anyone wishing to indulge in a closer examination will find all kinds of suggestive and surprising things.

The response to the existential graphs

We have already noted that, although Peirce saw his graphical logic as a continuation of his algebraic logic, many others saw it as a rather drastic break with the manner and method of 'ordinary' logic. Before we conclude this chapter, then, it is worth pausing to make one or two observations about how Peirce's graphical logic has been received.

First of all, there are obvious detractors. Quine's response to the existential graphs, for instance, was decidedly cold:

> One questions the efficacy of Peirce's diagrams, however, in their analytical capacity as well. Their basic machinery is too complex to allow one much satisfaction in analyzing propositional structure into terms of that machinery. While it is not inconceivable that advances in the diagrammatic method might open possibilities of analysis superior to those afforded by the algebraic method, yet an examination of Peirce's product tends rather, apagogically as it were, to confirm one's faith in the algebraic approach. (Quine 1935, 552)

Problematically, this was an early and influential review of Peirce's diagrammatic logic by one of the premier logicians of his age. It would be putting matters too strongly to say that the views of people such as Quine more or less blocked philosophers paying serious attention to Peirce's graphs during the first half of the twentieth century, but they certainly didn't help. Worse, much of the most fecund thinking about logic of that early period took place without paying attention to approaches such as Peirce's, and we are now constrained with a way of thinking about logical languages and logical calculi that makes the insights of the existential graphs even harder to see.

However, since serious work on Peirce's existential graphs began to emerge in the 1960s and 1970s with book-length treatments by Don Roberts (1973) and J.J. Zeman (1964), increasingly sophisticated and important work has continued to emerge.[22] With regard to the gamma graphs especially, there is lots of exciting research taking place, and as the dynamic and at times dialogical nature of the diagrammatic logic becomes clearer, the potential of this approach is increasingly realised.[23]

Summary

One of the most important areas of Peirce's philosophical output is in logic, and his work in the area is divided between two approaches – an earlier algebraic account and a later diagrammatic account.

- Peirce viewed logic in very broad terms, treating logic at its broadest as including many topics in language, epistemology and the philosophy of mind. Construed narrowly, he viewed logic in terms very similar to those we use to describe contemporary formal deductive logic.
- The most distinctive themes in Peirce's approach to logic are that it is normative – logic has a clear prescriptive element; it is anti-psychologistic – the study of mind and the psychology of reasoning can tell us nothing about logic; and it is anti-logicist – logic does not play a foundational role in mathematics, but mathematics is super-ordinate to logic.

- Peirce's work in algebraic logic is well known and very influential in the history of logic. His early work involved developing the logical work of George Boole and giving an account of the logic of relatives. Peirce developed this work in interesting ways, offering some of the first accounts of truth-functional propositional logic with truth tables and quantification.

- From the 1890s onwards, Peirce began to develop an account of logical diagrams called existential graphs. He described these as 'pictures of moving thought', and they were presented as a form of iconic logic using 'graphs' rather than simple algebraic symbol systems. He developed three portions of his existential graphs called alpha, beta and gamma, which correspond roughly to propositional logic, predicate logic and modal logic, respectively.

- Although the existential graphs were not widely taken up, Peirce's work in algebraic logic, especially his notation for quantification, directly influenced modern practice through the work of Schröder and Peano.

Further reading

As was emphasised, Peirce is recognised as an important founding figure in the growth of mathematical and formal logic, and he is still arguably under-appreciated. The best short and accessible accounts of Peirce's place and worth are to be found in Hilary Putnam's paper 'Peirce the logician' (1982) and Jaako Hintikka's 'The place of C.S. Peirce in the history of logical theory' (1997). Both papers provide good accounts of Peirce's importance to the development of modern logic, with Hintikka claiming Peirce as a crucial figure in the development of model-theoretic approaches to logic. Both focus primarily on his algebraic work.

In terms of simple and accessible accounts of Peirce's logic itself, Randall Dipert's excellent 'Peirce's deductive logic: its development, influence, and philosophical significance' (2004) gives a clear overview and summary of the key phases and interests in Peirce's philosophical work on logic. It also makes the developmental pressures on Peirce's logic clear, and it does this without getting bogged down in unnecessary symbolism or detail. This makes it an especially useful introduction.

Good introductions to Peirce's later logical work on existential graphs are to be found in Donald Roberts' *The Existential Graphs of Charles S. Peirce* (1973) and J.J. Zeman's *The Graphical Logic of C.S. Peirce* (1964). These two texts are good introductions, but they are not so simple that they do not need any logical background at all. They are also the seminal works in the secondary literature in the area. Even if the logic makes these texts daunting to the beginner, they are still worth consulting for their interesting speculations on the development of the existential graphs. Zeman in particular notes what he sees as the influence of Peirce's metaphysics on the development of the diagrammatic logic.

Two more-recent works on the existential graphs are also worth taking note of: Sun-Joo Shin's monograph *The Iconic Logic of Peirce's graphs* (2002) offers a reinterpretation of the alpha and beta portions of the existential graphs, and Ahti-Veikko Pietarinen's paper 'Peirce's contributions to possible-worlds semantics' (2006a) offers an exposition of the gamma portion, focusing on its relevance for discussions of modality and possible-worlds semantics.

Notes

1 To give the quote more fully:

> One can sum up these simple facts (which anyone can quickly verify) as follows: Frege certainly discovered the quantifier first [. . .]. But Leif Erikson probably discovered America 'first' [. . .]. If the effective discoverer, from a European point of view, is Christopher Columbus, that is because he discovered it so that it stayed discovered [. . .]. Frege did 'discover' the quantifier in the sense of having the rightful claim to priority; but Peirce and his students discovered it in the effective sense. The fact is that until Russell appreciated what he had done, Frege was relatively obscure, and it was Peirce who seems to have been known to the entire world's logical community. How many of the people who think that 'Frege invented logic' are aware of these facts?

2 See W2. 15 (1867) or CP3. 429 (1896), for example.

3 See NEM4. 235–263 (1904), for instance, or CP2. 93 (1902).

4 See Wittgenstein (1953, 38): 'F.P. Ramsey once emphasised in conversation with me that logic was a "normative science". I do not know exactly what he had in mind, but it was doubtless closely related to what only dawned on me later.'

5 See W1. 165–166 (1865), for example.

6 See Frege (1968) or Dedekind (1909).

7 In fact, Boole developed different notation across his four main logic texts. The example here is representative of what is found in Boole (1847/1951).

8 Boole (1854) suggests that, strictly speaking, the algebra of logic is just the same as the logic of 0 and 1. Indeed, as Dipert (2004, 294) notes, this makes Boole's work one of the earliest abstract algebras.

9 For example, in an 1893 manuscript, MS 946, we find a truth-table definition for the material conditional.

10 Peirce does not, in fact, state which connective his truth-table example is derived from, but it yields truth whenever its values agree in truth value and is false otherwise.

11 The three pages are found in MS 339, but they are reproduced in Max Fisch and Atwell Turquette's seminal paper, 'Peirce's triadic logic' (1966).

12 Peirce's note that addition in the last formula is non-relative multiplication suggests we should think of (l†b) in terms of the exclusive 'or' – i.e. everything is either loved by i or a benefactor of j, but not both.

13 This was first noted in Martin (1965).

14 See, for example, his 1909 paper 'Studies in meaning. The import of thought: an essay in two chapters' (MS 619).

15 See, for example, CP4. 372 (1901).

16 See Peirce's 1889 manuscript 'Notes on Kempe's paper on mathematical forms' (MS 714 (1889)), for instance.

17 Properly speaking, the assertion is a graph, but to keep matters simple we shall try to keep terms as familiar as possible in giving the rules.

18 This way of transforming the graph from [P v Q,~P] to [Q] is actually more complicated than need be. Three steps – deiteration, double cut and erasure – would have been enough, but this way shows more of the rules in action and in its last four figures shows the reasoning of modus ponens.

19 Peirce adds a fourth clause which allows us to 'close' any multiple lines crossing a cut as in clause (ii) and extending to the same graph. To keep matters simple, though, we'll omit this here.

20 Again, there is an additional clause relating to the fourth clause of Rule 3, but we shall omit that too.

21 There are places in Peirce's accompanying syllabus for his 1903 Lowell lectures where he seems to explicitly rule out applying iteration and deiteration rules in gamma graphs, but this is to a degree ambiguous since we don't know if he means only to rule out their use with broken cuts, or something stronger.

22 For instance, Shin (2002) gives us an alternative reading of Peirce's alpha and beta graphs. Burch (1997) gives us an account of Peirce's beta graphs in terms of Tarski-style semantics. Also, see Burch (1994) or Pietarinen (2011) for treatments of the graphs in game-theoretic terms.
23 A useful account of the kind of questions and challenges raised by Peirce's existential graphs is given in Pietarinen (2010).

Six
Metaphysics

Introduction

The final area of Peirce's philosophy that we will examine is his work on metaphysics. In many ways, Peirce's views on metaphysics are the least explored and least well-integrated area of his work, and even once we manage to get clear about what his ideas are there is still the difficult problem of understanding them in terms of the broader structure of his philosophy. What's more, understanding any relation between Peirce's views on metaphysics and either traditional or contemporary work in the area is a difficult task. Much of Peirce's work in metaphysics doesn't look like traditional metaphysics, nor do its concerns resonate closely with newer approaches developed in the late twentieth-century revival of the sub-discipline. There are overlaps, of course, but on the whole, the first impression of Peirce's metaphysics is that it is a rather strange affair.

Part of the problem with understanding Peirce's work in metaphysics is that we find his interests clustering into three broad areas which don't obviously overlap, either with each other, with traditional metaphysics, or with the rest of his philosophy. Further, we find two distinct attitudes to metaphysics emerging in his work, one negative and eliminativist, the other more positive and speculative.

With regard to the three areas of his work in metaphysics, at various points Peirce does attend to questions which are familiar to traditional metaphysicians, and he gives his views on such questions as the nature of time, the relationship between wholes and parts, essences, and many topics in religious metaphysics. This work is much more familiar to us as traditional metaphysics, but it is sparse and represents a very small portion of his output in the area. Instead, Peirce pays greater attention to two other areas, areas which will be the focus of this chapter. First, he worked throughout his career on various attempts to construct a system of *universal categories*, much in the manner of Aristotle or Kant. Second, in a series of articles in the 1890s he developed an interesting, but at first pass eccentric, account of *evolutionary cosmology*.

Peirce scholars have paid a great deal of attention to the account of the categories, and its place in Peirce's philosophy is well understood. Indeed, some Peirce scholars think Peirce's work on the categories is explanatorily crucial to other key areas of his work, such as his realism or his semiotics.[1] All the same, despite work on the categories representing a fairly traditional metaphysical enterprise, the way in which Peirce explains it can still seem alien when we first encounter it, as we shall see. Peirce's evolutionary cosmology, however, is even more alien and looks less familiar as a metaphysical enterprise. At the time he was producing it, in fact, his contemporaries worried for his sanity. His former student Christine Ladd-Franklin is said to have taken this work as evidence that he was losing his mind.[2]

All of these things – limited attention to familiar areas of metaphysics, difficult and unfamiliar accounts of the universal categories, an unusual evolutionary cosmology – are made all the more complicated by Peirce's espoused views on the value and importance of metaphysics. On the one hand, we find him making apparently critical comments about metaphysics, which he describes as being in a 'deplorably backward condition' (CP6. 2 (1898)) or as a 'puny, rickety, and scrofulous science' (EP2. 375 (1906)). On the other hand, we find him suggesting that all scientific views are underpinned by metaphysics, which must be subject to proper study and scrutiny (CP1. 129 (1906)). And, of course, we find him engaging in metaphysics and placing it within his architectonic. So how is this apparent schism to be explained?

A useful distinction made by Peirce in various places is that between two general approaches to philosophy, which he labels 'laboratory philosophy' and 'seminary philosophy' (CP1.129 (1906)). These two approaches are distinguished from each other by their practitioners and by the attitude of those practitioners to the methods common in science. In the first case, laboratory philosophy, we find scientifically inclined philosophers who think of philosophy as on a par with science and think of the discipline as having much to gain by using the experimental and observational methods common to science. In the case of seminary philosophy, we find 'theologians' (CP6. 3 (1898)) who are inclined to set philosophy and science apart from each other, treating philosophy as in some way better furnished with access to fundamental truths (CP1. 128 (1906)). This is a very cursory account of the distinction, but what follows from it is that these two approaches lead to two very different views of the role, value and nature of metaphysics.

One approach to metaphysics, the approach which comes from 'seminary' thinking, is what Peirce has in mind when he describes the discipline as 'puny' and 'scrofulous' and claims that its practitioners 'carry not the hearts of true men of science' (EP2. 375 (1906)). Indeed, he sees its lamentable state as being due precisely to its practitioners and their approach to the questions of metaphysics:

> In my opinion the chief cause of its backward condition is that its leading professors have been theologians. [. . .] The unfitness [. . .] would consist in those persons having no idea of any broader interests than the personal interests of some person or collection of persons. (CP6. 3 (1898))

For Peirce, this is metaphysics pursued in the manner of *a priori* inquiry, which he condemned as a poor method of investigation in his 1878 paper 'The fixation of belief'. On such a view, metaphysics is a difficult and abstract discipline which Peirce describes as being reduced to interminable scholastic disputes that render the discipline 'a mere amusement for idle minds, a sort of chess, – idle pleasure its purpose, and reading out of a book its method' (EP2. 339 (1905)). This is the kind of metaphysics that Peirce rejects. Indeed, in his later accounts of pragmatism, he states that he sees the *raison d'être* of his pragmatic maxim as being to 'show that almost every proposition of ontological metaphysics is either meaningless gibberish [...] or else is downright absurd' (EP2. 338 (1905)).

It is quite clear, then, that Peirce is opposed to this 'seminary' approach, but we have to guard against taking his rejection of 'ontological metaphysics' to be a rejection of metaphysics *tout court*. The idea that the pragmatic maxim is designed to dispense with metaphysical confusion leads to the often stated claim that Peirce is opposed to metaphysics entirely, in much the same manner as certain stripes of verificationism.[3] Indeed, we noted this connection in Chapter 2. However, Peirce sees the laboratory approach to philosophy as yielding an alternative approach to metaphysics which is acceptable and respectable in a way that seminary or ontological metaphysics is not and which the pragmatic maxim is designed to accommodate.

Metaphysics approached from a laboratory perspective takes the scientific mode of inquiry as the primary means of investigation in the field. Whilst Peirce was writing for a series of 1898 lectures called *Reasoning and the Logic of Things*, he produced a series of reflections on just what metaphysics conceived and pursued in a scientifically respectable manner would mean.[4] In that work he suggests that any abstractness to be found in the study of metaphysics makes it a straightforward discipline to develop, and that despite our inclination to think that its objects of study are unobservable entities, it should instead be thought of as an observational science:

> [M]etaphysics [...] really rests on observations, whether consciously or not; and the only reason that this is not universally recognized is that it rests upon kinds of phenomena with which every man's experience is so saturated that he usually pays no particular attention to them. (CP6. 2 (1898))

The proper way to engage in metaphysics, then, is by adopting a scientific attitude towards its study, acting in direct pursuit of the truth, and treating it as an observational science. Peirce suggests a laboratory approach to metaphysics should proceed as follows:

[I]t is worth trying whether by proceeding modestly, recognizing in metaphysics an observational science, and applying to it the universal methods of such science, without caring one straw what kind of conclusions we reach or what their tendencies may be, but just honestly applying induction and hypothesis, we cannot gain some ground for hoping that the disputes and obscurities of the subject may at last disappear. (CP6. 5 (1898))

Whilst Peirce thinks that metaphysics has not traditionally been conducted in this way, this scientific approach to the discipline is how he thinks it can be made into a respectable and fruitful object of study. Moreover, metaphysics pursued in the manner of science is exactly how Peirce sees his own work in this area. Put like this, then, we can see why Peirce makes negative and positive statements about metaphysics and why he seems to both reject and embrace it. He is negative towards and rejects *ontological metaphysics,* born of a seminary attitude to philosophy, but he is positive towards and embraces as a central part of his architectonic a *scientific metaphysics,*[5] born of a laboratory attitude to philosophy.

Brief overview

How Peirce thinks a scientifically respectable metaphysics should look is really what is of interest to us in this chapter. It is helpful to keep the distinction between ontological and scientific metaphysics in Peirce's work as clearly in mind as possible, precisely because it has a profound influence on the kind of metaphysical questions that he thinks we should engage in. For example, according to Peirce's view of scientific metaphysics, 'logic requires that the more abstract sciences should be developed earlier than the more concrete ones, for the more concrete sciences require as fundamental principles the results of the more abstract sciences' (CP6. 1 (1898)). Since, on the architectonic view, metaphysics is a more abstract discipline than the natural or social sciences, it is important that we have a well-developed and appropriately scientific body of metaphysical research in place. Indeed, Peirce claims explicitly that the 'immature condition of Metaphysics has very greatly hampered the progress of one of the two great branches of special science' (CP6. 2 (1898)). What this means is that treating metaphysics in an appropriately scientific manner requires that we adopt the methods of science in our metaphysical investigations, and that the questions we pursue play an appropriate role in supporting the proper pursuit of the more concrete sciences.

In terms of the topics of scientific metaphysics pursued in this chapter, we will see that Peirce is interested in examining the fundamental nature of experience. This is in many ways an examination of the observations that underpin scientific metaphysics, which, as we saw, he claims 'rests upon kinds of phenomena with which every man's experience is so saturated that he usually pays no particular attention to them' (CP6. 2 (1898)). This is a rather curt summary of the drive behind Peirce's various attempts to give an account of the universal categories of experience, but as we shall see, a very large portion of his scientific metaphysics is devoted to just that.

A further important topic in Peirce's scientific metaphysics – indeed, the area of his work which is most closely associated with the term 'scientific metaphysics' – is the explanation of a series of clearly observable facts about the universe, particularly the existence of laws and regularities (CP6. 613 (1893)). These observable facts about the universe are exactly the kind of thing which underpin more concrete sciences, sciences which would benefit from a scientifically conducted metaphysical analysis of such phenomena. For instance, Peirce suggests:

> To find out much more about molecules and atoms we must search out a natural history of laws of nature which may fulfill that function which the presumption in favor of simple laws fulfilled in the early days of dynamics, by showing us what kind of laws we have to expect[.] (CP6. 12 (1891))

And again, this kind of metaphysical study leads Peirce to develop his accounts of evolutionary cosmology. We shall spend a considerable portion of this chapter expanding on Peirce's views about evolutionary cosmology as a topic of scientific metaphysics, but it is enough here to note that, given Peirce's ideas about the appropriate means of conducting metaphysical inquiry, along with his architectonically informed view about the place and role of metaphysics within the broader structure of knowledge, his motivation for engaging in such work is clear.

Before we move on and begin to introduce Peirce's work on universal categories and evolutionary cosmology in more detail, it is worth pausing briefly to note that Peirce's metaphysics has often proved to be something of an 'interpretational' stumbling block. The general tone so far perhaps suggests that, once we have a clear sense of Peirce's distinction between ontological and scientific metaphysics to hand, the task of explaining his metaphysical work falls easily into place; it is simply a matter of revealing the detail and reminding ourselves regularly of the task Peirce has set for himself. Things are not so simple as this, though, and Peirce's metaphysics has traditionally been the source of deep disagreement. We shan't linger over the different interpretational positions, but needless to say, some find the work on metaphysics to be at the core of Peirce's wider philosophy and deeply resonant with such areas as his semiotic,[6] whilst others think it discordant with his more obvious scientific and naturalistic tendencies[7] in ways which make it difficult to accommodate. The view here is that we can make sense of much of his work in metaphysics in terms of his pragmatism, his logic, his architectonic and his semiotic, and it seems quite clear that Peirce thinks of his metaphysical work as entirely integral to his broader body of philosophy. All the same, we needn't think it is an entirely successful enterprise as it stands, and in the case of the evolutionary cosmology, we shall return briefly to this question of interpretation again at the close of the chapter since the problem of how we should judge this particular topic of scientific metaphysics against Peirce's broader body of work is (still) an important and contentious topic in Peirce scholarship.

In what follows, then, we shall begin by looking at Peirce's account of universal categories. As we shall see, the project of developing an account of the categories was something which concerned

Peirce throughout his life, and he made various attempts at a theory. We shall detail Peirce's three main attempts before examining the importance of the categories to the rest of his work. We shall then move on to examine Peirce's theory of evolutionary cosmology. We shall begin by looking at the origins of Peirce's views on cosmology from work in the 1880s before moving on to give an account of its motivation and the three main concepts at its core: tychism, synechism and agapism. Finally, we shall return to the problem just mentioned: what are we to make of the evolutionary cosmology in light of Peirce's broader body of work?

The categories

The first area of Peirce's metaphysics that we shall examine is arguably one of the most important features of his entire philosophy – his study of the universal categories. As we work our way through his various attempts at identifying and explaining what he takes the universal categories to be, it will quickly become apparent just how much of Peirce's thinking here emerges in other areas of his work. One of the most notable things about Peirce's thinking on the categories is that there are three of them present in all experience, and the tendency to treat things in threes is a common occurrence in Peirce's philosophy.[8] In the architectonic structure of the discipline, for instance, we find three branches of philosophy, three branches of normative science, three branches of logic, three areas of methodeutic, three areas of metaphysics and so on. Indeed, Paul Weiss, who edited the first six volumes of the *Collected Papers of Charles S. Peirce*, described the categories as being the very essence of Peirce's philosophy (Weiss 1940, 262). However, despite the importance to and presence in his broader philosophy, Peirce's accounts of the universal categories cannot be included amongst his easiest or most immediately graspable work. In many ways, this is a result of their abstractness as a subject of study, but it is also because, more than in any other area of his philosophy, Peirce returned to adjust his arguments and explorations of the categories in light of other interests or developments. There are, for example, at least three clear attempts at giving an account of the categories.

Peirce's first attempts come from early in his life, and there is evidence that work on the universal categories is amongst the first philosophical work that he undertook. As a young man of seventeen in 1857, for instance, he was preoccupied with the study of Kant and Schiller, and he produced papers identifying three categories with the terms 'I', 'It' and 'Thou'. This early Kantianism manifested itself in some of his most important early published work, and a paper we have already mentioned in connection with Peirce's semiotic, 'On a new list of categories' (EP1. 1–10 (1867)), gives his first established view of the universal categories. However, within twenty years, his focus had shifted away from Kant and towards his own work on the logic of relatives. This led him to produce a different account of the categories which he explained in terms of his work in logic; he still saw them in Kantian terms, but his focus had shifted. Finally, at the turn of the century, when Peirce had his clearest sense of the archi-tectonic structure of his work, he explained the categories in terms of phenomenology, which he placed as the first branch of philosophy. With such a variety of attempts and motivations, it is little wonder that the categories can seem bewildering at times. Yet, as we shall see, there is a surprising consistency across the various explanations. Most important, though, is that we see Peirce returning to his account of the categories throughout the course of his life and using it at all stages in the development of his philosophy. Whether or not Weiss is correct that they give us the very essence of Peirce's system of philos-ophy, it is clear that they are a prominent feature in his thinking.

In what follows, we shall look at Peirce's project of explaining the universal categories in the most general terms, introducing the core ideas of his account. We shall then look at the three different attempts to derive or argue for the categories just mentioned: his early Kantian derivation, his middle logical explanation and his later phenomenological account.

Peirce's categories

At the start of this chapter, we noted that Peirce's work in meta-physics isn't easily connected to either traditional or contemporary concerns. His long-standing preoccupation with giving an account of universal categories, however, does represent Peirce's engagement in a project with a distinguished heritage ranging from Aristotle to Kant, Hegel and Husserl, and whilst Peirce's own approach is quite distinct, we can still make sense of his project in terms of more traditional approaches.

In the hands of Aristotle (1963), the project of giving an account of categories is an attempt to give a classification of all entities at their highest level of generality. Whilst we aren't interested in the details of Aristotle's account, it is interesting that what we see is a kind of ontological project of adumbrating and enumerating what there is; the task of giving categories is metaphysics in its most straightforward form for Aristotle.

An equally important but different approach to uncovering a system of universal categories is found in Kant (1781/1958). Kant's account of the categories is still an attempt to give us a system of adumbrating and classifying things, but his concern is focused more squarely on explaining how the world is divided according to our experience and conceptual apparatus than with classifying what things there are. For Kant, the point of categories is to explain the world as it is filtered through the lens of our cognitive apparatus, and the categories are derived or explained in terms of *a priori* or transcendental conditions for cognition; the task of giving categories for Kant is a conceptual or phenomenal project.

In terms of Aristotle and Kant's approach to the question of universal categories, we can see that Peirce's interests are similar. However, as one might expect with Peirce, he leans more towards the Kantian concern with experience than towards the Aristotelian concern with ontology.

> [T]he Doctrine of the Categories, whose business it is to unravel the tangled skein [of] all that in any sense appears and wind it into distinct forms; or in other words, to make the ultimate analysis of all experiences the first task to which philosophy has to apply itself. (CP1. 280 (1902))

The point of giving an account of universal categories for Peirce, then, is to take unanalysed experience and find within it a set of classes or categories into which all experiences fit. This makes Peirce's concern very much on a par with Kant's project of using the raw material of our experiences of the world and deriving from them a system which explains the objects of our experience in terms of the categories we impose upon them in our experience (CP1. 286 (1904)).

Although this gives a sense of how abstract accounts of categories can be, there is another feature of Peirce's account which can make the project of explaining it even harder. Peirce thinks that, given the nature of the raw materials used in deriving a system of categories, that is, our experiences, or rather 'the phenomena with which every man's experience is so saturated that he usually pays no particular attention to them' (CP6. 2 (1898)), his role in explaining the categories can never be more than to give us some sense or guidance. Instead, the account of the categories is something that can only be fully or properly grasped once we have pursued it for ourselves:

> [E]very reader can control the accuracy of what I am going to say about [the objects of experience]. Indeed, he must actually repeat my observations and experiments for himself, or else I shall more utterly fail to convey my meaning than if I were to discourse of effects of chromatic decoration to a man congenitally blind. (CP1. 287 (1904))

This is an interesting feature of Peirce's account of the categories, not least because it shows his commitment to laboratory philosophy: we are to engage in the experiment too. However, a side effect of this is that Peirce's categories are often explained in a rather obscure and gestural way, with particular examples expected to take the explanatory weight. For example, the following definition is a rather typical example of Peirce's manner of introducing his categories:

> *Firstness* is that which is such as it is positively and regardless of anything else.

Secondness is that which is as it is in a *second* something's being as it is, regardless of any third.

Thirdness is that whose being consists in its bringing about a secondness.

There is no fourthness that does not merely consist in Thirdness.

(EP2. 267 (1903))

This is hardly enlightening, but it gives us the bare outline of Peirce's categories. We shall expand upon this below by looking at examples and clearer explanations from across Peirce's work, but it should be clear that the obscurity of the project of identifying universal categories from our phenomenal experiences is made worse by Peirce's suggestion that he can lead us only with suggestion and example.

Even from the rather obscure summary we have just examined, we can see that Peirce thinks there are three universal categories – *firstness, secondness* and *thirdness* – and any other experience which does not seem to belong to these three categories can, in fact, be reduced to thirdness. So what exactly does Peirce think these three categories of experience are? Let's look at each in turn.

Firstness for Peirce is often identified in terms of feeling or mere appearance (CP8. 329 (1904)), and it is meant to capture those elements of experience that are in some sense disembodied or best described in qualitative terms. For instance, Peirce gives the following examples of firstness:

Imagine me to make and in a slumberous condition to have a vague, unobjectified, still less unsubjectified, sense of redness, or of salt taste, or of an ache, or of grief or joy, or of a prolonged musical note. (CP1. 303 (1894))

Our sense of redness disembodied from what object it is that is red is the kind of experience that Peirce would suggest we should think of as a first. And whilst trying to see qualities and feelings as instances of firstness actually gives us a reasonable sense of what we should be attempting when we repeat Peirce's observations and experiments, it is also instructive to see how Peirce identifies first-ness elsewhere in his philosophy.

Recall that when we examined Peirce's semiotic, we mentioned his famous three-fold distinction of signs into icons, indices and symbols. Icons rely upon a shared quality between sign and object, indices rely on a shared physical or causal connection between sign and object, and symbols rely on a conventional or law-like connection between sign and object. In terms of universal categories, we can see that in that three-fold distinction, icons are firsts. A red colour swatch as a sign of the coloured paint I intend to buy functions through a shared quality, namely, the redness they have in common.

The next category, secondness, is often described by Peirce in such terms as 'struggle', 'existence' or 'resistance' (CP1. 325 (Undated)) and is meant to capture those elements of experience which are, in a sense, more brute, physical and existential. For instance, Peirce gives the following examples of secondness:

> [There is a category] which the rough and tumble of life renders most familiarly prominent. We are continually bumping up against hard fact.[. . .]. You get this kind of consciousness in some approach to purity when you put your shoulder against a door and try to force it open. You have a sense of resistance and at the same time a sense of effort. There can be no resistance without effort; there can be no effort without resistance. (CP1. 324 (1903))

Our sense of the physicality of the world we experience, then, is what Peirce wants us to search for in our own observations of secondness. In his own example of forcing open a door with your shoulder, the brute physical reality of the door, its resistance to your shoulder, the interplay of cause and effect in your attempt to force the lock, are all instances of secondness. And if we continue with the illustrative use of the icon/index/symbol trichotomy, we can see that just as icons are firsts, indices are seconds. Where smoke is a sign of fire, it is because of the causal relationship between smoke and fire that the latter signifies the former. Similarly, we can see that the smoke gives us less of a sense of the simple qualities of the fire and focuses our attention quite clearly on its simple physical existence.

The final category in Peirce's account is thirdness. Thirdness is often described by Peirce in terms of our experiences of 'connection', 'mediation', 'relation' and 'law' (CP1. 337 (1875)). In many ways, the category of thirdness is meant to capture those elements of our experience which involve synthesis or connection, especially in terms of mind and cognition (CP1. 537 (1903)). For example, Peirce suggests that the following concepts are primarily a matter of thirdness:

> Some of the ideas of prominent Thirdness which, owing to their great importance in philosophy and in science, require attentive study are generality, infinity, continuity, diffusion, growth, and intelligence. (CP1. 340 (1895))

The category of thirdness is deeply important to much of Peirce's work, but it is a difficult concept to grasp in many ways, even in relation to the other categories. If we take the idea that thirdness is our experience of synthesis, connection or growth, we can see how a concept such as law gives us an instance of thirdness by noting how it takes disparate events (or instances of secondness) and draws them together and describes them as falling under or according with a general form of behaviour or habit. Again, this is vague, but we must remember that Peirce is devoutly anti-nominalist, and so, for him, laws and habits are real. Our experience of some tendency or habit found in real instances is an experience of a real law and is an experience that falls under the category of thirdness.

Just as we associated icons with firstness and indices with secondness, we can see that the symbol is the corollary of thirdness in Peirce's icon/index/symbol division of signs. The word 'fire' is a symbol of object fire not because of a shared quality or because of a causal or physical connection (as with smoke), but because we developed the convention and habit of applying this type of sign to instances of fire. The two things – 'fire' and fire – are brought together or connected in cognition or thought, as it were. Indeed, if we extend the application of the categories further into Peirce's semiotic, we can see that the sign structure itself gives us examples of the three categories.

Recall that a sign is made up of a sign-vehicle, an object and an interpretant. Sign-vehicles function in respect of qualities they share with the object, objects are the distinct things which signs signify, and interpretants draw those sign-vehicles and objects together under the process of representation. This is firstness as a quality in the sign-vehicle, secondness as existence or resistance in the object, and thirdness as connection and synthesis in the interpretant.

This, in outline, is Peirce's account of the universal categories. For Peirce, all experiences can be divided into these three categories, and if we engage in the same process of investigating our experiences of the world, we will find that we, too, find these three categories in all of our experiences. There is much more that we could mention about Peirce's account of the categories, but in what remains of our discussion we will examine the three main ways in which Peirce attempted to derive the categories. What we won't spend time doing is developing any in-depth criticism of the categories, and this is primarily because of the nature of the study. For Peirce, the account of the categories is not to be proved through logical deduction or *a priori* reasoning; rather, it is a matter of observing or reflecting upon our observations and engaging in Peirce's project for ourselves. The only real objections to Peirce's account of the categories come from our ability to derive or discern them in our experience. So how does Peirce suggest that we derive his system of universal categories?

The early accounts of the categories

As we noted, Peirce was first drawn to the project of giving an account of universal categories by his early studies of Kant. What's more, just as we can see that the conceptual or phenomenological leanings of his categorical project are especially Kantian, his earliest attempts to derive categories follow a distinctly Kantian method. As Peirce himself notes:

In the early sixties I was a passionate devotee of Kant, at least as regards the *Transcendental Analytic in the Critic of the Pure Reason*. I believed more implicitly in the two tables of the Functions of Judgment and the Categories than if they had been brought down from Sinai. (RLT 124 (1898))

This devotion to Kant manifests itself in his earliest interesting attempt in 'On a new list of categories' (EP1. 1–10 (1867/1868)), where he derives an account of the categories by applying certain forms of logical analysis to our experiences. Peirce is especially interested in the idea that we can attempt to abstract away from our particular experiences to the most general features within them.

Peirce notes that there are three types of analysis or abstraction we might use: discrimination, dissociation and precision. Discrimination concerns the meaning of terms, so for instance I can 'discriminate' 'red' from 'blue', but not 'blue' from 'colour'. To invoke the more familiar terminology of analyticity, the meaning of 'colour' is contained in the meaning of 'blue', whereas the meanings of 'red' and 'blue' are quite separate. Dissociation concerns our ability to imagine or be conscious of one thing without being simultaneously conscious of another. So, for instance, I can 'dissociate' 'red' from 'blue' but not 'space' from 'colour'. The idea is that I can imagine something red without imagining something blue, but I cannot imagine something being coloured without also imagining it being extended in space. The final type of abstraction, precision, concerns our ability to attend to different elements of experience whilst diminishing our attention to others. Although the notion of precision isn't entirely clear, we see an instructive instance of it in Wittgenstein's discussion of 'pointing' in the *Philosophical Investigations*:

What does 'pointing to the shape', 'pointing to the colour' consist in? Point to a piece of paper. — And now point to its shape – now to its colour – now to its number (that sounds queer). – How did you do it? – [Y]ou will say you concentrated your attention on the colour, the shape, etc. (Wittgenstein 1953, 16)[9]

What we are doing here, by attending more to the shape, then more to the colour, and so on, is prescinding the different elements of our experience. All the same, Peirce takes it that some elements cannot be prescinded from others, so I can prescind space from colour but not colour from space. I can attend to space without having to attend to colour, but I cannot attend to something's colour without also attending to its spatial extension.

Of the three kinds of possible abstraction, Peirce thinks only precision is a suitable tool for uncovering universal categories from the content of experience. Discrimination relies more on the meanings of words than it does upon our analysis of cognition and experience, so its results may not give us an accurate account of what underlies all experience. Dissociation relies upon the peculiarities of our ability to imagine one thing without another. Precision, on the other hand, does not call for us to remove or withdraw the content of our experience, but only to attend to different elements in separation from each other.

In many ways, the division of these tools and the focusing upon prescinding to derive universal categories from experience is unclear, but from this method Peirce identifies five categories:

> The following five conceptions thus obtained [...] may be termed *categories*. That is,
>
> BEING
>
> Quality (reference to a ground)
>
> Relation (reference to a correlate)
>
> Representation (reference to an interpretant)
>
> SUBSTANCE (EP1. 6 (1967))

One of the first things we can see here is that these categories are clearly not firstness, secondness and thirdness. Moreover, instead of there being *three* categories, there are *five*. There are many interesting things that we might say about this particular derivation of the categories, not least that the tools that Peirce uses to analyse the contents of experience in its most general terms look, to modern eyes, idiosyncratic. Of course, this is due to the tradition that Peirce is working in, and he inherits these tools of analysis from ancient and scholastic philosophy. But all the same, quite how the method of precision leads to these categories is not well worked out. We know, for instance, that in this account of the categories, quality cannot be prescinded from relation, which cannot be prescinded from repre-sentation, but why this is so is not clear.

The final thing to note about this early account of the categories is that we see within it the seeds of the later three categories and, interestingly, the elements of a sign. Quality later becomes both the firstness and the sign-vehicle, relation later becomes both the sec-ondness and the object, and representation later becomes both the thirdness and the interpretant.

The logical derivation

The next clear account of the categories is in many ways the easiest to understand and rests on Peirce's ideas about the logic of relations. As Peirce's own research into Boolean logic and the logic of relatives became more established during the 1870s and 1880s, he began to recognise that his earlier accounts of the categories had relied on rather outmoded methods of analysis inherited from Kant and needed a better grounding in more modern developments in logic (CP1. 561 (1907)). From the 1870s onwards, then, we begin to find Peirce deriving the categories in logical terms. For instance, in an interesting paper, 'One two three: fundamental categories of the thought and of nature' (W5. 242–245 (1885)), we find him char-acterising the categories thusly:

> First, we find it necessary to recognize in logic three kinds of characters, three kinds of facts. First there are singular charac-ters which are predicable of single objects, as when we say that anything is white, large, etc. Secondly, there are dual characters which appertain to pairs of objects; these are implied by all rel-ative terms as 'lover,' 'similar,' 'other,' etc. Thirdly, there are plural

characters, which can all be reduced to triple characters but not to dual characters. Thus, we cannot express the fact that A is a benefactor of B by any descriptions of A and B separately; we must introduce a relative term. [. . .]

The three fundamental categories of fact are, fact about an object, fact about two objects (relation), fact about several objects (synthetic fact). (CP1. 371–372 (1885))

What we are seeing here is Peirce's identification with the universal categories of three types of logical relation: one-placed relations such as '— is thirsty', which hold of single objects; two-placed relations such as '— is taller than —', which hold of two objects; and three-placed relations which hold of three objects, such as '— gives — to —'. Firstness correlates with single-placed predicates, secondness with two-placed predicates, and thirdness with three-placed predicates.

This is as straightforward an explanation of the three categories of experience as one finds in Peirce's work, and it is interesting to see the suggestion that the content of our experiences might be divided in this way. Our experiences of qualities or feelings correlate with unsaturated monadic predicates; our experiences of brute existence or resistance correlate with dyadic predicates; our experiences of mediation, synthesis, and so on correlate with triadic predicates; and any other experience is in fact reducible to just these three kinds of relation. We can also see that Peirce has now reduced the number of categories he believes are needed from five to three, and in other papers from this period we see him applying the terms firstness, secondness and thirdness to these three categories.[10] This all seems much more familiar.

Before moving on to look at Peirce's final method of deriving the categories, however, it is worth noting that, when expressed in these terms, it becomes easier to see how one might argue more directly against Peirce's claims for the categories. Peirce may still maintain that this is a project which we cannot fully understand until we have engaged in it for ourselves, but it is clear that his claims here about the three kinds of logical relation must stand if they are to provide the support from logic that Peirce is looking for. That is, it must be the case that these three kinds of logical relation are necessary for our reasoning and that they cannot be reduced to either one-placed or two-placed relations alone. Additionally, it has to be the case that they are sufficient to explain our reasoning and that any relation greater than three can be reduced to a three-placed (or less) relation. If we either need more relations than this or can get by with fewer, then the logical basis of the categories looks flawed – either logic cannot be used to derive the categories or Peirce is wrong about which categories there are.

It is obvious that Peirce thinks that these three relations are *sufficient* for explaining the content of our experiences, and it doesn't seem too controversial to think that relations of four or greater can in fact be reduced to some complex of relations with smaller adicity. However, the claim that the three relations are *necessary*, that we cannot reduce triadic predicates to dyadic and/or monadic predicates, is more controversial. For example, it is something of a commonplace in the mainstream history of logic that predicate logic can function with two-placed predicates and that all relations of higher adicity can be reduced to dyadic relations.[11] If this is true, then Peirce's three-placed relations are not needed in logic and so look like a poor basis for deriving a third category of experience which is claimed to be universal; if 'thirdness' is not needed in logic, why assume it is needed in experience?

As it happens, there is extensive and persuasive support for Peirce's claims about the necessity of a three-placed relation in logic, and for the most part I think the work done in this area supports what is often called 'Peirce's reduction thesis',[12] that is, three-placed relations cannot be reduced to relations of smaller adicity. All the same, it is worth noting how the turn to logic to derive the categories results in such claims as these.

Phenomenology and the categories

The final clear attempt at deriving the categories comes from Peirce's work on phenomenology. As we have noted throughout, Peirce thought of his philosophy in systematic terms, and one his clearest expressions of this comes around the turn of the century when he suggested an architectonic structure for philosophy. As we know, he divided philosophy into three branches, the first of which he termed 'phenomenology'. This architectonic turn and the development of a science of phenomenology is the source of Peirce's final derivation of the universal categories of experience.

The precise content of the phenomenological derivation is much closer to the account of the categories that we outlined when we first introduced Peirce's project. In the phenomenological derivation, our aim is to account for the universal categories of experience by attending to the 'tangled skein' of our experience and giving an 'ultimate analysis of all experience' (CP1. 280 (1902)). This analysis turns out to give us the three universal categories we are familiar with: firstness, which is our experience of quality and feeling; secondness, which is our experience of reality and existence; and thirdness, which is our experience of law and mediation. The categories as derived from phenomenology, then, have been explained to some extent already. What we have not made sense of is why Peirce moves to a phenomenological explanation.

The first thing to note is that whilst there are obvious deficiencies in the manner of derivation used in both the early Kantian account of the 'new list' and in the logical derivation of the 1870s and 1880s, Peirce does not really abandon them by establishing phenomenology. The task facing the phenomenologist is still that facing the Kantian – to attend to the manifold of experience and to study 'the kinds of elements universally present in the phaneron; [that is], whatever is present at any time to the mind in any way' (EP2. 259 (1903)). Furthermore, the three categories derived in phenomenology are still closely tied with monadic, dyadic and triadic logical relations, and Peirce still describes thirdness, especially, in relational terms (CP8. 331 (1904)). The real difference with the phenomenological derivation, then, is not so much how it supposed we should derive the categories, or even their logical foundation, but where Peirce sees it in terms of his broader philosophy.

Phenomenology, as described by Peirce, is the first of the three branches of philosophy. In this sense, then, phenomenology is a more super-ordinate discipline than the normative sciences of aesthetic, ethics and logic, or the third branch of philosophy, metaphysics. The centrality of phenomenology to philosophy on this view is expressed quite clearly by Peirce at various points around the turn of the century. For instance, in a lecture delivered to Harvard in 1903 Peirce makes the following statement:

> Phenomenology, which simply contemplates the Universal Phenomenon, and discerns its ubiquitous elements, Firstness, Secondness, and Thirdness, together perhaps with other series of categories. The second grand division is Normative Science, which investigates the universal and necessary laws of the relation of Phenomena to Ends, that is, Truth, Right, and Beauty. The Third grand division is Metaphysics, which endeavours to comprehend the Reality of Phenomena. (EP2. 196–197 (1903))

The clear change here then is in terms of how we are to view the science of phenomenology and how it sits in relation to the rest of philosophy. As a science, it has no concern with truth, right, beauty or reality – those questions are taken up in subordinate disciplines – and instead studies mere appearance or experience. Moreover, it is the most basic and most super-ordinate philosophical discipline. This is an interesting shift in focus, on the one hand because it gives us a clearer sense of why we tend to see the universal categories emerge in so much of Peirce's other work, and on the other hand because it seems to suggest that Peirce has simply abandoned any drive to ground the derivation of the categories in anything else, except, of course, the most abstract discipline of all, mathematics. For some Peirce scholars, this is an unsatisfactory and *ad hoc* move on Peirce's part to insulate his sense that the categories are best expressed in terms of logical relations from the more problematic elements of that view:

> It is impossible to regard Peirce's phenomenological treatment of the categories as anything more than a quite unsuccessful sleight of hand. [. . .]

> It is obvious that Peirce does not regard the categories as simply the most convenient available system of classes, but his method

of classifying the sciences has now made it impossible for him to prove that his categories are either necessary or particularly important. (Murphey 1961, 368)

For Murphey, the move to explain the categories within phenomenology is unmotivated. An alternative view, however, is that Peirce was already familiar with the outcomes of pursuing phenomenology and already saw its apparent centrality to the rest of philosophy. T.L. Short makes just such a defence against Murphey's objection by claiming that Peirce 'already knew that the analysis of experience in relational terms was fruitful, that it permits a defence of his realism, and in other ways supports a coherent philosophy' (Short 2007, 65). I am inclined to think that Short is entirely correct here and that Peirce's move to establish a science which focuses on uncovering the categories universal to experience is a clear instance of scientific metaphysics. The results of phenomenology are no more than hypotheses based upon observations of our raw experience, which are then tested and investigated in the course of subordinate sciences.

Summary of the categories

We have seen in broad terms Peirce's account of the universal categories, in which he takes our experience to be generalisable into the three broad classes of firstness, secondness and thirdness. Firstness is most clearly associated with qualities, secondness with reality or existence, and thirdness with mediation or law. What's more, we've seen Peirce's various attempts to derive these categories, ranging from an early Kantian account through an attempt to base the categories on relational logic to a final account where the study of the categories is assigned the philosophically central science of phenomenology. This is a rather fast journey through Peirce's account of the categories, but it certainly gives us enough of a sense of what he thinks such a study should reveal and even why the division of phenomena into threes is such a common feature throughout the rest of his work. We shall now move on to look at the second main subject in Peirce's metaphysics – evolutionary cosmology.

Evolutionary cosmology

Finally, we turn to Peirce's evolutionary cosmology, a subject which has always been considered a rather problematic area of his work.[13] We shall examine some of the more philosophically motivated objections to the details of his theory below, but many objections to it are driven by concerns other than its philosophical content. For instance, many of the objections facing the evolutionary cosmology stem either from concerns about how obscure, vague and speculative it appears to be or from the worry that it fits so badly with the rest of Peirce's work. On the one hand, the problem is that the manner in which he writes about this subject is unclear, even by Peirce's standards, and on the other, that it is at times difficult to see how we are to understand this body of work in relation to the rest of his ideas and even why he thinks he must engage in this type of inquiry at all. We shall return to these interpretative problems below, but in short many of the issues raised against Peirce's evolutionary cosmology – that it looks wildly 'speculative' and seems much more in line with the kind of 'ontological metaphysics' he wants us to reject and replace – come from failing to appreciate the task that Peirce has set for his scientific metaphysics and how his cosmological work accords with that. As we shall see, Peirce views his evolutionary cosmology as entirely consistent with a scientific or laboratory approach to philosophy, and he would undoubtedly resist the claim that his cosmology is a form of ontological speculation. Nonetheless, as useful as keeping the distinction between ontological and scientific metaphysics in mind may be, closer examination of the evolutionary cosmology makes it clear that the work falls short of his scientific vision, even it isn't an example of metaphysics as 'a mere amusement for idle minds, a sort of chess'.

The origins of the cosmology

The best statements of Peirce's evolutionary cosmology are given in a series of five papers published in The Monist in the early 1890s. Indeed, The Monist metaphysical papers (EP1. 285–371 (1891–1893)) are the canonical statement of the evolutionary cosmology.

However, it is helpful to see how his ideas there emerge from other elements of his philosophy, in particular, his views on science and scientific metaphysics and a series of suggestive comments about the place of law and chance within the universe in an important paper from 1884, 'Design and chance'.

In terms of Peirce's views on science, we have already mentioned at the start of this chapter that he thought that we should try to adopt a laboratory attitude to philosophy and that from such an attitude a scientifically respectable body of metaphysical research would emerge. This laboratory sensibility is something that is found in Peirce's work even from his earliest writings. For instance, in an early paper from 1868, 'Some consequences of the four incapacities', we find a clear commitment to conducting philosophy in the manner of science:

> Philosophy ought to imitate the successful sciences in its methods, so far as to proceed only from tangible premises which can be subjected to careful scrutiny, and to trust rather to the multitude and variety of its arguments than to the conclusiveness of any one. (EP1. 29 (1868))

This commitment to philosophy conducted in the manner of science is not, however, a simple reductionism. Peirce is not committed to the view that philosophy must be reduced to science and our philosophical questions handed over to scientists. Instead, Peirce is suggesting that in order to answer our philosophical concerns we must proceed carefully, looking to the weight of evidence and building experimental confirmations to support our conclusions. As we saw at the beginning of this chapter, his long-standing commitment to this view of science, along with his experience as a practising scientist, led him to view a well-conducted metaphysics as connected to science in two ways. First, it is an observational discipline which can generate real progress by adopting such scientific methods as proposing and testing hypotheses (CP6. 2 and CP6. 5 (1898)). And second, the less abstract sciences need metaphysics to advance itself in order to clear the ground for research in those scientific fields (CP6. 1 (1898)). In short, metaphysics must adopt the methods of proper scientific investigation and should help support advances in less abstract sciences by establishing the core principles and assumptions of those sciences.

This two-way connection between metaphysics and science, on Peirce's view, although raised at various points throughout his writing, is made quite clear in his accounts of the architectonic structure of philosophy around 1903, where metaphysics is treated as the third branch of philosophy and stands in a super-ordinate position to various 'physical' and 'psychical' sciences. It is a task of metaphysics, then, to uncover and examine the underlying presuppositions of those sciences. But a further important point here is to note which presuppositions of science Peirce thought were the appropriate subjects for metaphysical inquiry.

As a practising scientist, Peirce was impressed by the manner in which science led to the progression and accumulation of ideas, as we well know from the role that scientific inquiry plays in his broader philosophy. However, a key element to scientific progress in the nineteenth century, as Peirce saw it, was the manner in which scientists had paid closer scrutiny to the laws of science and how existing scientific study had been made to fall under clearer and better general iterations of those laws. For instance, in material prepared for his lectures at Johns Hopkins University in 1882, Peirce describes the generalisation of methods from one discipline to those of another as 'what the greatest progress of the passing generation has consisted in' (CP7. 66 (1882)). For Peirce, the nature of laws and their development over time is a key presupposition of the sciences, and if anything constitutes the proper subject of scientific metaphysics, it is these presuppositions about the laws of science.

In a paper delivered to the Johns Hopkins Metaphysical Club in 1884, Peirce's ideas about scientific metaphysics and the proper study of the laws of nature begin to emerge into what is the first clear forerunner to his account of evolutionary cosmology. In that paper, 'Design and chance' (EP1. 215–224 (1884)), Peirce makes a series of conjectures about the nature of laws and what is most important for our questions about them, and he describes a general tendency amongst scientists 'to question the exact truth of axioms' as 'likely to teach us more than any other general conception' (EP1. 215 (1884)). This is, in short, Peirce engaging in scientific metaphysics by examining a key proposition of the concrete sciences, the nature of laws.

Peirce makes numerous claims in 'Design and chance' about the nature of scientific laws, many of which foreshadow the key ideas of his evolutionary cosmology. Whilst this work is interesting because it presents early and clear examples both of Peirce engaged in scientific metaphysics and of his evolutionary cosmology, it is three key ideas that are of immediate interest to us.

First, we find Peirce suggesting that it is crucial that we have an explanation of *laws*, and second, he suggests that these laws *evolve*:

> I maintain that the postulate that things shall be explicable extends to *laws* as well as to states of things. We want a theory of the evolution of physical law. We ought to suppose that as we go back into the indefinite past not merely special laws but *law* itself is found to be less and less determinate. (EP1. 218–219 (1884))

His first claim, that laws must also be explicable, is just an upshot of taking on the task of scientific metaphysics. His second claim, that laws evolve and become more determinate over time, or as he also puts it, that 'things must on the whole have proceeded from the Homogenous to the Heterogeneous' (EP1. 218 (1884)), is an upshot of his view that science is able to progress by making the applicability of its laws clearer by extending and increasing the precision of its axioms.

The third and final claim that Peirce makes is that the *evolution* of law is due to chance, and in particular to something he calls *absolute chance*.

He goes on to talk about the role of chance in the evolution of laws thusly:

> It has always seemed to me singular that when we put the question to an evolutionist [. . .] what are the agencies that have brought about evolution, he mentions various determinate facts and laws, but [. . .] he never once mentions *Chance*. Yet it appears to me that

> chance is the one essential agency upon which the whole process depends. [...] I suppose that on excessively rare and sporadic occasions a law of nature is violated in some infinitesimal degree; that may be called *absolute chance*. (EP1. 218–219 (1884))

Peirce's claim here, then, is that if we are to understand the evolution of law, we must posit some rare, minute and undetermined violation of a law of nature, something Peirce calls absolute chance.

We shall examine just how Peirce develops these themes into a fuller account of his evolutionary cosmology shortly, but immediately following the paper of 1884, it seemed to Peirce that this work in scientific metaphysics was a real landmark discovery. He wrote to his brother James in 1885 that he had 'a great and momentous thing to say on this subject. Without it, molecular science must remain at a stand-still' (W6. 595 (1885)). He wrote to William James at the same time that he had something which was 'an attempt to explain the laws of nature, to show their general characteristics and to trace them to their origin & predict new laws by the laws of the laws of nature' (W6. 595 (1885)). For Peirce, then, his views on the nature and purpose of scientific metaphysics seemed to call for an inquiry into the nature of the laws of science, and these laws seemed to Peirce to evolve through the existence of absolute chance. Moreover, this account, if properly worked out, seemed to him to provide the key to understanding the nature of science and scientific discovery, to offer the promise of uncovering new laws, and to be crucial to facilitating the future progress of science.

The cosmological picture

From the statements of 'Design and chance', where we find Peirce taking what look like the first steps towards an evolutionary account of the existence of laws, he moves within a few years to producing a full account of the evolution of the *universe* in his *Monist* metaphysical papers. That series consists of five papers which develop various theories in favour of Peirce's views about the nature of the universe and its development. The papers construct arguments against various explanations that Peirce thinks are either incorrect or incomplete accounts of the way the universe is. The project as a whole is often vague and rather enigmatically explained, but at the heart of these papers, Peirce's broad aim is to give an account of the evolution of the universe. He sees the universe as having moved from some past state of complete chaos to its present state, where we find the world governed by physical laws, and it will continue to evolve to some future state where all chance and randomness have disappeared. Rather interestingly, the clearest summary statements of the overall picture of evolutionary cosmology come from Peirce himself, with an especially clear account given in a letter to his former student Christine Ladd-Franklin. To quote at length:

> I may mention that my chief avocation in the last ten years has been to develop my cosmology. This theory is that the evolution of the world [. . .] proceeds from one state of things in the infinite past, to a different state of things in the infinite future. The state of things in the infinite past is chaos, tohu bohu, the nothingness of which consists in the total absence of regularity. The state of things in the infinite future is death, the nothingness of which consists in the complete triumph of law and absence of all spontaneity. Between these, we have on our side a state of things in which there is some absolute spontaneity counter to all law, and some degree of conformity to law, which is constantly on the increase owing to the growth of habit. The tendency to form habits or tendency to generalize, is something which grows by its own action, by the habit of taking habits itself growing. Its first germs arose from pure chance. There were slight tendencies to obey rules that had been followed, and these tendencies were rules which were more and more obeyed by their own action. (CP8. 317 (1891))

The picture presented here, then, is of the universe in a state of chaos where there is no habit and no regularities for law to explain. Amidst this chaos of the infinite past, we find that through chance occurrences the development of some general tendencies or regularities appear, perhaps one or two repetitions, which once started to lead to a more ingrained regularity. These developing regularities become habits and laws. The laws and habits become more engrained, and the tendency towards habit and law itself increases. And whilst these laws continue to evolve and develop, there still remain random instances of absolute chance which violate whatever habits, tendencies and laws have emerged from the chaos of the infinite past. Eventually, the universe will reach a state where no spontaneous violations of habits and laws occur, and the universe will have evolved to a state of complete determination. Peirce explains the process from chaos to complete determination in a similarly instructive passage in the first paper of The Monist metaphysical papers, 'The architecture of theories' (EP1. 285–297 (1891)):

> [I]n the beginning [. . .] there was a chaos of unpersonalized feeling, which being without connection or regularity would properly be without existence. This feeling, sporting here and there in pure arbitrariness, would have started the germ of a generalizing tendency. [. . .] Thus, the tendency to habit would be started; and from this [. . .] all the regularities of the universe would be evolved. At any time, however, an element of pure chance survives and will remain until the world becomes an absolutely perfect, rational, and symmetrical system, in which mind is at last crystallized in the infinitely distant future. (EP1. 297 (1891))

When we see Peirce's cosmological vision put like this, it can seem strikingly peculiar, and it is not hard to see why so many Peirce scholars have thought it much closer to the unscientific speculation of ontological metaphysics than to the scientifically respectable metaphysics that Peirce claimed to be pursuing. Nonetheless, Peirce certainly thought of this project as scientific metaphysics, and although it helps, of course, to have seen how this picture of evolutionary cosmology grew from his earlier speculations in 'Design and chance', it is important that we now turn to two important questions in order to make it clear how he thought this was a scientifically respectable enterprise. So, given that this is how Peirce thinks we should explain the evolution of the universe, firstly, why does he think we need such an account? And secondly, how does he intend to show that his account is correct?

With regard to why Peirce thinks we need an account of evolutionary cosmology in the manner presented, he suggests the following four reasons in a rejoinder to the editor of The Monist, Paul Carus:

> In my attack on 'The Doctrine of Necessity' I offered four positive arguments for believing in real chance. They were as follows:
>
> 1 The general prevalence of growth, which seems to be opposed to the conservation of energy.
>
> 2 The variety of the universe, which is chance, and is manifestly inexplicable.
>
> 3 Law, which requires to be explained, and like everything which is to be explained must be explained by something else, that is, by non-law or real chance.
>
> 4 Feeling, for which room cannot be found if the conservation of energy is maintained. (CP6. 613 (1893))[14]

Andrew Reynolds, one of the leading Peirce scholars on Peirce's scientific metaphysics and evolutionary cosmology, also notes the significance of this rejoinder to Carus in explaining Peirce's motivation for offering his account of cosmology. Reynolds (2002, 13) takes Peirce's justification here, then, to be that the following four things are readily observable in the universe and require some proper explanation: growth and complexity, variety and diversity, the laws of nature, and consciousness. Moreover, since these four things represent many of the axioms and presuppositions of the physical and psychical sciences, the proper task of a scientific metaphysics is to give a proper account of their existence. Peirce clearly takes his evolutionary cosmology to do just that.

If the purpose of the cosmological picture that Peirce suggests is to give us a scientifically respectable metaphysical account of growth, *diversity, law and consciousness,* then how does he intend to argue for this picture? So far, we are presented with a curiously Biblical picture of how things were in 'the beginning', but without support, this is simply a rather mystical 'just-so' story. However, Peirce attempts to argue for this cosmological picture with the use of three core arguments or theories: *tychism, synechism* and *agapism*. We shall examine these three ideas in more detail below, but in broad terms they are Peirce's accounts of chance, continuity and evolutionary love. Each of these concepts plays a role in Peirce's attempt to establish the cosmological picture presented above.

Tychism

In the second of *The Monist* metaphysical papers, 'The doctrine of necessity examined' (EP1. 298–311 (1891)), Peirce introduces his account of *tychism,* or absolute chance, and defends it against what he sees as the opposite view of *necessitarianism.* Necessitarianism is the rather simple, deterministic view that all events are causally determined according to immutable laws, that from any given present state, the set of immutable laws governing the universe will lead us to some determinate future state. As Peirce puts it:

> [G]iven the state of the universe in the original nebula, and given the laws of mechanics, a sufficiently powerful mind could deduce from these data the precise form of every curlicue of every letter I am now writing. (EP1. 299 (1891))

Tychism is Peirce's claim that this view is false and that 'absolute chance is a factor of the universe' (RLT 260 (1898)). Tychism, then, is simply the claim that genuine chance occurrences have a profound impact upon the way the universe has evolved and will continue to evolve. It is the role of tychism to explain 'the sporting feelings' that occur 'here and there in the pure arbitrariness', and in many instances Peirce alludes to the epicureanism of Democritus, who explained free will as the random swerving of atoms in the void (EP1. 299 (1891)). But why does Peirce think we should accept the tychist's commitment to the real influence of absolute chance over the necessitarian's commitment to determinism?

In 'The doctrine of necessity examined', Peirce presents a series of arguments against necessitarianism and in support of his tychist alternative. Peirce claims, for instance, that the deterministic picture which appeals to the necessitarian cannot be claimed as a postulate of scientific reasoning on the grounds that proper scientific reasoning is ampliative, and the key methods of ampliative reasoning – induction, abduction and analogy – have no need to assume postulates (EP1. 300–303 (1898)). Any necessitarian appeal to determinism as a postulate is modelled on an old-fashioned picture of the scientific method. Similarly, Peirce claims that no appeal to observational facts can support the necessitarian claim either, since the best that observation can afford us is merely the claim that there are regularities, not that they are born of accordance with universal or immutable laws (EP1. 303–305 (1898))

In terms of his support for the tychist picture, Peirce offers answers to a series of potential objections, including concerns that the notion of absolute chance can play no genuine causal role in the nature of the universe. The objection here is that what we might be inclined to think of as chance is really just a lack of knowledge about whatever causal factors are involved. Peirce rejects such concerns on the grounds that tychism offers better explanations of such phenomena as increased complexity or diversity. For Peirce, a deterministic picture seems to need all diversity and complexity built into the structure of the universe at the outset. The process of diversification or complexity accounted for mechanistically isn't really explaining how variety or complexity occurs at all. Instead, things are as they always were and such phenomena are more or less stipulated on the necessitarian view. This is a rather curt summary of Peirce's claims, and any assessment of how convincing these arguments for tychism are is unimportant here. Instead, what matters is that Peirce takes himself to be offering good scientific grounds for favouring an account of the universe which allows for absolute chance: it respects our best scientific practice of conjecturing and testing hypotheses inductively, it does not outrun what observation will support, and it has greater power to explain observed features of the universe.

In terms of Peirce's evolutionary picture itself and what he claims it must explain, we can see how tychism allows him to account for the presence of growth, diversity and law in the universe. As we noted, absolute chance is what accounts for the spontaneous 'sportings' in the 'pure arbitrariness' that characterises the chaos of the infinite past, but from these chance events, the undifferentiated arbitrariness becomes increasingly various and diverse. And by taking on a tendency towards habit, the universe becomes increasingly suffused with laws. Further, by the spontaneous violation of laws, it becomes increasingly complex and grows. But, interestingly, Peirce also sees the possibility of tychism explaining the existence of consciousness.

Peirce argues that necessitarianism must make mind a feature of the material world, which Peirce thinks commits the necessitarian to the view that consciousness is merely illusory. As Peirce puts it:

> Brain-matter is protoplasm in a certain degree and kind of complication – a certain arrangement of mechanical particles. Its feeling is but an inward aspect, a phantom. (EP1. 309 (1891))

Consciousness as an illusion is not a commitment of tychism. We shall see how Peirce thinks consciousness can be more fully explained on his view below, but it should be clear that, for Peirce, since an account of the universe must be able to explain growth, variety, law and consciousness, tychism must form part of the evolutionary cosmology.

Synechism

The second important theory used by Peirce to support his account of the evolution of the universe is *synechism*. Two of *The Monist* metaphysical papers are directly concerned with synechism: 'The law of mind' (EP1. 312–333 (1892)) and 'Man's glassy essence' (EP1. 334–351 (1892)). Although synechism is most relevant to his evolutionary cosmology, as we shall see, the concept is closely connected to various important ideas in Peirce's broader body of philosophy.

Defined as simply as possible, synechism is simply the philosophical doctrine that the concept of continuity is crucial to philosophy. As Peirce puts it in a definition written for *Baldwin's Dictionary of Philosophy and Psychology*:

> Synechism is that tendency of philosophical thought which insists upon the idea of continuity as of prime importance in philosophy and, in particular, upon the necessity of hypotheses involving true continuity. (CP6. 169 (1901))

Continuity is a concept of deep importance to Peirce and features at various points in his philosophy. His own accounts of continuity draw heavily on mathematics, and he sees his own views on the nature of continuity and the continuum as developed in contrast to the views of Cantor. Nonetheless, we find Peirce describing continuity in terms simplistic enough to make it clear what the synechist is supposed to be committed to:

> We all have some idea of continuity. Continuity is fluidity, the merging of part into part. But to achieve a really distinct and adequate conception of it is a difficult task [. . .]. I may say this, however. I draw a line. Now the points on that line form a continuous series. If I take any two points on that line, however close together, other points there are lying between them. If that were not so, the series of points would not be continuous. (CP1. 164 (1897))

Although Peirce was later less convinced that the Cantorian method of defining continuity in terms of points was correct,[15] this is nonetheless a useful account for showing what continuity is supposed to mean, indicating what synechists would have us believe is crucial to understanding philosophy, and, more importantly, proving the cosmological picture that Peirce posits by explaining growth, variety, law and consciousness. But whilst the metaphor of points on a line is helpful for understanding continuity and clarifying what lies at the heart of the synechist commitment, it is perhaps less clear why this theory supports Peirce's cosmological claims.

Three features of the synechist claim are important here. The first is what we might call *inexactitude*, in so far as, however determinate or accurate we might think an answer may be, there is always some greater precision we could extract. Peirce cites as an example our saying that the sum of angles in a triangle is equal to 180 degrees (EP2. 2 (1893)) and suggests that a commitment to synechism would not allow us to make such a statement. Rather, we must insist that the sum of angles in a triangle is close to 180 degrees, or 180 degrees plus or minus some exceedingly small figure. This is more or less a consequence of claiming that there is always some further division of the continuum that we can make, that there is always some more determinate, more precise answer we can give.

The second feature of synechism is what we might call 'anti-discreteness', in so far as there is a connectivity and 'flow' between things, which means that, in an important sense, discrete things are apparently linked together in the continuum. For example, Peirce talks of the apparent distinctness between *being* and *not-being*, suggesting that 'synechism flatly denies it, declaring that being is a matter of more or less, so as to merge insensibly into nothing' (EP2. 2 (1893)). Importantly, this feature of synechism is anti-dualist, treating all things as connected to each other along the flow of the continuum rather than as separate things. We shall return to this point shortly.

The third feature of synechism is its pervasiveness. Peirce describes synechism as the tendency to see continuity as of prime importance to philosophy, but synechism, in fact, seems to make the stronger claim that all phenomena are describable in terms of a continuum. For example, we find Peirce explaining the nature of ideas in terms of what he calls the 'law of mind':

> Ideas tend to spread continuously and to affect certain others which stand to them in a peculiar relation of affectibility. In this spreading they lose intensity, and especially the power of affecting

others, but gain generality and become welded with other ideas. (EP1. 313 (1892))

This is simply synechism applied to the mind. We also find him explaining the flow of time in similar terms (EP1. 323 (1892)). Of course, this ability to use synechism to describe such various phenomena leaves Peirce with an interesting philosophical tool for explaining philosophical issues such as the problem of other minds (EP2. 3 (1893)).

In terms of Peirce's evolutionary cosmology, however, synechism does two interesting things. First of all, it helps to explain, or least underpins, the tychist explanations of growth, variety, law and consciousness. Earlier states are connected to later states in the continuum; laws are made clearer and more precise in the flow from the infinite past to the infinite future as we look at and accommodate 'the points lying between' those we have already explained, so to speak. Perhaps most instructive in this regard, though, is how Peirce uses synechism to explain the existence of consciousness in the universe.

As we noted, the synechistic commitment to a continuum means that we can 'never abide dualism' (EP2. 2 (1893)). This doesn't mean that Peirce won't accept that we can differentiate between things, but only that things cannot, at a fundamental level, be divided into different classes. In terms of consciousness, then, Peirce suggests that:

> [T]he synechist will not admit that physical and psychical phenomena are entirely distinct [. . .] but will insist that all phenomena are of one character, though some are more mental and spontaneous, others more material and regular. (EP2. 2 (1893))

What Peirce means here is that mind and matter are the same kind of thing but are just at different points on the continuum. Mind, or consciousness, he characterises as being the same as body, or matter, except that the former is more spontaneous and the latter more bound down in habit. It is clear that the way in which Peirce divides the two leans heavily upon his cosmological account of the universe as moving from a state of chaos through random spontaneity and absolute chance to a more habit-bound state. In terms of an explanation of consciousness, then, Peirce seems to be suggesting that consciousness is the primary state of the universe and that matter emerges or flows out from consciousness along the continuum.

This account of consciousness – the claim that 'matter is effete mind' (EP1. 293 (1891)) – is described by Peirce as *objective idealism*, and it is something he takes to follow quite clearly from the untenability of both *materialism* and what he calls *neutralism*. On Peirce's view, the neutralist suggests that mental and physical phenomena have to be viewed as entirely distinct from each other, whilst the materialist suggests the physical is more basic and the mental derived from it. The neutralist position is ruled out by Peirce on the principle of Ockham's razor, whilst materialism is ruled out on the grounds that it requires us to accept the unpalatable claim that consciousness can develop from a purely mechanistic process. For Peirce, the only remaining plausible claim is that the mental is basic, or 'primordial', and the physical is derived from it. Whilst the claim that matter is merely mind that has lost its spontaneity by taking on habit leaves many uneasy about Peirce's arguments for the evolutionary cosmology, it is clear that for Peirce, synechism helps to explain the phenomena in the universe that any scientific metaphysics should explain.

The second thing to note about synechism in relation to Peirce's arguments for his particular cosmological picture is that it calls for an account of evolution, and in many ways it makes this account central to the explanation that he offers. Of course, we are attempting to explain Peirce's *evolutionary* cosmology, so it is barely surprising that an account of evolution is a crucial feature, but the point here is that synechism and tychism, as commitments to the presence of continuity and the role of absolute chance, are by themselves not enough to explain why the universe progresses to the fixed and completely determined state that it does in the infinite future. We can see quite clearly how evolution is closely connected to the view that chance produces changes which we can see running along a continuum, but the manner of evolution in Peirce's picture leads to a clear and determinate end state. This needs explanation, which of course leads us to the final element of Peirce's evolutionary cosmology, *agapism*.

Agapism

In the last of his five *Monist* metaphysical papers, 'Evolutionary love' (EP1. 352–371 (1893)), Peirce introduces his account of *agapism*. This is the third important element in Peirce's argument for his cosmological picture and leads to an account of 'evolution which every careful student of "The Laws of Mind" must see that synechism calls for' (EP1. 354 (1893)). In many ways, Peirce's account of agapism in 'Evolutionary love' is the vaguest and least satisfactory part of his evolutionary cosmology, often sounding the most mystical of any part of his account. Nonetheless, we can recover some sense of what Peirce thinks agapism is and why he thinks it is important for explaining the nature of the universe.

Put simply, agapism is the claim that love is an important operative feature of the universe. Just as tychism is a commitment to the presence and importance of absolute chance and synechism a commitment to the presence and importance of continuity, agapism is a commitment to the presence and importance of love. More specifically, agapism is the claim that growth or evolution comes from the operation of love:

> Everybody can see that the statement of St. John[16] is the formula of an evolutionary philosophy, which teaches that growth comes only from love, from – I will not say self-*sacrifice*, but from the ardent impulse to fulfil another's highest impulse. (EP1. 354 (1893))

As a statement of how the universe evolves, this is far from clear. We are supposed to see the continuity prevalent in the universe as leading clearly and directly to the claim that growth and evolution is the result of a form of self-sacrificing love directed towards the needs of others. Put like this, it is again clear why so many of Peirce's contemporaries and early commentators found the evolutionary cosmology so difficult to square with his more hard-headed scientific work.

However, Peirce compares evolution as a result of love with two other kinds of evolution operative in the universe, and this comparison is perhaps more instructive:

> Three modes of evolution have thus been brought before us: evolution by fortuitous variation, evolution by mechanical necessity, and evolution by creative love. We may term them *tychastic* evolution or *tychasm*, *anancastic* evolution, or *anancasm*, and *agapastic* evolution, or *agapasm*. [. . .] [T]he mere propositions that absolute chance, mechanical necessity, and the law of love are severally operative in the cosmos may receive the names *tychism*, *anancism*, and *agapism*. (EP1. 362 (1893))

For Peirce, tychastic evolution is simply change through chance, but such changes are so small and so random that they cannot account for the full extent of evolution and growth apparent in the universe (EP2. 365 (1893)). Anancastic evolution, on the other hand, is simply evolution by natural selection, much in the form of the Darwinian model we are so familiar with. Whilst this is clearly an operative form of evolution in the universe, and we can see the rate of change it gives rise to is much greater than tychastic evolution, it is still change without purpose and so cannot explain why we have increasing refinement and greater determination in our universe (EP1. 367 (1893)). The only form of evolution that can do this is agapastic evolution, which Peirce takes to be driven by the fulfilment of some 'higher impulse':

> The agapastic development of thought should, if it exists, be distinguished by its purposive character, this purpose being the development of an idea. We should have direct agapic or sympathetic comprehension and recognition of it, by virtue of the continuity of thought. (EP1. 369 (1893))

Peirce's argument, then, is that the only explanation for growth and development along the continuum is a form of evolution which, though allowing change through chance and mechanical means, has to be focused on the development and determination of ideas and laws themselves. It is purposeful, end-directed evolution. Agapism, then, as odd as it may sound when expressed in terms of evolutionary or creative love, is perhaps most easily thought of as a form of evolution which is essentially teleological and end directed – which, for Peirce, is required by both synechism and tychism.

Problems with the evolutionary cosmology

Although this is a fairly short treatment of Peirce's evolutionary cosmology, we can see what the account is supposed to be doing. Peirce thinks the universe has evolved, through the mechanism of random chance from a state of chaos to a state where habit and law are present. Random chance violations can still occur, but the universe will continue to develop to a final state where there is no longer any deviation from habit and law and the universe is fully determinate. Peirce's theories of tychism, synechism and agapism are all supposed to support this account of the cosmos. The presence of absolute chance gives us the agent of change, the presence of continuity gives us the mechanism of development and emergence, and the presence of agapism gives us a determinate direction and goal. Moreover, this is supposed to explain the existence of growth, variety, laws and consciousness. But what are we supposed to make of this in philosophical terms?

The evolutionary cosmology is, in fact, a short-lived project relative to Peirce's other philosophical work, not extending much past The Monist metaphysical papers without its ideas being dropped or transformed into other notions in later philosophy, and this makes it harder to judge his work here. The changes to his work from earlier to later have been something of a feature of the accounts we have given, and it has always been clear that in the later work details have been filled out more fully or clear problems addressed in some way. For the evolutionary cosmology, we cannot easily engage in such an exercise, and the work that we have is so programmatic that its value becomes difficult to really assess. Nonetheless, there are some obvious problems, three of which are mentioned here.

First of all, there are some clear internal incoherencies in the account as it is stated. For example, in the account of the cosmos, it is absolute chance that drags us from a primordial lawless state into a state where law and habit emerge. However, in some places Peirce describes absolute chance itself in terms of 'general law'. In a rejoinder to Paul Carus of The Monist, for instance, he says:

> [T]he *existence* of absolute chance, as well as many of its characters, are not themselves absolute chances, or sporadic events, unsubject to general law. On the contrary, these things *are* general laws. Everybody is familiar with the fact that chance has laws, and that statistical results follow therefrom. (CP6. 606 (1893))

This seems to present a difficulty that applies just as much to synechism and agapism as to the tychist commitment to absolute chance. Are these notions governed by laws or not? Agapism is described as 'the law of love', for instance, and if it is operative in the universe and is instrumental in explaining the move from the primordial state to the coalescence and increased determination of laws, then it too must be subject to the nature of the universe. In short, if laws govern the mechanisms that move us from the primordial lawless state to the development of laws, the existence of the laws governing tychism, synechism and agapism seem to be unexplained. This is troubling.

Second, if we are to take the architectonic seriously and respect the priority of phenomenology, there are many features in the account of evolutionary cosmology which seem to clash with Peirce's account of the universal categories. For example, we are supposed to treat the categories as universal – they are supposed to be a feature of all things and are found together. As Peirce puts it, the categories 'cannot be dissociated in imagination from each other' (CP1. 353 (1880)). We can *prescind* firstness from secondness or thirdness, but we cannot properly separate it. However, in positing a primordial state of chaos, of 'unpersonalised feeling' (EP1. 297 (1891)), Peirce posits only firstness. This seems to be a place where the categories are not, in fact, universal.[17] This is not the only clash between the categories and the cosmology.

A similar clash occurs in Peirce's phenomenological catego-
risation of the elements of the cosmological picture, which seem
strangely out of sorts with how we would normally think of them
given our usual understanding of the categories. For instance, Peirce
describes the key cosmological components in the following terms:

> Chance is First, Law is Second, the tendency to take habits is Third.
> Mind is First, Matter is Second, Evolution is Third. (EP1. 297 (1891))

But in more familiar work on Peirce's phenomenology, we are led
to identify *possibility* with firstness, *actuality* with secondness and,
importantly, *law* with thirdness (EP2. 160–178). There are two clear
incongruities here. First, *chance* cannot be a matter of feeling or possibility, as it would need to be if it were an archetypal instance of
firstness, since it depends upon events and actual occurrences. Indeed,
even within the cosmological picture, an instance of absolute chance
has to be an *actual* instance. This makes it look as though chance is
much more suited to the category of secondness. The second incongruity is that law is clearly an instance of thirdness in Peirce's broader
phenomenology and looks to be misplaced as an example of secondness in the cosmology.[18] Even if we defend this by noting that at the
time of writing *The Monist* metaphysical papers, Peirce was still developing full statements of his architectonic and his phenomenological
account of the categories, the incongruity is still problematic.

The third and final worry about the evolutionary cosmology is
that it isn't clear that it really fulfils its own stated aims of giving
us a *scientific metaphysics* that explains observed phenomena in the
universe and supports the advance of less abstract sciences. I shan't
elaborate much on this worry, but, in short, it is hard to see how
the evolutionary cosmology is really an example of scientific metaphysics in the sense that Peirce suggests since it isn't clear how it
really gives us a proper scientific explanation of everything it pur-
ports to. For example, how does it explain all laws? How does it
help us to identify new laws? Indeed, how are its claims themselves
empirically testable? Take, for instance, the claim that matter is effete
mind and that consciousness is explained in this way as having

been the primordial state from which matter emerges by taking on habits of action. Peirce gives us arguments, of course, but these look like logical deductions allied with methodological preferences about plausibility, and they certainly don't follow the notion that metaphysics should work by giving hypotheses and proceeding by observation and inductive testing.

These are only a few of the kinds of problems that are raised against the evolutionary cosmology, and with a more developed picture of Peirce's theory, they may, in fact, be easily accommodated. However, as we have frequently noted, the details of the cosmology are vague and it is hard to construct answers and responses without speculating far beyond anything Peirce wrote. What is clear about the cosmology, though, is that as it stands it is not satisfactory or convincing as a piece of scientific metaphysics. Nonetheless, it is a deeply puzzling and enigmatic part of Peirce's broader philosophy which poses interesting problems in terms of the philosophical claims it makes and in terms of how we should understand it in relation to his entire body of work. Indeed, the extent of the problem of understanding how it fits in relation to the rest of his work is a feature of the evolutionary cosmology shared by none of Peirce's other work, and it is by looking briefly at this problem that we will conclude this chapter.

Summary of evolutionary cosmology

In the first chapter, we noted that we were going to use Peirce's architectonic as an interpretative tool, along with his commitment to logic and science. In this way we can see where the evolutionary cosmology is supposed to sit, namely, as the third branch of scientific metaphysics, physical metaphysics. Whether it is well placed there or fulfils the role that Peirce has given it is, as we've seen, a rather different matter, but on the face of it this seems to be where we should see the evolutionary cosmology in the broader scheme of Peirce's philosophy. Highly prominent Peirce scholars[19] have taken the work on evolutionary cosmology to represent a side to Peirce's philosophy that is at once mystical, transcendentalist and completely at odds with his work on logic and pragmatism. Murray Murphey, for instance, writes:

From first to last, Peirce was a metaphysician [. . .]. So much of Peirce's writing is so bizarre that the reader tends to cling for dear life to those few doctrines which, like pragmatism, have an aura of reasonableness about them. (Murphey 1965, 12–13)

Others are either deeply sympathetic to placing Peirce's metaphysics closer to the core of his philosophical enterprise, or they make little mention of how problematic the account of evolutionary cosmology really is.[20] However, the more interesting and, I believe, accurate view of the cosmology is that it is something that Peirce saw a distinct place for in his philosophy and that we can make sense of in light of Peirce's scientific and logic leanings, but we have to view his attempt to fill in the details in a satisfying way as a failure. This is a view which can be found amongst leading interpreters of Peirce's metaphysics, including Andrew Reynolds (2002, 179–180), W.B. Gallie (1952, 236), and, more recently, T.L. Short (2010, 522). There is still debate amongst these figures about what the failure of the evolutionary cos-mology amounts to. Reynolds, for instance, sees it as an admirable attempt to engage in scientific metaphysics and views the apparent schism as coming more from Peirce's failure to see the incompati-bility with his more clearly scientific work. T.L. Short, meanwhile, thinks Peirce never proceeded further than sketching out a program of cosmology which he quickly abandoned. However, what is clear is that the view of Peirce's cosmology as 'the black sheep or the white elephant of his philosophical progeny' (Gallie 1952, 216), which Gallie noted was widespread amongst early Peirce scholars, is no lon-ger so prevalent, and we are much better placed than we once were to see the work as connected to Peirce's philosophy as a whole.

Summary

Peirce produced interesting but controversial work in various topics in metaphysics. His most interesting metaphysical ideas, however, were his development of an account of universal categories and an evolutionary cosmology.

- Peirce viewed the traditional practice of metaphysics as being responsible for a lack of progress in the discipline and for its apparent lack of relevance for other disciplines. Peirce himself thought that traditional metaphysics – or ontological metaphysics – was the result of taking a seminary approach to philosophy.
- As an alternative to seminary philosophy and ontological metaphysics, Peirce thought a laboratory approach to philosophy could yield a scientific metaphysics, which would allow progress in metaphysics and give support to subordinate disciplines in the physical and psychical sciences.
- Peirce's account of the universal categories was an attempt to describe what is general or universal in our phenomenal experience. He identified the three categories of firstness, secondness and thirdness. These were broadly described in terms of feelings or qualities, existence or objects, and habits or laws.
- Peirce made three separate attempts to derive these universal categories: an early account based on Kant's account of the categories; an account from the 1870s and 1880s based upon three logical relations; and an account from around 1903 which made the discovery of categories a matter of the first branch of philosophy, phenomenology.
- Peirce's evolutionary cosmology is an account of the universe in which the universe grows and develops from a primordial state of chaos to a state where laws are present but are still contravened by spontaneous chance events, and finally to state where laws and habits have made the universe fully determinate.
- Three concepts are key to explaining this cosmological picture: tychism, the view that chance is really operative in the universe; synechism, the view that continuity is fundamental to the universe; and agapism, the view that creative love operates as a teleological form of evolution in the universe.
- All of Peirce's metaphysical views are controversial, but the evolutionary cosmology has led many commentators to see it as anomalous within Peirce's philosophy. However, as a form of scientific metaphysics, we can understand what motivates it.

Further reading

Peirce's work on the universal categories is a common element in any exegesis of his work, but a good, clear account can be found in Chapter 3 of Christopher Hookway's 1985 *Peirce*. The topic can be presented quite obscurely, but Hookway offers an accessible account, explaining the nature of the categories, Peirce's various attempts to give a theory of them, and their importance to other areas of his philosophy. A similarly useful account is Andre de Tienne's 1988 paper 'Peirce's search for a method of finding the categories'. It is shorter than Hookway's chapter but harder to obtain. Finally, David Savan's 1952 paper 'On the origins of Peirce's phenomenology', although older, is well worth attending to. Savan gives an illuminating explanation of Peirce's development of phenomenology as a philosophical subject and its importance as a discipline used purely for the study of the categories.

Work on Peirce's evolutionary cosmology is less plentiful than that in other areas, and good, well-written, extended treatments of it are rare. All the same, Andrew Reynolds' *Peirce's Scientific Metaphysics: The Philosophy of Chance, Law and Evolution* (2002) is a useful explanation of Peirce's work. In particular, Reynolds works hard to establish the scientific credentials of Peirce's cosmology. Two articles giving accounts of the development of Peirce's cosmology are Paul Forster's 'The logical foundations of Peirce's indeterminism' (1997) and Christopher Hookway's 'Design and chance: the evolution of Peirce's evolutionary cosmology' (1997a). Forster's article explains Peirce's tychism of the 1890s in terms of earlier work in the 1860s and gives a developmental account for the whole of the evolutionary metaphysics

Finally, it is worth mentioning two papers which are sceptical of the overall relevance or cogency of Peirce's evolutionary cosmology. First, Walter Bryce Gallie's classic statement of scepticism about the cosmology is to be found in Chapter 9 of his 1952 book, *Peirce and Pragmatism*. Gallie offers a dated but still worthwhile account of Peirce's metaphysics even though he sees serious problems with it. Second is T.L. Short's recent paper, 'Did Peirce have a cosmology?' (2010).

This offers an interesting reading of the cosmology and suggests that Peirce in fact gave up on what quickly revealed itself to be a philosophical dead end.

Notes

1 See, for example, Esposito (1980) or Savan (1988).
2 See W8. xcvi.
3 A.J. Ayer (1968), for instance, thought Peirce's maxim was an anti-metaphysical forerunner to verificationism.
4 See CP6. 1–6. 5 (1898).
5 The term 'scientific metaphysics' is an interesting one. It is very often attributed to Peirce, and Volume 6 of the *Collected Papers* is called 'Scientific metaphysics', but so far as I can tell, Peirce never uses the term. All the same, it is common currency in the secondary literature.
6 See Sheriff (1994).
7 See Murphey (1961).
8 Peirce was aware of this tendency himself and referred to it later in his life as an affliction which should be called 'triadomany' (CP1. 568 (1910)).
9 Of course, Wittgenstein raised these worries to question the notion of ostensive definition, but the process of 'attending' to different things in the imagination here strikes me as a good example of how precision is meant to work.
10 See, for instance, his 1887 paper 'A guess at the riddle' (EP1. 245–279 (1887)).
11 See, for example, Quine (1954).
12 For those interested in the arguments in favour of Peirce's claims here, Burch (1991) is indispensable.
13 See, for example, Gallie (1952, 215), who notes that many Peirce scholars see the work as 'the black sheep' or 'white elephant' of his work.
14 Strictly speaking, Peirce offers these arguments as justifications or 'positive reasons' (CP6. 614 (1893)) for his account of tychism or absolute chance. We shall examine tychism in detail below, but given the role that tychism plays in the evolutionary picture, these reasons also explain what we need Peirce's entire cosmological picture for.
15 See NEM3. 780 (1899), for instance.
16 'A new commandment I give unto you, that ye love one another; as I have loved you, that ye also love one another' (John 13:34).
17 This point is also made in Gallie (1952, 225).
18 This same issue is explored by T.L. Short (2010, 534–535) and Bernard Suits (1979), amongst others.
19 See, for example, Goudge (1950) or Murphey (1961).
20 For instance, Esposito (1980) or Anderson (1995).

Seven
Influence

Introduction

How important a philosophical figure is C.S. Peirce? How influential is his work? These are questions of abiding interest to Peirce scholars, especially since we tend to see a disparity in the answers. On the one hand, Peirce's importance and philosophical ability tend to be widely recognised. Bertrand Russell judged him to be 'one of the most original minds of the later nineteenth century, and certainly the greatest American thinker ever' (Russell 1959, 276). Hilary Putnam states, 'I regard Peirce as a towering giant among American philosophers' (Putnam 1990, 252). Karl Popper declares Peirce 'the great American mathematician and physicist and, I believe, one of the greatest philosophers of all time' (Popper 1972, 212). High praise indeed. On the other hand, however, the extent of Peirce's influence is not nearly so clear cut. His work *is* influential, as we shall see below, but one cannot help feeling that Peirce's work is yet to be taken up to the extent that it should be, and that a rich and untapped vein of important Peircian ideas are yet to find their way into contemporary debates.

Such a claim may well sound dramatic, especially when we consider the extent of Peirce's influence in very simple terms. We have noted his founding role in the development of pragmatism, his importance in the rise of modern logic, his development of a pragmatist theory of truth and a forerunner of logical empiricism, his foundational role in semiotics, and so on. And these are just the areas we have focused on during the course of this book. There are areas we haven't mentioned, such as Peirce's views on science and his interest in the study of abductive reasoning, all of which are deeply influential. Of course, this influence isn't restricted to philosophy.

Robert Burch (2010), for instance, notes the many intriguing influences that Peirce's work has had on Russian and Soviet Union era computer science and information theory. Other interesting examples include anthropologists such as Milton Singer (1978), Michael Silverstein (1985) and Richard Parmentier (1994) using Peirce's semiotics to analyse the development of culture and communication in such diverse times and places as Micronesia and medieval Europe. Indeed, *Semiotic Anthropology,* the sub-discipline developed by these anthropologists, draws heavily and unapologetically on Peirce's work. Even in areas such as dance or music, we can find theorists who think that Peirce's work provides valuable insight. The late music theorist and violinist Naomi Cumming, for instance, makes use of Peirce's semiotics and his belief/doubt model of inquiry in her book, *The Sonic Self* (2000). We even find her making use of Peirce's early anti-Cartesianism to explain the intelligibility of musical experience (Cumming 2000, 58).[1] There are many more examples besides, but this is not our concern here. Rather, we are interested in how we can claim, in light of the obvious and broad influence that Peirce's work enjoys, that he may yet be under-appreciated or under-utilised in contemporary philosophical work.

It is, of course, rare that scholars of important historical figures in philosophy think there is no more insight to be had from that philosopher's work, but in the case of Peirce, there are areas of his philosophy that do seem to be genuinely under-explored or under-utilised. This harks back to the issues mentioned in Chapter 1 about the availability and accessibility of Peirce's work: we are still waiting for a published version of his entire body of philosophy, and the effect of his academic isolation makes interpreting what we do have a specialist's task. Consequently, as the primary literature emerges and the secondary literature deepens, we are gaining new insight into his ideas all the time. The further step of applying these ideas to the questions and problems that interest philosophers today, whilst a common endeavour, still needs careful handling. Peirce scholarship is healthy in its readiness to find new applications and influences for his work and ideas and equally ready to see where such exercises become procrustean, but we have room to be more evangelical than we are. What this means is that whilst we can see clear strands of influence for Peirce's work, there are also areas where further use of his ideas would prove fruitful, or where some Peircian development or turn in the research might be decisive or groundbreaking. As such, the exploration of Peirce's influence in this chapter will frequently include some suggestion of where a Peircian turn suggests promise, or where greater exploration of his work might have an important bearing on the directions of our current concerns.

In what follows, then, we shall chart where and how far Peirce's work influenced, and has continued to exert an influence on, some of the main areas we have covered in previous chapters. We shall begin by looking at how far he influences and remains significant in work on pragmatism. We shall then examine the influence of his accounts of truth and inquiry, before moving on to look at the influence of his semiotics in philosophy. We will then conclude with an examination of his work in logic. Throughout, we will draw attention not only to where Peirce influenced and influences work in philosophy, but also to the avenues for greater influence and relevance to contemporary work.

Pragmatism

Since Peirce is widely considered to be the founding father of pragmatism, it is unsurprising that we can find his work exerting a considerable influence in the various stages of the movement. Notably, though, Peirce's continued role in the pragmatist cannon is frequently subject to some controversy, and the extent of his influence is often in question. In what follows, we shall review Peirce's influence over three discernible stages, or waves, in the history of pragmatist philosophy: the first wave of classical pragmatism and the period directly after it; the second wave of neo-pragmatism characterised most prominently by the work of Richard Rorty and Hilary

Putnam; and a more recent third wave of pragmatism, christened 'new pragmatism' by Cheryl Misak.

The early influences

The most prominent influence Peirce's work on pragmatism has exerted is on the early and founding work of the movement. In the hands of James and Dewey, pragmatism became the predominant philosophical movement in American universities up until the rise of analytic philosophy from the 1930s onwards, and Peirce's influence is clear. However, pragmatism was not simply an American movement, and in Europe there were pragmatist schools of thought where Peirce's work exercised an influence. We shall look at Peirce's influence on pragmatism outside of the United States, but let's begin by looking at the extent of his influence on the work of James and Dewey.

As we saw in Chapter 1, James was quick to name Peirce as the foundational figure for pragmatist philosophy. In the second chapter of his seminal *Pragmatism: A New Name for Some Old Ways of Thinking*, he declares:

> It was first introduced into philosophy by Mr. Charles Peirce in 1878. In an article entitled 'How to Make Our Ideas Clear' in the 'Popular Science Monthly' for January of that year. (James 1907, 29)

We have already examined just how Peirce's maxim influenced James' pragmatism and how the pragmatic maxim became an approach to philosophy in the hands of James. This shift from a methodological tool to a philosophical outlook is what gives pragmatism its initial impetus as a philosophical movement, but of equal importance is that James' interpretation of the maxim drew a corresponding philosophical response from Peirce, giving us the later, more developed accounts of the pragmatic maxim examined in Chapter 2.

With regard to Dewey, the influence of Peirce's pragmatism is in many ways tempered by James' expansion of the pragmatic maxim. Dewey was well aware of the differences between the two founding figures' accounts of pragmatism,[2] and he certainly thought favourably of Peirce's account of the maxim. Nonetheless, Dewey saw pragmatism as being more than a mere methodological tool. His own expansion of pragmatism, which he preferred to call 'instrumentalism', was perhaps much closer to Peirce than it was to James,[3] but it drew upon Peirce's work on inquiry and scientific progress far more than it drew upon the pragmatic maxim. For his part, Peirce was aware of Dewey's work – indeed, Dewey was briefly a student of Peirce's at Johns Hopkins in the 1880s – but was troubled by some of the more psychologistic and descriptivist tendencies in Dewey's program. All the same, Peirce's presence in the philosophical thinking of the early pragmatists is clear.

As we mentioned, though, the seeds of pragmatism took hold outside of the United States too, and there were early, prominent exponents of pragmatism in Europe. In Great Britain, for instance, the Oxford philosopher F.C.S. Schiller developed a humanist account of pragmatism but thought Peirce to be committed to a 'narrower', less useful version of the theory. Schiller also thought Peirce's work irrelevant to the movement in virtue of his [Peirce's] 'extensive inability to follow the later developments' (Schiller 1907/1912, 5). Elsewhere in Europe, though, Peirce's work was taken more seriously.

Also around the turn of the century, a group of young, politically active Italian philosophers in Florence self-identified as pragmatists. James had a particular influence over many of these Italian pragmatists, Giovanni Papini and Giuseppe Prezzolini being the most prominent, but other important figures in the Florentine School were deeply influenced by Peirce's pragmatism. Giovanni Vailati and Mario Calderoni were especially taken with Peirce's methodological and scientific approach. Sadly, the Italian school of pragmatism as a whole burned out quickly, with the Peircian-influenced arm of the Florence school curtailed by the early deaths of Vailati in 1909 and Calderoni in 1914.

Although there are many other examples of the early influence of Peirce's pragmatism, two are especially instructive and interesting: its influence on the work of economist Thorstein Veblen and philosopher C.I. Lewis. Peirce's influence on Veblen and Lewis is important since it shows how, even early on, his philosophical work bridges the gap into other disciplines, and also how it comes to be viewed as more amenable or commensurate with the sensibilities of analytic philosophers.

Thorstein Veblen studied logic under Peirce at Johns Hopkins in 1881 after enrolling at the university the previous year to take a doctorate in philosophy. Veblen is best known for his work *The Theory of the Leisure Class* and the concept of 'conspicuous consumption'. Although Veblen never explicitly references Peirce, the Peircian and pragmatist overtones of much of his work are very clear, and scholars have spent considerable time tracing out the precise influence of Peirce on Veblen's work.[4]

C.I. Lewis, on the other hand, worked at Harvard and was given an office in 1920 next to Peirce's papers, partly in the hope that he might perform some of the editorial work that the manuscripts so badly needed. Lewis is an important figure in terms of the development of logic and as a bridging figure between the older pragmatist tradition of Peirce, James and Dewey and some of the newer, more pragmatically minded analytic philosophers that so dominated American philosophy from the 1930s onwards; Willard Van Orman Quine and Nelson Goodman both studied with Lewis during their time at Harvard, for instance. Moreover, Lewis speaks candidly of the influence of Peirce's pragmatism upon his work:

> [I]t became my duty and privilege to turn over the numerous papers of Charles Peirce. Though I was not specially conscious of it, this was perhaps the means of stirring up old thoughts of the time when I had listened to James, and reminding me also of what Royce used to call his 'absolute pragmatism. [. . .] Peirce's 'conceptual pragmatism', turning as it does upon the instrumental and empirical significance of concepts rather than upon any non-absolute character of truth, was at some points consonant with my own reflections where James and Dewey were not. (Lewis 1970, 12)

What all this amounts to is the simple observation that Peirce's influence is clearly discernible during the early life of pragmatism. As pragmatism's prominence in the academic landscape began to wane during the 1940s and 1950s, however, so too did Peirce's centrality to the movement, so much so that by the time pragmatism re-emerged through the work of Richard Rorty in the 1980s and Hilary Putnam in the 1990s, Peirce is considered as a secondary influence at best.

The second wave

A common assumption is that pragmatism was simply left behind in the growing professionalization of philosophy in the early twentieth century and was replaced by analytic philosophy. Whilst this isn't an entirely accurate picture – pragmatism tempered the views of many important analytic figures – it is true that it did not predominate in the way it once had. However, from the late 1970s onwards pragmatism came to prominence again in a series of debates and exchanges focused mainly on the work of Richard Rorty and Hilary Putnam. And whilst both Rorty and Putnam were keen to draw connections between their work and the insights of the classical pragmatists, neither claimed a strong inheritance from Peirce. Indeed, with the exception of important neo-pragmatists such as Susan Haack and Nicholas Rescher, very few pragmatists of the second wave looked beyond James and Dewey when claiming forerunners for their view.[5]

Rorty and Putnam

Of the two prominent figures, Rorty is perhaps the least sympathetic to claims for Peirce's influence or relevance. We have already seen that Rorty suggests Peirce's best claim to being a pragmatist is to have given the movement a name and to have influenced William James. Rorty gives clear reasons for this rejection of Peirce's influence and relevance to the second wave of pragmatism. In part, he sees Peirce's philosophy as being in some measure responsible for the wider neglect of James and Dewey, especially since he takes analytic philosophers to be overly impressed with Peirce's work in logic and to take the mistaken view that his semiotics is a prescient attempt to place language at the centre of philosophy (Rorty 1982, 160–161).

More importantly, though, Rorty sees Peirce as being deeply traditionalist and committed to the view that philosophy promises us an absolute answer, 'a view from nowhere'. Peircian pragmatism, then, simply could not feature in Rorty's linguistic pragmatism and the reconstruction of philosophy that followed from it.

Putnam, on the other hand, is far more sympathetic to Peirce and, as we have noted, sees him as a 'towering giant among American philosophers'. Nonetheless, where Putnam's pragmatism takes ideas from the classical pragmatists, it is primarily from James. For example, Putnam describes himself as attempting to give an epistemic model of truth, but he clearly disavows any interest in pursuing the kind of project Peirce was interested in (Putnam 1990, 223). Rather, he sees his project as continuing and scrutinising issues concerning

> the relationship of truth, warranted assertability, permanent credibility, what, if anything, inquiry must converge to if conducted the right way etc. – [all issues which] figure today in books and papers by the Putnams, Michael Dummett, Nelson Goodman, Richard Rorty, and Bernard Williams. (Putnam 1995, 11)

For Putnam, though, all of these philosophers are engaging with pragmatism in a Jamesian, not a Peircian, manner, often unintentionally. Whilst there is some argument about how Peircian Putnam really is, it is clear that, like many pragmatists of the second wave, he sees a narrow range of relevance for Peirce.

The third wave

Although the reprisal found in the neo-pragmatist work of Rorty and Putnam never really died down, there has been another more recent surge of interest in pragmatism. Philosophers such as Robert Brandom and Huw Price have increasingly expressed a willingness to describe themselves as pragmatists and to pursue important pragmatist themes in their work. Cheryl Misak has called this third wave of pragmatism 'new pragmatism', and we can see it as marked by two things. First, it recognises (not always intentionally) the key insights of the early pragmatists, especially their anti-metaphysical and anti-representational sensibilities, and second, it is marked by the notion that our philosophical inquiries have to be confined by and answerable to human concerns. However, unlike second wave pragmatists, who are also sympathetic to these views, new pragmatism finds Rorty's reconstruction of philosophy unsettling. Rorty would dismiss the concern with objective elements of inquiry such as truth or reality as quixotic; new pragmatists are inclined to think that the pursuit of objective answers and properly domesticated concepts of truth and reality are as much a human concern as any other element of inquiry. The second feature of much new pragmatist work is that the body of philosophers it claims as relevant and influential are often not card-carrying pragmatists. We find Wittgenstein, Ramsey, Hegel, Bernard Williams, Wilfrid Sellars, Heidegger and many others treated as the most relevant influences for third wave pragmatists.

In terms of the relevance and influence of Peirce in this third wave, however, these two features prove to be interesting. On the one hand, philosophy as bound down in human inquiry but with a commitment to the pursuit of truth (appropriately explicated) is deeply Peircian. Of course, it is more in line with Peirce's views on inquiry and truth than with his pragmatic maxim per se, but it is Peircian nonetheless. On the other hand, the recognised canon of the third wave sidelines Peirce in favour of philosophers that we would barely recognise as pragmatists at all. It looks as though Peirce should be clearly relevant to the third wave, but for many he is absent.

What further role for Peircian pragmatism?

An interesting feature of the foregoing survey of Peirce's influence over the various waves of pragmatism is that he is in many respects sidelined. James, though deeply influenced by Peirce's ideas, took them in a direction that was counter to Peirce's intentions. No sooner had James drawn attention to Peirce's place as a central figure in the tradition than we find Schiller sidelining him as 'pre-pragmatic' and narrow. In the great second wave revival of pragmatism, Rorty sees no place at all for Peirce in the pragmatist pantheon; Putnam is more welcoming but places James and Dewey ahead of him. And even in the third wave, work by such central figures as Robert Brandom and Huw Price more or less bypasses Peirce's philosophy. Of course, there have always been important pragmatists who are Peircian and see pragmatism as a movement that needs the influence of Peirce. All the same, I think it is not unfair to say that pragmatism and pragmatists have been less influenced by Peirce than by James or Dewey or even Wittgenstein. Before moving on to look at Peirce's influence in other areas, however, it is worth pausing to say something about where more Peircian pragmatist strands are emerging, especially in relation to third wave pragmatism.

There are, in fact, many ways in which we might suggest some fruitful outcomes for a strongly Peircian turn in third wave pragmatism. This is to be expected since, as Jeffrey Stout notes, this most recent approach to questions of pragmatism, whilst according 'some kind of philosophical priority to human practices', tries to formulate its approaches 'in a way that makes sense of the ways in which inquirers show concern for things distinct from themselves and from the practices in which they engage' (Stout 2007, 8–9). This is very Peircian, and Stout rightly notes that many would see Peirce as pursuing pragmatism in just this vein (Stout 2007, 29 fn 9).[6] For our purposes, though, we shall note just two interesting strands of research connecting Peirce to the third wave.

The first interesting strand comes from work connecting Peirce's pragmatism to what we might call 'Cambridge pragmatism'. To elaborate, an especially interesting strand of the most recent incarnation of pragmatism attaches closely to philosophers and philosophy at Cambridge University. The expressivism of Simon Blackburn and, more importantly, what is sometimes called the subject naturalism of Huw Price is central to this branch of the pragmatist third wave that we looked at above. Moreover, much of this work draws on, or runs parallel to, the research of an earlier generation of Cambridge philosophers including Ludwig Wittgenstein and Frank Ramsey. Intriguingly, there has always been an interest amongst Peirce scholars about just how deep the connections between Peirce and the early Cambridge philosophers run.

Speculation by Charles Hardwick (1979) or Jaime Nubiola (1996), for instance, is quite typical of the suggestion that Peirce could have had a deep influence on the more pragmatist themes in the work of the later Wittgenstein and F.P. Ramsey.[7] In terms of the future influence of Peircian pragmatism, however, recent developments, especially in the work of Cheryl Misak, promise to make both historical and future philosophically significant connections clear. Recent explorations by Misak of Peirce's influence on Ramsey, and the potential this has for our understanding of contemporary pragmatist questions of truth and inquiry, promises to reintroduce a strongly Peircian turn to the most recent return to pragmatism.

The second interesting strand, though in a sense more promissory than Misak's work on the Cambridge connection, comes from Catherine Legg's work drawing connections between Peirce's early anti-Cartesianism and Robert Brandom's inferentialism. In the work that gave rise to Peirce's early account of thought-signs and infinite semiosis, as well as proto-statements of his pragmatic maxim[8] from the 1860s, Legg sees a form of what she calls 'hyper-inferentialism' – the claim that all mental content is inferential rather than referential. Brandom's own form of inferentialism adopts a slightly weaker position, allowing that some content is non-inferential. Robert Brandom's inferentialist program marks an especially prominent form of third wave pragmatism, and if Legg's work here is right, then there is clear scope for a Peircian contribution to this approach to pragmatism.

Truth and inquiry

The next interesting area in charting Peirce's influence and relevance is with his account of truth and inquiry. In some ways, it can be artificial to look at how Peirce's views here influence contemporary accounts of truth without also considering his influence on pragmatism. As we've seen, pragmatists tend to see accounts of truth and inquiry as more important to their views than any examination of methodological principles such as Peirce's 'maxim'. Nonetheless, to keep matters reasonably discrete, we'll leave pragmatism aside here and focus more centrally on theories of truth and just how far Peirce's account has any influence on them. As we shall see, the account of truth from Peirce's work has not been taken up very widely, and in part because of either mischaracterisation or limited readings, it is seen as unpromising.

Peirce is, of course, a pragmatist. His account of truth first emerges from a pragmatist explication of reality, and so we see what is in effect a pragmatist account of truth. However, it is well known that pragmatist accounts have a poor reputation, and for the most part they have been sidelined in ongoing research into the nature of truth. Even when they are not mischaracterised as permitting us to believe whatever useful thing takes our fancy, there is still a widespread uneasiness about the close identification of truth with epistemic constraints such as those found in Peirce's account – that truth is the belief found at the end of an inquiry carried sufficiently far. Even those who think there is something importantly epistemic about truth find the Peircian view unconvincing, and we have in Chapter 3 already noted Crispin Wright's concerns about Peirce's account. And as we have noted above, even Hilary Putnam, who many take to be giving a Peircian account of truth,[9] considers Peirce's approach to be wrong. For Putnam, it is acceptable to view truth as an idealisation of such notions of warranted assertion, but Peirce's view commits him to what Putnam calls the 'One Complete and Consistent Theory of Everything', an idealist's 'Utopian fantasy' which is unnecessary for pragmatist theorising about truth (Putnam 1990, 223). The problem, though, is that this all sells Peirce's views on truth short.

As we saw in Chapter 3, Peirce's early statements about truth are under-described and leave room for all kinds of potential problems. Later developments to the account of truth and inquiry, however, show numerous subtleties that bypass many of those problems. Indeed, properly understood, Peirce's later, more developed views on truth ought to show how unfounded much of the uneasiness expressed by Putnam or Wright really is. But sadly, Peirce is forever associated with the early picture of truth given in his *Popular Science Monthly* papers of the 1870s.

Peirce's ongoing influence upon debates about the nature of truth, then, has been restricted largely as a result of taking too limited a view of his account. For those of a non-pragmatist persuasion, he is too much the pragmatist and his identification of the truth with the fruits of human endeavour is problematic. For those more inclined towards the pragmatist view of truth, Peirce associates truth too closely with an independent state of things which lies beyond the limit of human practice. For Wright, it relies on our being in an epistemic state that we could never know has obtained (Wright 2001); for Putnam, it relies on our attaining a fantastical state which contains the truth about every single question (Putnam 1990).

All of this suggests that Peirce's views of truth aren't influential at all. However, it is important to note that in recent years there has been important clarificatory work on Peirce's views of truth and inquiry, and that with this careful charting out of the Peircian territory there is now the possibility of a fertile re-engagement with his ideas. Just to give the clearest examples of recent attempts to reinvigorate Peirce's account of truth, we can point to important work by Mark Migotti, Christopher Hookway and Cheryl Misak, all of whom provide clear reasons for taking a Peircian approach to truth seriously.

Migotti (1998), for instance, gives a careful analysis of Peirce's views on truth, considering many of the later developments to his account and suggesting that Peirce's account, properly analysed, is a 'double-aspect' view of truth – making truth a matter importantly *independent* of us and yet essentially *accessible* to us. If Migotti is right, then those of an anti-pragmatist disposition can re-engage with Peirce's view since it is 'compatible with a robustly "realist" acknowledgement that the realm of truth might well outstrip the realm of possible human knowledge' (Migotti 1998, 76). Similar points are made by Hookway (2004a), whose careful charting of the development of Peirce's views shows reason for thinking realists and pragmatists alike have been far too quick to set Peircian accounts aside.

Where we can see Migotti as providing grounds for the 'realist' to engage with Peirce and Hookway as giving reason to think pragmatists such as Putnam or Brandom should re-engage, work by Cheryl Misak (1991) suggests clear grounds for those who identify truth with an epistemic constraint to take a Peircian view seriously. Along with Hookway, Misak's work on Peirce's theory of truth has pushed our understanding of his views to a point where it is no longer acceptable to merely identify Peirce's account with the platitudes of the *Popular Science Monthly* papers. Most interesting here, though, is the clear case she makes for thinking that certain minimalist views of truth, especially those of Crispin Wright, are much more in line with Peirce's account than most would seem to think. Indeed, her arguments make it clear that there is an obvious, albeit unacknowledged, Peircian strand of argument alive and well in many minimalist approaches to truth. Moreover, Misak's careful tracing of the connections between pragmatism and deflationist approaches offers the clearest avenue of contemporary relevance for Peirce yet.

In a recent paper (2007), Misak offers a pragmatic account of truth drawing directly from Peirce's approach to truth and inquiry. In that account, Misak stakes out clear grounds for a Peircian contribution to the debate on truth along the lines of deflationary theories. As she notes, the deflationary platitudes of minimalist, prosententialist and disquotationalist accounts of truth are given similar treatment in Peirce's work, where it is clear that our engagement with truth should not aspire to giving a *theory* of truth, but instead should aim at merely giving an explication of truth. As Misak notes, though, beyond the various expressions of this deflationary platitude, we find missing or unsatisfactory attempts to work out a series of important questions which remain – most notably, how we account for our assertoric practices and the connections between truth and practice. For many deflationists, to note the thinness of truth is to do all that we need to do, but for the Peircian, this is to stop well short of answering the important questions about truth. This line of research, extending a deflationary approach beyond the deflationary platitude is, I would contend, an area of real interest and one where Peirce's account or a broadly Peircian sensibility can do much work. As Misak notes:

> Peirce's project of getting leverage on the concept of truth by exploring its connections with practice is the project we must engage in. Not only does it give us an account of truth that best

makes sense of the full range of practices concerning assertion, belief, reason giving, and inquiry, but it makes sense of and promises some headway in our long-standing philosophical debates about realism and anti-realism. (Misak 2007, 88)

As we generate clearer views of Peirce's accounts of truth and inquiry and their development in his later work, applications such as Misak's will become more prominent and more numerous. There are many other avenues for Peirce's accounts to become involved in these debates in ways that do justice to his philosophical work on truth. It strikes me that we are only now emerging from the delete-rious and restrictive effects that limited readings and stalking-horse renderings of his accounts have had on the prominence and influence of his views.

Signs

In terms of influence exercised in philosophy, the situation with Peirce's semiotics is perhaps even more perplexing than it is with pragmatism or truth. In the appraisal of Peirce's importance to prag-matism mentioned above, Rorty suggests that Peirce's standing with analytic philosophers is high, primarily because his semiotics is taken to be a forerunner of a language-first philosophy. Yet amongst ana-lytic philosophers, and especially analytic philosophers of language, his sign theory is hardly taken up at all. What is clear to most Peirce scholars, though, is that the sign theory holds enormous promise and potential for dealing with many of the problems and questions of contemporary analytic philosophy of language and mind.

The lack of engagement from mainstream analytic philosophy with Peirce's semiotic can be divided into two broad stripes – virtual neglect and unhelpful selectiveness. Moreover, I think we can see the two areas of mainstream analytic philosophy one would most likely expect to engage with Peirce's semiotics – the philosophy of language and the philosophy of mind – as adopting precisely these two attitudes. In the philosophy of language, one sees virtual neglect everywhere; in the philosophy of mind, one occasionally sees some unhelpful selectiveness. As such, much of what we shall suggest below points at the areas where Peirce's semiotic can do more work and seems to offer interesting new approaches to long-standing problems in the philosophy of language and mind. But before we look at these areas of possible influence and relevance, it is perhaps worth pausing over the question of why Peirce's semiotics is either absent or only anaemically present in much analytic philosophy of mind and language. Two answers or reasons present themselves.

In his recent and important introduction to Peirce's semiotic, T.L. Short (2007) opens his book with the following observation:

> Peirce's theory of signs, or semiotic, misunderstood by so many, has gotten in amongst the wrong crowd. It has been taken up by an interdisciplinary army of 'semioticians', whose views and aims are antithetical to Peirce's own. (Short 2007, ix)

Short's statement is controversial in so far as most of the people engaging with Peirce's semiotic do so from beyond the disciplinary borders of philosophy, and their enterprises are made no less respectable by that. Nonetheless, Short's observation picks up on something important: semiotics and the study of signs is something that is strongly associated with non-analytic modes of philosophy. From the viewpoint of mainstream analytic philosophers, then, Peirce's semiotic is part of the stock-in-trade of 'the wrong crowd', and as Short goes on to suggest, the effect on sign theory is that 'it has been shunned by those philosophers who are working in Peirce's own spirit on the very problems to which his semiotic was addressed' (Short 2007, ix). One reason for the lack of engagement, then, is a perception problem.

A second reason, I would contend, is the preferred tools and machinery of contemporary analytic philosophy of language and mind. Indeed, the case in the philosophy of language is quite instructive. Just as with modern logic, there has been a long-standing preoccupation with the tools and methodology of Frege in the philosophy of language. Even those who have rejected his 'descriptivism' have carried on with a set on constraints and conditions that are distinctively Fregean and which have contributed in many ways to the sidelining of a Peircian semiotic approach. For instance, the Fregean approach to philosophy of language takes itself to be mapping the connections between words and the world and has little truck with the vagaries of language users and minds. In the context of such a sensibility, a semantic framework that incorporates an interpretant and makes meaning a broadly triadic and inferential matter looks as though it is engaged in an altogether different enterprise. In short, with a century of Russellian and Fregean machinery in place, Peirce's semiotic simply doesn't look like 'normal science'.

Semiotics and the philosophy of language

Having already suggested that the influence of Peirce's semiotic in philosophy is characterised by a lack of engagement, and that in the philosophy of language that lack of engagement is characterised by virtual neglect, I still think it is worth emphasising that this is one area where it is clear that the relevance of Peirce's work is yet to be properly explored. There are traces of recognition that Peirce's interests overlap with some of our more recent philosophical concerns, and that he even offered proto-accounts of phenomena that concern contemporary philosophers of language. For instance, there is a general awareness that Peirce originated the terms 'index' and 'indexical' and may even have had a theory that runs close to Hans Reichenbach's account of token-reflexivity.[10] But the real promise of Peirce's semiotic doesn't come from such piecemeal nods to history. Instead, it is through the many key differences in approach that Peirce's work holds such promise.

We have already noted that in the Russellian and Fregean idiom Peirce's work can look strange, but this strange appearance is often founded on important differences. For instance, an attempt to bypass the vagaries of language use not only leads Frege to avoid any talk of minds and users, but also leads to an artificial abstraction towards a perfect language. This often tends to generate a picture of meaning and semantics as *static* – we theorise about language from idealised snapshots. This runs counter to what is perhaps the greatest insight to be had from Peircian semiotics, that meaning and language as expressed through signs and symbols are *dynamic*. Or as Peirce puts it, *symbols grow*:

> Symbols grow. They come into being by development out of other signs [...]. If a man makes a new symbol, it is by thought involving concepts. So it is only out of symbols that a new symbol can grow. [...] A symbol once in being, spreads among the peoples. In use and in experience, its meaning grows. (EP2. 10 (1898))

This dynamic picture imbues Peirce's semiotics with a range of machinery and theory for solving or dissolving many of the problems that analytic philosophers of language have occupied themselves with. Indeed, there is plenty of Peirce scholarship exploring Peircian answers to the perennial problems of the philosophy of language. For example, David Boersema (2002, 2009) and David Agler (2011) have explored the relationship between Peirce's semiotic and the *direct reference* or *causal theories* of names and meaning, showing that Peirce is able to give compelling solutions to problems such as empty reference, or reference determination. Similarly, Atkin (2008a) suggests how Peircian semiotic can be used to solve the *problem of cognitive significance*, or *Frege's problem*, as it is sometimes called. Key to all of these putative solutions, however, is the dynamic element of Peirce's semiotic.

Mainstream analytic philosophers of language have, of course, realised that by moving away from some of the core presuppositions of the field there are insights to be had. We have long seen attempts to include and accommodate language *use* within our accounts of meaning, and approaches which emphasise the dynamic, informational and communicational aspects of meaning and language are common. It seems clear, then, that Peirce's semiotic ought to be brought to bear on some of these discussions and developments. Indeed, two recent and interesting accounts of meaning from within the body of traditional philosophy of language show remarkably Peircian sensitivities and are worth brief comment.

John Perry's critical referentialism (Perry 2001) takes its cue from Peirce-inspired work by Arthur Burks (1949) and develops a multi-propositional account of meaning. As an account of meaning, it is both Peircian and fit for further development along Peircian lines.[11] Similarly, François Recanati's recent book, *Mental Files* (Recanati 2012), attempts to recast traditional debates in the philosophy of language by giving what he calls an *indexical model* of meaning. In that account, mental informational files take the central role in his account of non-descriptivist meaning. Recanati himself places Kaplan, Reichenbach *and Peirce* (Recanati 2012, 58–59) at the heart of this indexical model, but the informational picture is perhaps more Peircian than even he seems aware. Again, this contemporary account is fit for further Peircian development and an exploration of Peirce's potential relevance.

Cognitive science and the philosophy of mind

In terms of the philosophy of mind, Peirce's semiotic seems especially useful, and the generation of an account of thought and mind was one of the primary purposes that he had intended for his account of signs. Indeed, as T.L. Short notes, primary amongst the 'problems to which his semiotic was addressed' was 'to construct a naturalistic but nonreductive account of the human mind' (Short 2007, ix). Unsurprisingly, then, there has been a wealth of work connecting Peirce's sign theory to the problems of cognition and mind, but they come from outside the discipline of philosophy. Newer disciplinary approaches such as *bio-semiotics* and *cognitive semiotics* take Peirce's work, amongst that of others, and address many of the questions that are familiar to us from Peirce's work and from the contemporary mind sciences. Although there are philosophers amongst this group of interdisciplinary researchers, it is not a body of work which mainstream philosophers are broadly engaged with. We have already speculated about the reasons for this and it doesn't pay to continue the lament, but the presence of such work makes it quite clear that many see something fruitful in Peirce's sign theory.

Within the narrow confines of mainstream analytic philosophy of mind, things are not very much different from within the philosophy of language; there is some recognition that Peirce generated some terms and maybe even had the beginnings of theory here and there, but that is all. The nearest and clearest uses are from philosophers, such as Ruth Millikan, who take a teleosemantic approach to questions of mind. Indeed, allusions to Millikan's Peircianism are quite common, and her adoption of a more tripartite analysis of representation draws comparison with Peirce's own sign/object/interpretant account of signs. Nonetheless, it is clear that even the best of the teleosemanticists don't draw nearly so heavily on Peirce as they might, and Peirce scholars have produced interesting suggestions for where more fruitful engagement is to be had. For instance, one of T.L. Short's main aims in his recent book has been to improve mainstream engagement with Peirce's semiotic, and he devotes work to elaborating possible connections with the work of Millikan and others (Short 2007, 303–309).

Similarly, there seems to be a much greater openness to engagement with Peirce amongst the growing stream of cognitive scientists looking for useful models of representation. The most well-known example is Terrence Deacon (1997), who uses Peirce's icon/index/symbol division of signs to explain the emergence of symbolic communication and the co-evolution of language and brain. According to Deacon, we see iconic representation in such instances of animal communication as camouflage and indexical representation in such instances as vervet monkey calls, and whilst neither of these are instances of symbolic communication, their iconic and indexical structure are part of the scaffolding that leads to the symbolic communication one sees in human language. Although there are differences in the precise use of Peirce's theories, we see other examples in the work of Barbara Von Eckardt (1993) and even William Ramsey (2007). However, the primary focus across all of this work seems to remain the icon/index/symbol trichotomy.

It is encouraging that cognitive scientists see some value in Peirce's model of representation, especially given its potential to provide a unifying model for all kinds of communicative interaction and informational exchange. Nonetheless, it seems obvious, especially in light of what we know about the breadth and depth of Peirce's model of semiotics, that taking only one very small trichotomic division from his work is unnecessarily limiting. The potential for a broader engagement and for exploring the relevance of Peirce's wider accounts of semiotic to the mind sciences is quite clear.

Logic

The final area of relevance and influence we shall examine is Peirce's account of logic. Of course, we have already seen that his achievements in logic are remarkable, deeply influential and still relevant, but in many ways the story of Peirce's influence and relevance in logic is one of the clearest instances of just why these questions are so fraught. Here we have an example of someone whose work stands at the heart of the development of modern logic, who developed many of its key ideas and tools, who is widely recognised for making these contributions, and who is still arguably under-valued and his ideas under-used. We have already seen that Peirce's contribution is under-valued, in large part because the orthodox history of the rise of modern logic sidelines the Boolean approach that he was conversant in. Moreover, we have seen that his diagrammatic approach to logic was described by Quine as an apagogic confirmation of a more conventional symbolic approach (Quine 1935, 552). This is strong condemnation by one of the most influential founding figures of analytic philosophy. Little wonder, then, that for all of his important achievements, Peirce's work in logic was and still is under-appreciated.

In what follows, we shall examine Peirce's influence and the opportunity for increased engagement by looking first at his graphical or diagrammatic logic and then at his algebraic work. It may seem obvious from what we have already said in Chapter 5 how this narrative is likely to go. The algebraic logic, under-appreciated but deeply influential, is now more or less quarried out as modern logic moves well beyond its beginnings in the age of formalisation and quantification; the graphical logic is far from influential but is ripe for new insight and engagement. Although this is true to a degree, we shall see that Peirce's graphical logic is already exerting some influence and showing relevance, and the algebraic logic is far from quarried out.

The influence and potential of the graphs

Ordinarily, Peirce's graphical logic is thought of as lacking in influence, often pursued only by those with esoteric interests in (re) invigorating under-explored areas of his work. Many of the landmarks in the interpretation of his graphical logic make it clear why such a view has prevailed. We waited thirty to forty years after the publication of the Collected Papers for in-depth and well-informed treatments of the existential graphs to begin to appear in the work of Donald Roberts (Roberts 1973) and J.J. Zeman (1964). Prior to that, Peirce's graphs laboured under the influence of Quine's quick dismissal, as we noted, and also struggled with a peculiarly poor reception from such important Peirce scholars as Thomas Goudge. Indeed, Goudge's reaction to the existential graphs is, I suspect, still quite pervasive:

> One can hardly avoid the conclusion that in the end Peirce permitted his graphs to become [. . .] a 'plaything'. The fascination they exerted led to a steady increase in their internal complexity, without any corresponding increase in their positive results. (Goudge 1950, 119)

Understandably, this leads to the view that the graphical logic showed no obvious lines of influence and presented no grounds for future relevance. Despite this, there are two clear avenues of influence where we see Peirce's work on graphical logic having an effect. The first is more philosophically oriented and the second more a matter of logic and its application.

In terms of philosophically oriented work on the existential graphs, certain Peirce scholars are attempting to reapply that work back to questions of philosophical concern. For instance, a central piece of Ahti-Veikko Pietarinen's recent work (Pietarinen 2006b) is to make use of Peirce's graphical logic to explain his game-theoretical and semiotic reading of meaning and language. Along similar lines, Frederik Stjernfelt (Stjernfelt 2007) uses the existential graphs to model an account of diagrammatic reasoning and thought to answer questions in semiotics and phenomenology, amongst other things. And whilst this philosophical application of Peirce's graphical logic is growing, a more clearly established area of application and influence is to be found in work on logic and its application.

Whilst we have noted that it took time for full-length treatments of Peirce's existential graphs to appear, there were earlier, shorter treatments that gave reasonable accounts of the work. More interesting, though, is that they tended to come from researchers interested in logic and machine reasoning rather than from Peirce scholars. Martin Gardner's (1958) *Logic Machines and Diagrams*, for instance, shows an interest in some of Peirce's extensions to Venn's system of diagrams and gives a quick and tentative account of the existential graphs. Whilst Gardner's own view of the diagrams is perhaps closer to that of Goudge, it is clear that from the viewpoint of alternative accounts of reasoning and information processing, Peirce's work looks interesting. Indeed, we often find Peirce's graphs mentioned in interdisciplinary work on diagrammatic reasoning,[12] and interesting cases have been made for Peirce's existential graphs offering contributions to debates on visual processing (Shin 2002, Chapter 1) and the representation of knowledge and discourse (Sowa 2000).

Whilst these contributions, influences and grounds for relevance do not mirror the impact of his algebraic logic, they certainly suggest that, as unorthodox as the existential graphs may seem, they are not the lost and uncharted feature of Peirce's logic that they sometimes appear to be. Rather, they have had some influence, and the possibility of finding genuine insight from them for areas such as game-theoretic logic, formal accounts of visual processing, diagrammatic reasoning, and the representation of knowledge systems is not lost on the wider intellectual community. There is much work to be done here and, certainly, greater influence to be had, but we are at a point with the existential graphs where some of the old prejudices are falling away and much of the excellent work done in the area over the last fifty years is finally being recognised in broader terms.

The scope for algebraic work

The algebraic logic, of course, is in many senses the best testament to Peirce's enduring value as a philosopher and thinker. We have already listed the many discoveries and firsts, examined the profound influence he exerted on the rise of modern logic, and gestured at some of the many areas where the promise of further pre-emption of crucial ideas in modern logic glimmer beneath the idiosyncrasies that fill his manuscripts. But there is an approach to the work on algebraic logic, best exemplified by Randall Dipert, that cautions us to pause for a moment and reassess just where this need to hammer home Peirce's significance comes from and what it does to future work on Peirce's algebraic logic. The worry, as Dipert sees it, is simply that the need to establish Peirce's primacy in the founding of modern logic manages to distract us from the very real task of examining how his approach to matters of logic might provide new insights. As Dipert puts it:

> Many, including myself, have been especially interested in Peirce as logical discoverer, and strains of this motivation are evident in much work on Peirce, with a sometimes fevered attempt to establish his [Peirce's] place in the pantheon of logical greats still dominated by Frege, Cantor, Russell, and others. [...] Yet I do not now see enormous benefits or value in this line of inquiry. (Dipert 1995, 32–33)

And in a more recent paper (Dipert 2004), Dipert picks up on this concern and notes that, in many ways, we have been lulled into a false sense of security by our extensive understanding of Peirce's algebraic logic and the increased recognition that Peirce is well placed in the pantheon of logical greats:

> Even if its details are now relatively clear, do we yet grasp the leading ideas of Peirce's logic and philosophy? Have we thoroughly examined them, and extended them as our own exercise in doing philosophy? I do not think so. [...][T]here is some truth to the claim that the most important work on Peirce's logical philosophy remains to be done. (Dipert 2004, 318–319)

My sense is that Dipert's attitude here is entirely correct. Work on uncovering and establishing the importance of Peirce's work in algebraic logic has been hugely important, but seeing widespread recognition of Peirce's significance in the founding of modern mathematical logic can easily give us the sense that our work here is done. The influence and importance is traced out, his significance is assured – what is left to be done? But, in fact, we have to be aware that Peirce arrived at many of his ideas about the nature of logic from a very different set of philosophical starting points.

We noted in Chapter 5 that much of what Peirce says about logic can seem warm and familiar – he is anti-psychologistic, he sees logic as normative, he is anti-logicist but draws deep connections between logic and mathematics – but beneath the surface, these views rest on some strange and unfamiliar ideas. The connection between logic and semiotic, for instance, is something that we can all too easily pass over as though it is of no great importance. Similarly, the underlying role of architectonic structures on determining the normativity of logic or the dependence of logic upon mathematics are often passed over in silence once we have established that the surface-level ideas aren't too far away from, say, familiar Fregean themes. But these connections between familiar surface-level claims and the deeper, underlying philosophy are perhaps more important than we have credited, and we should be turning now to an examination of them. Indeed, it seems clear that an examination of these areas could well yield new avenues of research and relevance for Peirce's logic.

There is no space here to trace out what such work would look like, but certain questions do present themselves as ready areas of study and promising sources of further insight from Peirce's logic. Dipert, for instance, notes that the famous Peircian reduction thesis (Dipert 2004, 319) – the claim that all relations of a higher adicity than three can be reduced to three-placed relations – though well known thanks to such work as that by Burch (1991), is still given less attention that it deserves. Dipert also notes the need to properly explore the source of Peirce's anti-logicism (Dipert 2004, 318), and I would suggest that related to this is the need to explore Peirce's suggestive claims about the connections between metaphysics, logic and mathematics:

Metaphysics in its turn is gradually and surely taking on the character of a logic. And finally logic seems destined to become more and more converted into mathematics. (EP2. 39 (1898))

Clearly, there is much more work we can do in relation to Peirce's algebraic logic. It is true that in many ways his contribution to logic is the crowning glory of his work, and such claims would no doubt have been a source of great pleasure to him, but it would be a mistake to think that there is little else left to glean in his logical work.

Conclusions

It may seem that as a conclusion to a book on a significant historical figure, the message of this chapter is a curious one. The founding father of pragmatism is not nearly so influential amongst second and third wave pragmatists as he should be; his distinctive accounts of truth and inquiry seem to have either been lumped into a pastiche of the pragmatist view or dismissed because of our realist sensibilities about lost facts; his account of signs is neglected by philosophers of language and used in an unhelpfully selective way by philosophers of mind; his graphical logic is rich with ideas but under-used; his achievements in algebraic logic have lulled us into a false sense of security and important research needs taking up with fresh vigour. There are also numerous instances highlighting how all of this work is finding its way into contemporary debates on pragmatism, truth, language, thought, logic, reasoning and so on, but all the same it all sounds very pessimistic. So let me conclude by noting three things that I take this state of affairs to suggest.

First, throughout the book we have seen the details of Peirce's work, how it developed across the course of his philosophical life, and how this development deals with many of the questions and concerns that are often raised against it. It is because of this philosophical work – the founding of pragmatism, the pragmatic account of truth and inquiry, the account of signs, the accounts of logic, the universal categories and evolutionary cosmology – that Peirce is a deeply important figure in nineteenth- and twentieth-century philosophy and a thinker worth paying close attention to. Even setting aside the complexity and range of his work, he is an interesting figure simply because of where he stands in the history of philosophy; many of his philosophical concerns and sensibilities are familiar to us, but many of his methods are deeply traditional. He is both a contemporary philosopher and a traditional philosopher; both familiar and alien. The value of his work alone, then, makes him a philosophical figure worthy of close attention.

Second, his influence has been profound in terms of pragmatism, truth, semiotics, logic, and much else besides, and even though his work has been given less attention at various points than it deserves, his insights have endured. He is still a source for insights into the most contemporary work on questions of pragmatism, truth, language, thought, logic and reasoning, as we have frequently noted. It seems strikingly apt to describe Peirce with such apparently conflicting terms and phrases as 'influential, yet under-appreciated' and 'sidelined, yet still relevant'. The ability to somehow remain influential and relevant is testimony to his abiding philosophical value.

Third, far from being pessimistic, I think the range of areas where Peirce's work can clearly offer new insights and new avenues of research is grounds for acute optimism. Throughout, we have highlighted how Peirce's approach to various issues seems to promise answers to questions raised in contemporary pragmatism: how can we have pragmatism without narcissism? In the study of truth: how can we be deflationists but still acknowledge the importance of truth in human practices? In language and mind: how does reference or representation really work? And even in logic: do diagrammatic and topological logics give us a better resource for applied questions of logic? That Peirce's work is still so rich with potential for continued relevance and insight stands testimony to his greatness as a philosopher.

What I would hope we have established is that Peirce is a philosopher whose body of work is impressively deep and wide, who has been influential in the rise of modern philosophy, who remains relevant to many of modern philosophy's most interesting questions, and whose work continues to hold clear promise of future insights for those prepared to give it the attention it deserves.

Further reading

As already suggested, work on Peirce is usually readily connectable to other work in philosophy, so it is quite easy to find suggestions of influence or relevance. The best work on tracing out the influence and relevance of Peirce's work, though, is usually found in relation to pragmatism. As a general statement of Peirce's relevance, Sami Pihlström's 'Peirce's place in the pragmatist tradition' (2004) is an especially useful and readable summary. Christopher Hookway's 'Logical principles and philosophical attitudes: Peirce's response to James' pragmatism' (1997b) offers a useful and detailed comparison of the work of James and Peirce, making their different motivations for using pragmatism clear. A slightly more speculative but still useful paper exploring the potential influence of Peirce on Wittgenstein is Charles Hardwick's 'Peirce's influence on some British philosophers: a guess at the riddle' (1979). Additionally, a useful collection of papers edited by Kenneth Ketner, *Peirce and Contemporary Thought* (1989), contains numerous efforts at drawing connections between Peirce's theories and more familiar or contemporary work.

Finally, it may be helpful for anyone interested in examples where Peirce's work is developed and extended into contemporary debates to attend to the following papers by Catherine Legg. Legg's paper 'Making it explicit and clear: from "strong" to "hyper-" inferentialism in Brandom and Peirce' (2008b) makes some interesting comparisons and explorations of Peirce's relevance to Robert Brandom's recent pragmatist program of inferentialism, and her paper 'The problem of the essential icon' (2008a) takes Peirce's notion of icons and iconic representation and makes an argument parallel to John Perry's claims about the essential place of indexical reference, claiming that some essential iconic element may be present in signification too. Although it is at least a little immodest to mention it, my own paper 'Peirce, Perry and the lost history of critical referentialism' (2008a) draws connections between Peirce's semiotic and the work of John Perry, and my 'Peirce's final account of signs and the philosophy of language' (2008b) suggests some Peircian solutions to common puzzles in modern philosophy of language. Finally, it is well worth noting Cheryl Misak's important paper 'Pragmatism and deflationism' (2007), which shows how a broadly Peircian account of truth can give us a ready explication which improves upon the contemporary deflationist and minimalist accounts of such philosophers as Paul Horwich, Dorothy Grover and Crispin Wright.

Notes

1 Catherine Legg (2002) gives an extensive and helpful review of Cumming's book.
2 Dewey (1916) gives a good early analysis of the two founding pragmatists' different accounts of pragmatism.
3 Putnam (2010, 53) makes what strikes me as a rather important observation: 'It has become fashionable in recent decades to associate Dewey with James and to isolate Peirce. Without at all denying the importance of Dewey's relation to James, or James' relation to Peirce, it is, I think, time for another study of Dewey's relation to Peirce.'
4 Especially useful are Dyer (1986) and Griffin (1998).
5 Susan Haack and Nicholas Rescher are both prominent and vehement defenders of the need to retain a Peircian sensibility in our pragmatism. Nonetheless, they are in the minority when it comes to the second wave of pragmatism.
6 Third wave approaches are characterised by what Stout calls 'pragmatism without narcissism', that is, pragmatism which avoids 'anthropomorphism of a sort that loses sight of the objective dimension of inquiry' (Stout 2007, 9). Most Peirce scholars will see this lack of narcissism in Peirce's work; he might agree with James that the trail of the human serpent is over everything, but he may well add that the *everything* it is over matters too.
7 Even Richard Rorty (1961) notes the parallels between Peirce and the Wittgenstein of *The Philosophical Investigations*.
8 See EP1. 24 (1868), where Peirce says 'the meaning of a term is the conception it conveys'.
9 See Wright (1992, 45–48), for example.
10 See, for example, Kaplan (1989, 490) or García-Carpintero (1998, 532–533).
11 See Atkin (2008b) for some suggestions here.
12 See, for example, Barwise and Hammer (1996).

abduction One of the three main forms of inference identified by Peirce. Peirce also calls this concept *hypothesis* or *retroduction* and treats it as a form of guessing or inference to the best explanation. Peirce makes the following suggestion of its form:

The surprising fact, C, is observed;

But if *A* were true, C would be a matter of course;

Hence there is reason to suspect that *A* is true.

(CP5. 189 (1903))

aesthetic ideal The aim of aesthetics, the first branch of normative science, treats the growth of concrete reasonableness as the ultimate aesthetic ideal.

agapism The commitment to the view that creative love really is operative in the universe. Along with **tychism** and **synechism**. one of the three key concepts in Peirce's evolutionary cosmology.

architectonic The systematic structure of knowledge. For Peirce, this is the division of philosophy into three branches: phenomenology, normative science and metaphysics. These branches are also divided into sub-branches.

belief A settled state of habit, based on Alexander Bain's dispositionalist view of belief as that upon which we are prepared to act.

categories The universal categories of experience divide all of our phenomenological experiences into the three general classes of *firstness, secondness* and *thirdness.*

critical logic One of the three sub-sub-branches of the logic sub-branch of normative science in Peirce's architectonic. Critical logic is divided into the three branches of *abductive logic, deductive logic* and *inductive logic* and studies the conditions under which such arguments are valid or inductively/abductively strong.

cut The equivalent of negation in Peirce's existential graphs. A cut is a complete boundary placed around some area of the sheet of assertion which effectively states that the content of that area does not exist. In the beta portion of the graphs, a broken cut is used to represent possible negation.

doubt Doubt is the state of unease that arises when belief faces recalcitrance. It consists in the disturbance of a habit of action – we do not know how or if to continue in some previously established habit – and the stimulation to settle belief once more.

existential graph Existential graphs are the main examples of Peirce's diagrammatic logic. Three systems – *alpha, beta* and *gamma* – were developed, giving us accounts of propositional, predicate and modal logics that used iconic and diagrammatic structures rather than algebraic symbols.

firstness The first of Peirce's three universal categories. It is the general category of our experience that captures feelings, qualities and potentials.

grades of clearness Instrumental to Peirce's account of pragmatism and the pragmatic maxim, he claims that our understanding of any concept has three grades. The first grade, clarity, represents our unreflective familiarity with a concept; the second grade, distinctness, represents our ability to give a definition of some concept; the third grade, expressed by the pragmatic maxim, represents our ability to understand the practical import of holding some concept to be true.

icon A common feature of Peirce's sign divisions, the icon is a form of sign that relies on a shared qualitative connection between the sign-vehicle and the object.

incognisable A sign that lies beyond the scope of understanding, interpretation or translation is incognisable. Peirce's semiotic will not tolerate incognisables, since they would need signs without interpretants, which by definition are not signs at all.

index A common feature of Peirce's sign divisions, the index is a form of sign that relies on a shared physical or causal connection between the sign-vehicle and the object.

inquiry The process of moving from doubt to a settled state of belief is simply the process of inquiry.

intellectual hope A common feature of Peirce's later work on truth and pragmatism is to treat such principles as truth and the end of inquiry as assumptions which we must make in order to begin investigations or attempt to answer questions. We proceed in the hope that truth can be had and inquiry can, in principle, reach an end point.

interpretant The third important element of Peirce's triadic account of sign structure. The interpretant is the representational or interpretational process of taking the sign/object relation to be significant. Every sign must have an interpretant and be a potential interpretant for some preceding sign.

intuition A first sign, or a sign without any preceding signs, is an intuition. Again, Peirce's semiotic will not tolerate intuitions, since a first sign is a sign which cannot be a potential interpretant for some preceding sign, and so by definition it is not a sign at all.

logic (broad vs narrow) As a branch of the normative sciences, Peirce's view of logic contains both broad and narrow elements. Logic broadly construed includes semiotic, science, pragmatism and inquiry. Logic narrowly construed is simply the study of deductive and formal logic.

method of a priori system building One of four proposed methods of settling belief when confronted with doubt and recalcitrance. One formulates a set of axioms according to taste and fashion and judges beliefs by how well they accord with the system.

method of authority One of four proposed methods of settling belief when confronted with doubt and recalcitrance. One appeals to some authority, such as the church or political doctrine, to define one's beliefs on any given matter.

method of science One of four proposed methods of settling belief when confronted with doubt and recalcitrance. One subjects one's beliefs to the process of science, taking on board the fallible belief suggested by the best evidence of science.

method of tenacity One of four proposed methods of settling belief when confronted with doubt and recalcitrance. One maintains one's preferred beliefs come what may, simply dismissing evidence of their falsehood.

methodeutic That sub-branch of the normative science of logic that deals with the methods which best provide answers and scientific progress. This branch of the architectonic is where we find the pragmatic maxim and other principles of inquiry.

nominalism In Peirce's philosophy, nominalism is a wide-ranging term, but it is usually applied to any theory or idea which is not committed to the reality of laws, universals and generals.

normative sciences The second branch of philosophy which contains aesthetics, ethics and logic. Described by Peirce as investigating 'the universal and necessary laws of the relation of Phenomena to Ends, that is, Truth, Right, and Beauty' (EP2. 196–197 (1903)).

phaneroscopy After 1904, Peirce used the term 'phaneroscopy' to describe the first branch of philosophy, phenomenology, because it was a less theoretically loaded term.

phenomenology The first branch of philosophy, devoted to the study of what is universal and general in the content of experience, and the source of the three universal categories.

pragmatic maxim The third grade of clearness; identifies the meaning of a concept with the practical effects of holding it true. The canonical statement of Peirce's pragmatism: 'Consider what effects, which might conceivably have practical bearings, we conceive the object of our conception to have. Then, our conception of these effects is the whole of our conception the object' (EP1. 130 (1878)).

secondness The second of Peirce's three universal categories. It is the general category of our experience that captures existence, resistance and reality.

semiosis The process by which signs develop and translate, with each sign's interpretant functioning as a further sign for the object and so generating a further interpretant.

speculative grammar An alternative name for *critical logic*.

speculative rhetoric That sub-branch of logic devoted to studying the nature of signs and semiotic. This is where Peirce's sign theories are placed within the architectonic structure of his philosophy.

symbol A common feature of Peirce's sign divisions, the symbol is a form of sign that relies on convention or law-like connections between the sign-vehicle and the object.

synechism A commitment to the view that continuity really is operative in the universe. Along with **tychism** and **agapism**, one of the three key concepts in Peirce's evolutionary cosmology.

thirdness The third of Peirce's three universal categories. It is the general category of our experience that captures connection, mediation, synthesis and representation. Often associated with habit and law in Peirce's philosophy.

tincture A feature of the gamma portion of Peirce's existential graphs. Different areas of the sheet of assertion are given different colours according to different modalities.

tychism A commitment to the view that absolute chance really is operative in the universe. Along with **synechism** and **agapism**, one of the three key concepts in Peirce's evolutionary cosmology.

'would-bes' Often used to describe possibilities which, contrary to **nominalism**, Peirce took to be robustly real.

Bibliography

Agler, David W. (2011). 'Peirce's direct, non-reductive contextual theory of names'. *Transactions of the Charles S. Peirce Society.* 46 (4): 611–640.

Anderson, Douglas. (1995). *Strands of system: the philosophy of Charles Peirce.* West Lafayette: Purdue University Press.

Aristotle. (1963). *Categories.* Trans. J.L. Ackrill. Oxford: Clarendon Press.

Atkin, Albert. (2005). 'Peirce on the index and indexical reference'. *Transactions of the Charles S. Peirce Society.* 41 (1): 161–188.

Atkin, Albert. (2008a). 'Peirce's final account of signs and the philosophy of language'. *Transactions of the Charles S. Peirce Society.* 44 (1): 63–85.

Atkin, Albert. (2008b). 'Peirce, Perry and the lost history of critical referentialism'. *Philosophia.* 36 (3): 313–326.

Ayer, A.J. (1936). *Language, truth and logic.* London: Victor Gollancz Ltd.

Ayer, A.J. (1968). *The origins of pragmatism: studies in the philosophy of Charles Sanders Peirce and William James.* San Francisco: Freeman, Cooper.

Barwise, Jon and Hammer, Eric. (1996). 'Diagrams and the concept of logical systems'. In *Logical reasoning with diagrams.* Eds. Gerard Allwein and Jon Barwise. Oxford: Oxford University Press. 49–78.

Bergman, Mats. (2009). *Peirce's philosophy of communication.* London: Continuum.

Boersema, David. (2002). 'Peirce on names and reference'. *Transactions of the Charles S. Peirce Society.* 38 (3): 351–362.

Boersema, David. (2009). *Pragmatism and reference.* Cambridge: MIT Press.

Boole, George. (1847/1951). *The mathematical analysis of logic, being an essay towards a calculus of deductive reasoning.* Oxford: Blackwell.

Boole, George. (1854). *An investigation of the laws of thought on which are founded the mathematical theories of logic and probabilities.* London: Macmillan.

Brent, Joseph. (1998). *Charles Sanders Peirce: a life.* Bloomington: Indiana University Press.

Bridgman, P.W. (1927). *The logic of modern physics.* New York: Macmillan Press.

Buchler, Justus. (1954). 'One Santayana or two?' *Journal of Philosophy*. 51 (2): 52–57.

Burch, Robert. (1991). *A Peircean reduction thesis: the foundations of topological logic*. Lubbock: Texas Tech University Press.

Burch, Robert. (1994). 'Game-theoretical semantics for Peirce's existential graphs'. *Synthese*. 99: 361–375.

Burch, Robert. (1997). 'A Tarski-style semantics for Peirce's beta-graphs'. In *The rule of reason: the philosophy of Charles Sanders Peirce*. Eds. Jacqueline Brunning and Paul Forster. Toronto: University of Toronto Press. 81–95.

Burch, Robert. (2010). 'Charles Sanders Peirce'. *The Stanford encyclopaedia of philosophy* (Fall 2014 Edition). Ed. Edward N. Zalta. <http://plato.stanford.edu/archives/fall2014/entries/peirce/>.

Burks, Arthur. (1949). 'Icon, index, symbol'. *Philosophical and Phenomenological Research*. IX: 673–689.

Carnap, Rudolf. (1936). 'Truth and confirmation'. In *Readings in philosophical analysis*. Eds. Herbert Feigl and Wilfrid Sellars. New York: Appleton Century Crofts. 119–127.

Comte, Auguste. (1858/2009). *The positive philosophy of Auguste Comte*, Vol. 1. Trans. Harriet Martineau. Cambridge: Cambridge University Press.

Cumming, Naomi. (2000). *The sonic self: musical subjectivity and signification*. Bloomington: Indiana University Press.

de Tienne, Andre. (1988). 'Peirce's search for a method of finding the categories'. *Versus*. 49: 103–112.

Deacon, Terrence. (1997). *The symbolic species: the co-evolution of language and the brain*. New York: W.W. Norton.

Dedekind, Richard. (1909). 'The nature and meaning of number'. *Essays on the theory of numbers*. La Salle: Open Court Press. 21–58.

Dewey, John. (1916). 'The pragmatism of Peirce'. *The Journal of Philosophy, Psychology and Scientific Methods*. 13 (26): 709–715.

Dipert, Randall. (1984). 'Peirce, Frege, the logic of relations, and Church's theorem'. *History and Philosophy of Logic*. 5: 49–66.

Dipert, Randall. (1995). 'Peirce's underestimated place in the history of logic: a response to Quine'. In *Peirce and contemporary thought*. Ed. Kenneth Laine Ketner. New York: Fordham University Press. 32–58.

Dipert, Randall. (2004). 'Peirce's deductive logic: its development, influence, and philosophical significance'. In *The Cambridge companion to Peirce*. Ed. Cheryl Misak. Cambridge: Cambridge University Press. 287–324.

Dyer, Alan. (1986). 'Veblen on scientific creativity: the influence of Charles S. Peirce.' *Journal of Economic Issues*. 20 (1): 21–41.

Elkins, James. (2003). 'What does Peirce's sign theory have to say to art history?'. *Culture, Theory and Critique*. 44 (1): 5–22.

Esposito, Joseph. (1980). *Evolutionary metaphysics: the development of Peirce's theory of categories*. Athens: Ohio University Press.

Farias, P. and Queiroz, J. (2003). 'On diagrams for Peirce's 10, 28, and 66 classes of signs'. *Semiotica*. 147 (1/4): 165–184.

Feigl, Herbert. (1949). 'Logical empiricism'. In *Readings in philosophical analysis*. Eds. Herbert Feigl and Wilfrid Sellars. New York: Appleton Century Crofts. 3–28.

Fisch, Max and Turquette, Atwell. (1966). 'Peirce's triadic logic'. *Transactions of the Charles S. Peirce Society*. 2 (2): 71–85.

Forster, Paul. (1997). 'The logical foundations of Peirce's indeterminism'. In *The rule of reason: the philosophy of Charles Sanders Peirce*. Eds. Jacqueline Brunning and Paul Forster. Toronto: Toronto University Press. 57–80.

Frankfurt, H.G. (1958). 'Peirce's account of inquiry'. *Journal of Philosophy*. 55 (14): 588–592.

Frege, Gottlob. (1879). *Begriffsschrift, eine der arithmetischen nachgebildete Formelsprache des reinen Denkens*. Halle: Louis Nebert.

Frege, Gottlob. (1968). *Foundations of arithmetic*. Trans. J.L. Austin. Oxford: Blackwell.

Frege, Gottlob. (1979). *Posthumous writings*. Eds. Hans Hermes, Friedrich Kambartel and Friedrich Kaulbach. Trans. Peter Long and Roger White. Oxford: Blackwell.

Gallie, W.B. (1952). *Peirce and pragmatism*. Harmondsworth: Penguin Books.

García-Carpintero, Manuel. (1998). 'Indexicals as token-reflexives'. *Mind*. 107 (4): 529–563.

Gardner, Martin. (1958). *Logic machines and diagrams*. New York: McGraw-Hill.

Gentry, George. (1952). 'Habit and the logical interpretant'. In *Studies in the philosophy of Charles Sanders Peirce*. Eds. Philip P. Wiener and Frederic H. Young. Cambridge: Harvard University Press. 75–92.

Goudge, Thomas. (1950). *The thought of C.S. Peirce*. Toronto: Toronto University Press.

Goudge, Thomas. (1965). 'Peirce's index'. *Transactions of the Charles S. Peirce Society*. 1 (2): 52–70.

Griffin, Robert. (1998). 'What Veblen owed to Peirce: the social theory of logic'. *Journal of Economic Issues*. 32 (3): 733–757.

Gu, J.-J., Montealegre-Z, F., Robert, D., Engel, M.S., Qiao, G.-X., and Ren, D. (2012). 'Wing stridulation in a Jurassic katydid (Insecta, Orthoptera) produced low-pitched musical calls to attract females'. *Proceedings of the National Academy of Sciences of the United States of America*, 109 (10): 3868–3873.

Haack, Susan. (1976) 'The pragmatist theory of truth'. *The British Journal for the Philosophy of Science*. 27 (3): 231–249.

Hardwick, Charles. (1979). 'Peirce's influence on some British philosophers: a guess at the riddle'. In *Peirce Studies*. 1: 25–29. Lubbock: Institute for Studies in Pragmaticism.

Hintikka, Jaakko. (1997). 'The place of C.S. Peirce in the history of logical theory'. In *The rule of reason: the philosophy of Charles Sanders Peirce*. Eds. Jacqueline Brunning and Paul Forster. Toronto: Toronto University Press. 13–33.

Hookway, Christopher. (1985). *Peirce*. London: Routledge.

Hookway, Christopher. (1997a). 'Design and chance: the evolution of Peirce's evolutionary cosmology'. *Transactions of the Charles. S. Peirce Society*. 33 (1): 1–34.

Hookway, Christopher. (1997b). 'Logical principles and philosophical attitudes: Peirce's response to James' pragmatism.' In *The Cambridge companion to William James*. Ed. Ruth Anna Putnam. Cambridge: Cambridge University Press.

Hookway, Christopher. (2000). *Truth, rationality, and pragmatism: themes from Peirce.* Oxford: Oxford University Press.

Hookway, Christopher. (2004a). 'The principle of pragmatism: Peirce's formulations and examples'. *Midwest Studies in Philosophy.* 28 (1): 119–136.

Hookway, Christopher. (2004b). 'Truth, reality, and convergence'. In *The Cambridge companion to Peirce.* Ed. Cheryl Misak. Cambridge: Cambridge University Press.

Houser, Nathan. (1992). 'The fortunes and misfortunes of the Peirce papers'. In *Signs of humanity*, Vol. 3. Eds. Michel Balat and Janice Deledalle-Rhodes. Berlin: Mouton de Gruyter. 1259–1268.

James, William. (1907/1975). *Pragmatism: a new name for some old ways of thinking.* Cambridge: Harvard University Press.

Jappy, A. (1989). 'Peirce's sixty-six signs revisited'. In *Semiotics and pragmatics.* Ed. Gerard Deledalle. Amsterdam: John Benjamins. 143–153.

Jevons, W.S. (1881). 'Recent mathematico-logical memoirs' *Nature.* 23: 485–487.

Kant, Immanuel. (1781/1958). *Critique of pure reason.* Trans. Norman Kemp Smith. London: Macmillan.

Kaplan, David. (1989). 'Demonstratives'. In *Themes from Kaplan.* Eds. Joseph Almog, John Perry and Howard Wettstein. Oxford: Oxford University Press. 481–563.

Katz, Jerrold. (1987). 'Descartes' *cogito'. Pacific Philosophical Quarterly.* 68 (3,4): 175–196.

Kempe, A.B. (1886). 'A memoir on the theory of mathematical form'. *Philosophical Transactions of the Royal Society.* 177: 1–70.

Kenny, Anthony. (1966). 'Cartesian privacy'. In *Wittgenstein: the philosophical investigations, a collection of critical essays.* Ed. George Pitcher. New York: Doubleday. 352–370.

Kent, Beverley. (1987). *Charles S. Peirce: logic and the classification of the sciences.* Kingston: McGill-Queen's University Press.

Ketner, Kenneth (ed). (1989). *Peirce and contemporary thought.* New York: Fordham University Press.

Kragh, Helge. (2009). 'The green line: a chapter in the history of auroral physics'. *Astronomy and Geophysics.* 50 (5): 5.25–5.28.

Legg, Catherine. (2002). 'Review of Naomi Cumming, *The sonic self: musical subjectivity and signification'. Semiotic Inquiry.* 22: 313–327.

Legg, Catherine. (2008a). 'The problem of the essential icon'. *American Philosophical Quarterly.* 45 (3): 207–232.

Legg, Catherine. (2008b). 'Making it explicit and clear: from "strong" to "hyper-" inferentialism in Brandom and Peirce'. *Metaphilosophy.* 39 (1): 106–123.

Lenzen, Victor. (1965). 'The contributions of Charles S. Peirce to metrology'. *Proceedings of the American Philosophical Society.* 109 (1): 29–46.

Leonard, Henry. (1937). 'The pragmatism and scientific metaphysics of C.S Peirce'. *Philosophy of Science.* 4 (1): 109–121.

Lewis, C.I. (1918). *A survey of symbolic logic.* Berkeley: University of California Press.

Lewis, C.I. (1970). *Collected papers of C.I. Lewis.* Eds. John D. Goheen and John L. Mothershead, Jr. Stanford: Stanford University Press.

Liszka, James. (1996). *A general introduction to the semiotic of Charles Sanders Peirce.* Bloomington: Indiana University Press.

Locke, John. (1975). *Treatise concerning human understanding.* Ed. Peter Nidditch. Oxford: Clarendon Press.

Martin, R.M. (1965). 'On Peirce's icons of second intention'. *Transactions of the Charles S. Peirce Society.* 1 (1): 71–76.

Meyer, Leonard. (1956). *Emotion and meaning in music.* Chicago: Chicago University Press.

Migotti, Mark. (1998). 'Peirce's double-aspect theory of truth'. In *Pragmatism: Canadian journal of philosophy.* Suppl. Vol. 24. Ed. Cheryl Misak. Calgary: University of Calgary Press. 75–108.

Migotti, Mark. (2005). 'The key to Peirce's view of the role of belief in scientific inquiry'. *Cognitio.* 6 (1): 43–55.

Misak, Cheryl. (1991). *Truth and the end of inquiry: a Peircean account of truth.* Oxford: Clarendon Press.

Misak, Cheryl. (1995). *Verificationism: its history and prospects.* London: Routledge.

Misak, Cheryl. (2004). 'C.S. Peirce on vital matters'. In *The Cambridge companion to Peirce.* Ed. Cheryl Misak. Cambridge: Cambridge University Press. 150–174.

Misak, Cheryl. (2007). 'Pragmatism and deflationism'. In *New pragmatists.* Ed. Cheryl Misak. Oxford: Oxford University Press. 68–90.

Morris, Charles. (1938). *Foundations of the theory of signs.* Chicago: Chicago University Press.

Müller, R. (1994). 'On the principles of construction and the order of Peirce's trichotomies of signs'. *Transactions of the Charles S. Peirce Society.* 30 (1): 135–153.

Murphey, Murray. (1961). *The development of Peirce's philosophy.* Cambridge: Harvard University Press.

Murphey, Murray. (1965). 'On Peirce's metaphysics'. *Transactions of the Charles S. Peirce Society.* 1 (1): 12–25.

Nubiola, Jaime. (1996). 'Scholarship on the relations between Ludwig Wittgenstein and Charles S. Peirce'. In *Studies on the history of logic: proceedings of the III Symposium on the History of Logic.* Berlin: Mouton de Gruyter. 281–294.

Parmentier, Richard. (1994). *Signs in society: studies in semiotic anthropology.* Bloomington: Indiana University Press.

Peirce, C.S. (1870/1873). 'Description of a notation for the logic of relatives, resulting from an amplification of the conceptions of Boole's calculus of logic'. *Memoirs of the American Academy of Arts and Sciences.* 9. 317–378.

Peirce, C.S. (1880). 'On the algebra of logic'. *American Journal of Mathematics.* 3: 15–57.

Peirce, C.S. (1883). *Studies in logic by members of the Johns Hopkins University.* Ed. Charles S. Peirce. Boston: Little Brown.

Peirce. C.S. (1885) 'On the algebra of logic: a contribution to the philosophy of notation'. *American Journal of Mathematics* 7 (2): 180–202.

Peirce, C.S. (1897). 'The logic of relatives'. *The Monist.* 7 (2): 161–217.

Perry, John. (2001). *Reference and reflexivity.* Stanford: CSLI.

Pietarinen, Ahti-Veikko. (2006a). 'Peirce's contributions to possible-worlds semantics'. *Studia Logica.* 82 (3): 345–369.

Pietarinen, Ahti-Veikko. (2006b). *Signs of logic: Peircean themes on the philosophy of language,
games, and communication.* Dordrecht: Springer.

Pietarinen, Ahti-Veikko. (2010). 'Challenges and opportunities for existential
graphs'. In *Ideas in action: proceedings of the Applying Peirce Conference.* Eds. M. Bergman,
S. Paavola, A.-V. Pietarinen and H. Rydenfelt. Nordic studies in pragmatism 1.
Helsinki: Nordic Pragmatism Network. 288–303.

Pietarinen, Ahti-Veikko. (2011). 'Moving pictures of thought II: graphs, games, and
pragmaticism's proof'. *Semiotica.* 186: 315–331.

Pihlström, Sami. (2004). 'Peirce's place in the pragmatist tradition'. In *The Cambridge
companion to Peirce.* Ed. Cheryl Misak. Cambridge: Cambridge University Press.
27–57.

Popper, Karl. (1972). *Objective knowledge: an evolutionary approach.* Oxford: Clarendon.

Putnam, Hilary. (1982). 'Peirce the logician'. *Historia Mathematica.* 9: 290–301.

Putnam, Hilary. (1990). *Realism with a human face.* Cambridge: Harvard University Press.

Putnam, Hilary. (1995). *Pragmatism: an open question.* Oxford: Blackwell.

Putnam, Ruth Anna. (2010). 'Dewey's epistemology'. In *The Cambridge companion to
Dewey.* Ed. Molly Cochran. Cambridge: Cambridge University Press. 34–54.

Quine, Willard Van Orman. (1935). 'Review of the collected papers of Charles
Sanders Peirce, volume 4: *The simplest mathematics*'. *Isis.* 22 (2): 551–553.

Quine, Willard Van Orman. (1954). 'Reduction to a dyadic predicate'. *Journal of Symbolic Logic.* 19 (3): 182–184.

Quine, Willard Van Orman. (1995). 'Peirce's logic'. In *Peirce and contemporary thought.*
Ed. Kenneth Laine Ketner. New York: Fordham University Press. 23–31.

Ramsey, William. (2007). *Representation reconsidered.* Cambridge: Cambridge University
Press.

Ransdell, Joseph. (1977). 'Some leading ideas in Peirce's semiotic'. *Semiotica.* 19: 157–178.

Recanati, François. (2012). *Mental files.* Oxford: Oxford University Press.

Rescher, Nicholas. (1997). *Profitable speculations.* Oxford: Rowman & Littlefield.

Restall, Greg. (2006). *Logic: an introduction.* London: Routledge.

Reynolds, Andrew. (2002). *Peirce's scientific metaphysics: the philosophy of chance, law and evolution.* Nashville: Vanderbilt University Press.

Roberts, Donald. (1973). *The existential graphs of Charles S. Peirce.* The Hague: Mouton.

Robin, Richard. (1967). *Annotated catalogue of the papers of Charles S. Peirce.* Amherst:
University of Massachusetts Press.

Robin, Richard. (1997). 'Classical pragmatism and pragmatism's proof'. In *The rule
of reason: the philosophy of Charles S. Peirce.* Eds. Jacqueline Brunning and Paul Forster.
Toronto: Toronto University Press. 139–152.

Rorty, Richard. (1982). *Consequences of pragmatism.* Minneapolis: University of
Minnesota Press.

Rorty, Richard. (1961). 'Pragmatism, categories and language'. *The Philosophical Review.* 70 (2): 197–223.

Royce, Josiah. (1885/1965). *The religious aspect of philosophy.* Gloucester: Peter Smith.

Royce, Josiah. (1899). *The world and the individual.* New York: Macmillan Press.

Russell, Bertrand. (1939). 'Dewey's new logic'. In *The philosophy of John Dewey.* Ed. Paul A. Schilpp. New York: Tudor. 137–156.

Russell, Bertrand. (1959). *Wisdom of the West.* Garden City: Doubleday.

Sanders, G. (1970). 'Peirce sixty-six signs?'. *Transactions of the Charles S. Peirce Society.* 6 (1): 3–16.

Saussure, Ferdinand de. (1916/1974). *Cours de linguistique générale.* Trans. Wade Baskin. Glasgow: Fontana Collins.

Savan, David. (1952). 'On the origins of Peirce's phenomenology'. In *Studies in the philosophy of Charles Sanders Peirce.* Eds. Philip P. Wiener and Frederic H. Young. Cambridge: Harvard University Press. 185–194.

Savan, David. (1988). *An introduction to C.S. Peirce's full system of semeiotic.* Toronto: Toronto Semiotic Circle.

Scheffler, Israel. (1974). *Four pragmatists.* London: Routledge Keegan Paul.

Scheffler, Israel. (2009). *Worlds of truth: a philosophy of knowledge.* Oxford: Blackwell.

Schiller, F.C.S. (1907/1912). *Studies in humanism.* London: Macmillan.

Schlick, Moritz. (1936). 'Meaning and verification'. *Philosophical Review.* 45 (4): 339–369.

Sheriff, John. K. (1994). *Charles Peirce's guess at the riddle: grounds for human significance.* Bloomington: Indiana University Press.

Shin, Sun-Joo. (2002). *The iconic logic of Peirce's graphs,* Cambridge: MIT Press.

Short, T.L. (2004). 'The development of Peirce's theory of signs'. In *The Cambridge companion to Peirce.* Ed. Cheryl Misak. Cambridge: Cambridge University Press.

Short, T.L. (2007). *Peirce's theory of signs.* Cambridge: Cambridge University Press.

Short. T.L. (2010). 'Did Peirce have a cosmology?'. *Transactions of the Charles S. Peirce Society.* 46 (4): 521–543.

Silverstein, Michael. (1985). 'Language and the culture of gender: at the intersection of structure, usage, and ideology.' In *Semiotic mediation: sociocultural and psychological perspectives.* Eds. Elizabeth Mertz and Richard J. Parmentier. Orlando: Academic Press. 219–259.

Singer, Milton. (1978). 'For a semiotic anthropology'. In *Sight, sound and sense.* Ed Thomas A. Sebeok. Bloomington: Indiana University Press. 202–231.

Sowa, John. (2000). *Knowledge representation: logical, philosophical, and computational foundations.* Belmont: Brooks/Cole.

Stjernfelt, Frederik. (2007). *Diagrammatology: an investigation on the borderlines of phenomenology, ontology, and semiotics.* Dordrecht: Springer.

Stout, Jeffrey. (2007). 'On our interest in getting things right: pragmatism without narcissism'. In *New pragmatists.* Ed. Cheryl Misak. Oxford: Oxford University Press. 7–31.

Suits, Bernard. (1979). 'Doubts about Peirce's cosmology'. *Transactions of the Charles S. Peirce Society.* 15 (4): 311–321.

Sylvester, J.J. (1878). 'Chemistry and algebra'. *Nature*. 17: 284.

Tarski, Alfred. (1956). *Logic, semantics, metamathematics: papers from 1923 to 1938*. Trans. J.H. Woodger. Oxford: Oxford University Press.

Van Heijenoort, Jean (ed). (1967). *From Frege to Gödel: a sourcebook in mathematical logic*. Cambridge: Harvard University Press.

Venn, John. (1883). 'Review of *Studies in logic by members of the Johns Hopkins University*'. *Mind*. 8: 594–603.

Von Eckardt, Barbara. (1993). *What is cognitive science?* Cambridge: MIT Press.

Weiss, Paul. (1940). 'The essence of Peirce's system'. *Journal of Philosophy*. 37 (10): 253–264.

Weiss, Paul and Burks, Arthur W. (1945). 'Peirce's sixty-six signs'. *Journal of Philosophy*. 42: 383–388.

Wiggins, David. (2004). 'Reflections on inquiry and truth arising from Peirce's method for the fixation of belief'. In *The Cambridge companion to Peirce*. Ed. Cheryl Misak. Cambridge: Cambridge University Press. 87–126.

Wittgenstein, Ludwig. (1953). *Philosophical investigations*. Trans. Elizabeth Anscombe. Oxford: Blackwell.

Wright, Crispin. (1992). *Truth and objectivity*. Cambridge: Harvard University Press.

Wright, Crispin. (2001). 'Minimalism, deflationism, pragmatism, pluralism'. In *The nature of truth: classic and contemporary perspectives*. Ed. Michael Lynch. Cambridge: MIT Press. 751–787.

Zeman, J.J. (1964). *The graphical logic of C.S. Peirce*. Unpublished Ph.D. Dissertation. University of Chicago. <http://www.clas.ufl.edu/users/jzeman/graphicallogic/>.

Index